Apple TV™ For Dummies®

D0817881

Home Theater Display Technology

Technology Name	Relative Cost	Typical Maximum Size	Pros	Cons
CRT	Very inexpensive	40 inches	Great color quality, no viewing angle problems, can display 1080i HDTV	Bulky, mediocre image detail
LCD	Average to high	52 inches	Thin, lightweight, low power, good image detail, handles most HDTV signals	Mediocre color quality, limited viewing angle, blurring or ghosting on cheaper sets
Plasma	Very expensive	70 inches	Thin, lightweight, great image detail, great color quality, handles all HDTV signals	Fragile, slight chance of burn-in, brightness degradation, sensitive to high altitudes, limited viewing angle
Rear-projection	Average to high	60 inches	Good to great image detail, good to great color quality, handles most HDTV signals	Bulky, may require adjustment and maintenance, limited viewing angle, requires a dark room
Front-projection	Average	200 inches	Good color quality, handles most HDTV signals	Requires a separate wall or screen, mediocre image quality, requires a dark room

TV Resolutions in a Nutshell

Name	Signal Type	Number of Scan Lines	Aspect Ratio	Resolution
SDTV	Analog	480	4:3	720 x 480
DTV	Digital	480	4:3 or 16:9	704 x 480 or 640 x 480
HDTV	Digital	1080i (interlaced) or 720p (progressive)	16:9	1920 x 1080i (interlaced) or 1280 x 720p (progressive)

For Dummies: Bestselling Book Series for Beginners

Apple TV™ For Dummies®

Cheat Sheet

Mark's Common Multimedia Format Guide

Name or Extension	Type of File	Good For
AIFF	Audio	Sound effects and archival audio in Mac OS X
AVI	Video	Playing video clips in Windows
M4A	Audio	Tracks you've ripped from audio CDs using the default iTunes settings
M4P	Audio	Playing music from the Apple iTunes Music Store
BMP	Image	Archival storage of images on CD or DVD
JPEG	Image	Sending photos in e-mail or displaying on the Web
MOV	Video	Playing video clips on PCs and Macs
MP3	Audio	Playing music on your hard drive or MP3 player
MPEG	Video	Playing video on PCs, Macs, and Linux computers
OGG	Audio	Sharing music on PCs, Macs, and Linux computers
PDF	Document	Sharing and printing high-quality documents online
PNG	Image	Displaying images on a Web page
RAR	Archive	Archiving and compressing multiple files into one file
TIFF	Image	Sharing images on PCs, Macs, and Linux computers
WAV	Audio	Sound effects and archival audio in Windows XP
WMA	Audio	Playing music on your hard drive or MP3 player
WMV	Video	Playing video clips in Windows
ZIP	Archive	Archiving and compressing multiple files into one file

Apple TV Syncing versus Streaming

Method	Library	Stored on Apple TV Hard Drive	802.11b Support	Source Computer Must Stay On	Photo Features	Buffering Pauses	Capacity
Syncing	1	Yes	All media	No	Yes	No	32GB maximum
Streaming	Up to 5	No	No video	Yes	No	Yes	Unlimited browsing

For Dummies: Bestselling Book Series for Beginners

Apple TV™ FOR DUMMIES®

by Mark L. Chambers

BICENTENNIAL
1807
WILEY
2007
BICENTENNIAL

Wiley Publishing, Inc.

Apple TV™ For Dummies®

Published by
Wiley Publishing, Inc.
111 River Street
Hoboken, NJ 07030-5774

www.wiley.com

Copyright © 2007 by Wiley Publishing, Inc., Indianapolis, Indiana

Published by Wiley Publishing, Inc., Indianapolis, Indiana

Published simultaneously in Canada

For general information on our other products and services, please contact our Customer Care Department within the U.S. at 800-762-2974, outside the U.S. at 317-572-3993, or fax 317-572-4002.

For technical support, please visit www.wiley.com/techsupport.

Wiley also publishes its books in a variety of electronic formats. Some content that appears in print may not be available in electronic books.

Library of Congress Control Number: 2007932468

ISBN: 978-0-470-17362-6

Manufactured in the United States of America

10 9 8 7 6 5 4 3 2 1

WILEY

About the Author

Mark L. Chambers has been an author, computer consultant, BBS sysop, programmer, and hardware technician for more than 20 years — pushing computers and their uses far beyond "normal" performance limits for decades now. His first love affair with a computer peripheral blossomed in 1984 when he bought his lightning-fast 300 BPS modem for his Atari 400. Now he spends entirely too much time on the Internet and drinks far too much caffeine-laden soda.

With a degree in journalism and creative writing from Louisiana State University, Mark took the logical career choice: programming computers. However, after five years as a COBOL programmer for a hospital system, he decided there must be a better way to earn a living, and he became the Documentation Manager for Datastorm Technologies, a well-known communications software developer. Somewhere in between writing software manuals, Mark began writing computer how-to books. His first book, *Running a Perfect BBS*, was published in 1994 — and after a short decade or so of fun (disguised as hard work), Mark is one of the most productive and best-selling technology authors on the planet.

Along with writing several books a year and editing whatever his publishers throw at him, Mark has also branched out into Web-based education, designing and teaching a number of online classes — called *WebClinics* — for Hewlett-Packard.

His favorite pastimes include collecting gargoyles, watching St. Louis Cardinals baseball, playing his three pinball machines and the latest computer games, supercharging computers, and rendering 3D flights of fancy with *TrueSpace* — and during all that, he listens to just about every type of music imaginable. Mark's worldwide Internet radio station, *MLC Radio* (at www.mlcbooks.com), plays only CD-quality classics from 1970 to 1979, including everything from Rush to Billy Joel to the *Rocky Horror Picture Show*.

Mark's rapidly expanding list of books includes *MacBook For Dummies, iMac For Dummies,* 4th Edition; *Mac OS X Tiger All-in-One Desk Reference For Dummies; Building a PC For Dummies,* 5th Edition; *Scanners For Dummies,* 2nd Edition; *CD & DVD Recording For Dummies,* 2nd Edition; *PCs All-in-One Desk Reference For Dummies,* 2nd Edition; *Mac OS X Tiger: Top 100 Simplified Tips & Tricks; Microsoft Office v. X Power User's Guide; BURN IT! Creating Your Own Great DVDs and CDs; The Hewlett-Packard Official Printer Handbook; The Hewlett-Packard Official Recordable CD Handbook; The Hewlett-Packard Official Digital Photography Handbook; Computer Gamer's Bible; Recordable CD Bible; Teach Yourself the iMac Visually; Running a Perfect BBS; Official Netscape*

Guide to Web Animation; and *Windows 98 Troubleshooting and Optimizing Little Black Book.*

His books have been translated into 15 different languages so far — his favorites are German, Polish, Dutch, and French. Although he can't read them, he enjoys the pictures a great deal.

Mark welcomes all comments about his books. You can reach him at mark@mlcbooks.com, or visit MLC Books Online, his Web site, at www.mlcbooks.com.

Dedication

This book is dedicated with love to Frank and Vera Judycki. They might have started out as my in-laws, but now they're MawMaw and PawPaw.

Author's Acknowledgments

Once again, the good folks at Wiley Publishing have made things easy on a demanding technology author! It's time to send my appreciation to those who helped make this book a reality.

As with all my books, I'd like to first thank my wife, Anne; and my children, Erin, Chelsea, and Rose; for their support and love — and for letting me follow my dream!

No project gets underway without the Composition Services team. Starting with my words and adding a tremendous amount of work, Composition Services has once again taken care of art, layout, and countless other steps that I can't fathom. Thanks to each of the team members for a beautiful book.

Next, my appreciation goes to editorial manager Leah Cameron as well as to my technical editor Dennis Cohen, who checked the technical accuracy of every word — including that baker's dozen of absurd acronyms that crops up in every technology book I've ever written. Their work ensures that my work is the best it can be!

Finally, I come to my hardworking project editor, Rebecca Senninger, and my top-of-the-line acquisitions editor Melody Layne: My heartfelt thanks to both of them, for without their support at every step, this book wouldn't have been possible. With their help, yet another *For Dummies* title was guided safely into port!

Publisher's Acknowledgments

We're proud of this book; please send us your comments through our online registration form located at www.dummies.com/register/.

Some of the people who helped bring this book to market include the following:

Acquisitions, Editorial, and Media Development

Project Editor: Rebecca Senninger

Acquisitions Editor: Melody Layne

Copy Editor: Jennifer Riggs

Technical Editor: Dennis Cohen

Editorial Manager: Leah Cameron

Editorial Assistant: Amanda Foxworth

Sr. Editorial Assistant: Cherie Case

Cartoons: Rich Tennant
(www.the5thwave.com)

Composition Services

Project Coordinator: Heather Kolter

Layout and Graphics: Carl Byers, Joyce Haughey, Shane Johnson

Proofreaders: Jessica Kramer, Todd Lothery, Charles Spencer, Christine Sabooni

Indexer: Potomac Indexing, LLC

Anniversary Logo Design: Richard Pacifico

Publishing and Editorial for Technology Dummies

Richard Swadley, Vice President and Executive Group Publisher

Andy Cummings, Vice President and Publisher

Mary Bednarek, Executive Acquisitions Director

Mary C. Corder, Editorial Director

Publishing for Consumer Dummies

Diane Graves Steele, Vice President and Publisher

Joyce Pepple, Acquisitions Director

Composition Services

Gerry Fahey, Vice President of Production Services

Debbie Stailey, Director of Composition Services

Contents at a Glance

Table of Contents

Introduction

Some computer owners still consider their machine a *tool:* That is, they use a computer to check their e-mail, figure out their budget, and occasionally visit a Web site or two. Heck, some folks even bring work home from the office and subject their poor digital friend to nothing but Quicken and Excel! No photos, no music, no podcasts, no movies. *No fun.*

Okay, I'll admit that today's PCs and Macs are darn good productivity tools. But then again, you'd have to be living under a rock to have missed out on all the revolutionary changes that can transform your living room into a digital entertainment center — stuff like widescreen, high-definition televisions, and incredible surround-sound speaker systems. Your computer wants to be a part of that!

Thanks to your new Apple TV unit, your PC or Mac can take advantage of the latest in TV technology! You can send movies, photos, music, and videos directly from your computer to that state-of-the-art HDTV in your living room . . . or your office, or your bathroom, if a suitable TV is in there. Apple TV uses a wired or wireless Ethernet connection to *stream* (or receive) your media from a Mac or PC running iTunes straight to your television, giving you full control with (yet another) handy remote.

And you're not limited to just what you buy on the iTunes Store, either: You can edit your own video, build a huge collection of CD-quality music on your computer's hard drive, or organize all your digital photographs and send them to your Apple TV.

In league with your Apple TV, this book is your ticket to the digital media lifestyle. Welcome to the wireless entertainment revolution!

About This Book

Each chapter in this book covers a different aspect of owning an Apple TV, including installation, specific features, maintenance, and troubleshooting. (And yes, *you* can troubleshoot, too.) I also demonstrate how to use popular applications to create videos, rip audio from your CDs, and tackle your ever-growing collection of digital images.

You can start at any point — each chapter is self-contained — although the chapters are arranged in a somewhat linear order that I recommend that you follow. The book also includes a glossary of computer terms, which comes in handy if you're not familiar with the alphabet soup of engineer-speak.

Conventions Used in This Book

From time to time, I might ask you to type a command within Windows or Mac OS X (or one of the applications I demonstrate). That text often appears in bold like this: **Type me.** Press the Enter or Return key to process the command.

I list menu commands with this format: File⇨Open. For example, this short-hand indicates that you should click the File menu and then choose the Open menu item.

From time to time, I mention messages that you should see displayed onscreen by an application or the operating system. Those messages look like this: `This is a message displayed by an application.`

Although you don't really need to know a great deal of technical information to enjoy an Apple TV, you might be curious about the technical details that surround computers and the hardware and software that you're using. This technical information is usually formatted as a sidebar (in a separate box) to separate it from the stuff that you really *have* to know.

Should I Jump in Anywhere?

If you're interested in using a particular feature, such as playing a video or configuring your TV, you can jump directly to the chapter that describes that feature and start reading. Every chapter includes detailed instructions that familiarize you with the software and hardware involved.

On the other hand, if you haven't yet bought your Apple TV (or it's still sitting in its attractive box), start with Chapter 1 and follow the chapters in order; you can also skip to other chapters whenever necessary for information that you might need.

Foolish Assumptions

Here's a friendly warning: You might run across one or two doubting Thomases when you announce that you'll create a wireless connection betwixt your computer and your TV. Those folks probably make lots of foolish assumptions about the real level of technical expertise required! Here's the *truth:*

✔ You *don't* have to be a computer technician with years of training, and you don't need a workshop full of expensive tools. In this book, no assumptions are made about your previous knowledge of computers, the Internet, connecting your TV, or long division.

✔ No experience? Don't let that stop you! I introduce you to each of the applications supplied by Microsoft and Apple so you can read what they do as well as how you use them, including advanced technology that would make a technoid green with envy.

✔ You *don't* have to be a professional graphic artist, video editor, or photographer to display fantastic videos and photographs on your home theater screen! Owning an Apple TV is *fun,* and you can exercise your imagination and creativity without attending a single class in Advanced Thakamology.

Now that I've put those myths to rest, it's time for the good stuff!

How This Book Is Organized

I divided this book into seven major parts. The seven parts are made up of a number of chapters, and each chapter is further divided into sections. You find all the nasty acronyms and abbreviations, menu and button names, and relevant items in the index; important topics and information that appear elsewhere in the book are cross-referenced to make them easier to find.

Part 1: The Beginning of a Beautiful Relationship

In Part I, I introduce you to your Apple TV unit — including how to install it with a minimum of hassle and how to configure it for your TV and computer system.

Part 11: Connecting Your Apple TV

In Part II, you set up the required Ethernet network within both Windows Vista and Mac OS X, and you connect your Apple TV to your TV set and speakers. You can celebrate by watching a DVD movie from your iTunes collection on your home entertainment system!

Part III: Exploring Your Apple TV

In Part III, I show you how to use the Apple Remote Control, as well as how to sync your Apple TV to your iTunes library and how to connect to the latest streaming Internet music and video.

Part IV: Creating Your Own Media

In Part IV, you jump into image, video, and audio editing. I also provide tips and tricks for iPhoto and iMovie HD on the Mac, and iTunes for both Windows Vista and Mac OS X.

Part V: Apple TV Tricks and Troubleshooting

In Part V, I show you how to customize your Apple TV for your preferences, how to organize and maintain your media library, and how to troubleshoot problems that you might encounter with your Apple TV unit.

Part VI: The Part of Tens

In Part VI, you find chapters that offer a quick reference of tips and advice on several topics related to digital media and your Apple TV.

Part VII: Appendixes

In Appendix A, I discuss some of the software available for your Apple TV that can expand its usefulness: With the right program, you can use your Apple TV for business presentations, convert video from other formats, and even shape up with a video workout!

Computers and the world of today's high-end, high-definition equipment are chock-full of tech terms, engineering-speak, and some of the most ridiculous acronyms ever devised — luckily, you can refer to the glossary in Appendix B for honest-to-goodness English translations.

Icons Used in This Book

Some things that you encounter while using your Apple TV and computer are just too important to miss. To make sure that you see certain paragraphs, they're marked with one of the following icons.

These are important. Consider my maxims to be the stuff you'd highlight in a college textbook. These facts and recommendations would make good tattoos because they're universal and timeless in scope. (No, really, I'm not kidding. You'll see.)

Information marked with this icon is the printed equivalent of those sticky notes that decorate the front of some computers. You might already know this stuff, but a reminder never hurts.

If you're like me and you're curious about what's happening behind the scenes — you know, if you're the kind of person who disassembled alarm clocks as a kid — this icon is for you. The Technical Stuff icon highlights information that you don't really *need* to use your Apple TV, but which you might find interesting. This information can also be blissfully ignored.

The Tip icon makes it easy to spot information that saves you time and trouble (and sometimes even money).

As you can imagine, the Warning icon steers you clear of potential disaster. *Always* read the information under this icon first!

Where to Go from Here

Before you turn the page, grab a pencil and some scratch paper for taking notes — or throw caution to the wind and write directly in the book. If you need help on a particular application, jump to the right chapter; if you need to start from the beginning, start with Part I.

A Final Word

I want to thank you for buying this book, and I hope that you find *Apple TV For Dummies* valuable. With this book in hand, you're ready to make the Content Connection!

Part I
The Beginning of a Beautiful Relationship

The 5th Wave   By Rich Tennant

"Apple TV? I thought it was the largest iPod ever made."

In this part . . .

This three-chapter introduction to your Apple TV begins with a discussion of content itself — what it is and how your Apple TV receives it from your computer. Next, I demonstrate how you can install it yourself . . . no fancy techno-guru technician necessary! Finally, I demonstrate how you can configure your Apple TV in just a few easy steps.

Chapter 1

Shaking Hands with Apple TV

Are you considering purchasing an Apple TV unit? Or are you nervous about that unopened box lounging on your desk? I understand completely! After all, just what do all those tech terms mean, and what specifications are really important when deciding whether to upgrade your system? Questions like these can strike fear into the strongest of men and women.

Dear reader, I have good news: Don't despair because this chapter is your first step in becoming an Apple TV and streaming content expert! I can *guarantee* you that by the time you finish this short chapter, you'll know what the Apple TV unit looks like and what it does. You also become familiar with the specific connectors, and I introduce you to the Apple Remote that you use to control your Apple TV from the comfort of your living room couch.

Are you prepared to dive into the world of Apple TV? Come on in, the water's fine!

Starting with . . . a Definition, of Course!

I owe my high school English teacher, Mrs. Stancil, a big vote of thanks. She used to say, "When confronted with explaining something that is potentially confusing, *always* begin your description with a definition. What is it made of? What does it look like? Is it edible?" That rule has never led me astray. She was a wonderful teacher!

In this section, I define your Apple TV and its lifelong mission of Content Connector. (Oh, and it's not edible, just in case you wondered.)

What's an Apple TV?

Figure 1-1 illustrates the front of an Apple TV unit — if you're reminded of a silver plastic sandwich protector, you're spot-on (at least appearance-wise). At first glance, this thin box certainly doesn't look revolutionary. For those of us who've invested in digital media, however, an Apple TV is *the* link between your PC or Mac system and your home entertainment system.

Figure 1-1: Can the Apple TV be called *beautiful?* Of course, it can!

Figure 1-2 provides the road map between those two systems and shows where the Apple TV fits in. Here's the syncing process, step-by-step:

1. You use iTunes to select which digital media (or *content,* which I discuss in the next section) is sent to your Apple TV.

2. The selected media is sent over a wired/wireless network connection by your Mac or PC to your Apple TV (a process called *streaming*).

3. Your Apple TV stores the content on its local hard drive.

4. You select what you want to play or view by using your Apple Remote and the Apple TV onscreen menu system.

5. The content is sent directly from your Apple TV through a hard-wired connection to your TV or A/V receiver.

Now, of course, your Apple TV does additional stuff and much more that you need to know about it . . . but essentially, that's the primary task for your new silver plastic sandwich protector!

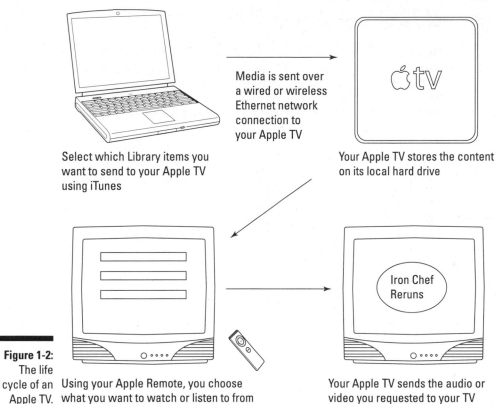

Media is sent over a wired or wireless Ethernet network connection to your Apple TV

Select which Library items you want to send to your Apple TV using iTunes

Your Apple TV stores the content on its local hard drive

Iron Chef Reruns

Figure 1-2: The life cycle of an Apple TV.

Using your Apple Remote, you choose what you want to watch or listen to from the Apple TV menu on your TV

Your Apple TV sends the audio or video you requested to your TV over a hard-wired cable connection

The Content Connection

So what exactly is this *content* I keep yammering about? Well, virtually any digital media you collect on your PC or Mac over the years can be enjoyed across your home or office. Content can include

- ✔ **Digital photographs** from your digital camera, scanner, or the Web
- ✔ **Music** ripped from your audio CDs or downloaded from the Web
- ✔ **Full-length movies** you buy from the iTunes Store, convert from DVDs, or download from the Web
- ✔ **Podcasts** downloaded from the iTunes Store
- ✔ **Audiobooks** downloaded from the iTunes Store

- ✔ **Movie trailers** downloaded automatically (by your Apple TV) from the Apple Web site
- ✔ **YouTube videos** downloaded from the YouTube Web site
- ✔ **Music videos** downloaded from the iTunes Store or the Web

Sure, you've been enjoying this stuff for years on your computer — perhaps you've invested in a widescreen computer monitor for your video or a great set of multimedia computer speakers for your music. Ah, but that's also the rub: In order to enjoy your stuff, you've been tied to your computer or your iPod, while that incredible 42-inch plasma big-screen TV and surround sound audio system in your living room have been sitting idle and helpless!

No matter what type of media you've been collecting on your computer, it's all sent wirelessly in the same manner — naturally, a 3MB MP3 song takes far less time to stream than a 1GB movie file, but they both travel through the same Content Connection. Your Apple TV works automatically in the background, synchronizing the stuff you want to watch and listen to between your Mac or PC and that local storage in your living room or conference room.

In upcoming chapters, I show you how to buy content from the iTunes Store, as well as how to download and convert content from the Web, and how to create your own content with Mac applications and PC programs.

The Major Stuff Sprouting from the Box

Ready for the grand tour? It's time to identify and explain the components that make up the Apple TV. Figure 1-3 illustrates the connectors along the back of the unit.

Most of us are used to one of two different kinds of computer video connectors, both of which are shown in Figure 1-4 (as they appear on a PC video adapter card):

- ✔ **The analog *VGA* (Video Graphics Array) *port:*** The cable from a traditional analog CRT monitor — those clunky monitors that remind you of an old-style heavy TV set — was plugged into this port.

- ✔ **A speedy digital DVI-I (Digital Video Interface-Integrated) connector:** For use with the latest flat panel LCD computer monitors. (Many Mac and PC owners also use a DVI-I to HDMI adapter cable to display graphics on their televisions.)

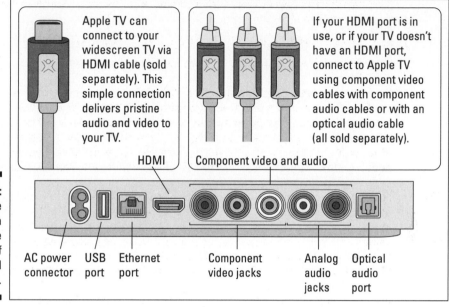

Apple TV can connect to your widescreen TV via HDMI cable (sold separately). This simple connection delivers pristine audio and video to your TV.

If your HDMI port is in use, or if your TV doesn't have an HDMI port, connect to Apple TV using component video cables with component audio cables or with an optical audio cable (all sold separately).

HDMI

Component video and audio

Figure 1-3: Your Apple TV sprouts a veritable forest of ports and connectors.

AC power connector   USB port   Ethernet port   Component video jacks   Analog audio jacks   Optical audio port

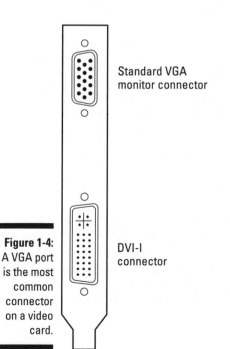

Standard VGA monitor connector

DVI-I connector

Figure 1-4: A VGA port is the most common connector on a video card.

Your Apple TV is designed for use with televisions; however, you find different ports in play. In this section, I describe each port, moving from left to right along the back of your Apple TV. I describe most of these connectors in detail in Chapter 7 — for now, I provide just an introduction.

The AC power connector

Of course, your Apple TV needs power to do its job, and the cable from a nearby AC plug connects here. Apple provides the power cord with the unit . . . and no, there's no ugly-looking transformer brick because the unit has internal power hardware.

The USB port

You're probably already familiar with USB peripherals, and your Apple TV sports a USB 2.0 port for software upgrades and servicing. (At the time of this writing, there's no support for connecting any external peripherals to your unit's USB port; however, that could certainly change in the future if additional functionality is added to your Apple TV's firmware.)

The Ethernet port

"Wait just a doggone minute, Mark — I thought you said that my Apple TV uses a wireless connection to my computer!" Indeed I did, good reader, but what if your PC or Mac doesn't have wireless hardware installed? You can either install a wireless network card, or you can run a standard 10/100BASE-T Ethernet cable from your Ethernet switch or router to your Apple TV. Kudos to Apple for providing both wired and wireless connectivity for the Apple TV.

As you might imagine, a wireless Ethernet connection is far more convenient than running Ethernet cabling from your office or computer room to your TV. However, many houses these days are wired already for Ethernet hardware in every room, and most offices have been Ethernet-ready for years. Plus, there's one very important advantage to making a wired network connection to your Apple TV: You get faster transfer speeds than most wireless connections can provide, with no worries about distance from your computer/wireless base station and no interference from sources, like your microwave oven or wireless phone.

The HDMI port

Oh, yes . . . if you're familiar with today's latest home entertainment hardware, you already know this puppy. Virtually all high-definition TVs and A/V receivers have an *HDMI port,* which carries both the video and audio signals to today's state-of-the-art home entertainment components.

Always use an HDMI connection to your Apple TV whenever possible.

'Nuff said — at least until Chapter 7.

The component video jacks

If your TV or A/V receiver doesn't have HDMI, you still can connect your Apple TV by using the component video connectors (sometimes called *RGB,* for the red/green/blue colors used to identify each signal). Although a component video signal doesn't offer quite the quality of an HDMI connection, most of us are hard-pressed to tell the difference.

The analog audio jacks

Most folks call these old favorites *RCA stereo* jacks — one cable for the left channel, one for the right. Analog audio is truly a common denominator, offered on just about anything from your super-powerful A/V receiver to your family's $50 boombox.

The optical audio port

Today's best audio systems rely on optical audio cabling — actually fiber optic — to transmit Dolby Surround and Dolby Digital signals between your A/V receiver (or your Apple TV) and your high-end sound system. This cable is often called a TOSLINK cable.

The front of your Apple TV is considerably less crowded: You find the I/R sensor for the Apple Remote as well as a power indicator/status light.

What's Inside the Box, Anyway?

It's a mystery. No one knows.

Sorry, I couldn't resist. Here's the real skinny on the major components inside your Apple TV's svelte exterior.

The hard drive

Your Apple TV stores the content that it receives from your computer on its own internal hard drive so that your photos, video, and audio are ready on demand. At the time of this writing, the Apple TV's hard drive stores about 40GB, which is about 50 hours of video or 9,000 songs stuffed into that little box.

The Intel CPU

Yep, Intel is inside your Apple TV. Like the latest Macs, the Apple TV unit has its own processor for handling your content requests, as well as overseeing the streaming and syncing between the unit and your computer.

The wireless hardware

Your Apple TV includes the same 802.11n super-fast wireless hardware that's used in today's Macs so that it can join just about any wireless network you set up.

And Here's Your Apple Remote

If you're an owner of a recent Mac computer, you've likely been introduced already to the unique Apple Remote. Like the Front Row menu software that allows you to control your Mac from several feet away, the Apple TV unit has a menu system that you use with the Apple Remote.

I discuss the Apple Remote in detail in Chapter 9 — for now, just avoid getting it mixed up with a pack of gum (or a first-generation iPod Shuffle).

Chapter 2

Installing Your New Entertainment Superstar

In This Chapter

▶ Verifying the minimum requirements

▶ Unpacking your Apple TV properly

▶ Installing iTunes

▶ Choosing the correct spot

▶ Calling for help if you need it

*I*f you're familiar with installing stereo components or external computer toys, like hard drives, you might need only to skim this installation chapter. Fair enough . . . after all, your Apple TV is designed to be plug-and-play.

But are you sure that your TV and your computer are ready for Apple TV? Do you have iTunes installed already on your PC? And what if you need help? No book that's complete would leave you hanging when it comes to installation.

Never fear, this chapter is here just in case! I lead you through the entire process, and you come out smelling like a rose.

Making Sure You Have the Minimum Requirements

Although Apple designed the Apple TV unit to be as compatible and simple as possible, your TV and computer still have to meet certain requirements for you to start streaming. Before you unpack your new toy, check to make sure you have the following:

- ✔ **Mac or PC with a CD or DVD-ROM drive:** You need your computer to buy, download, rip, and convert your media, of course — and a minimum of a CD-ROM drive to rip audio CDs into your iTunes library.

- ✔ **iTunes 7.1 (or higher):** Gotta have it. iTunes not only stores and organizes your content, you use it to specify what to stream to your Apple TV (and to listen and watch stuff on your computer as well).

- ✔ **Mac OS X 10.3.9 or Windows XP Service Pack 2 (or higher):** Your computer must be using the correct operating system. (If not, consider upgrading your operating system to meet the required version.)

- ✔ **An HD (high-definition) or ED (enhanced-definition) TV:** You find more on what constitutes HDTV and EDTV in Chapter 6.

- ✔ **Cables to connect stuff:** Usually this is an HDMI cable, or a combination of a component video cable and either RCA or optical audio cables.

- ✔ **A broadband connection to the Internet:** Okay, so perhaps this isn't an absolute requirement: You can use your Apple TV without buying anything from the iTunes Store and without downloading any content from Web sites. But is that really as much fun? I think not.

- ✔ **Wireless or wired Ethernet network:** Your computer needs either a wireless or wired Ethernet network to stream content to your Apple TV. (If you don't currently have a wireless network set up or you only have a single computer, you can still set up a wireless network if your PC or Mac has wireless Ethernet hardware.)

Oh, and I want to add one more minimum requirement to Apple's list: hard drive space. Lots and *lots* of hard drive space. If you're just getting started building your media library on your computer with iTunes, you'll find that all that music, video, and photographs takes up a considerable amount of space! If you find yourself running short on space, consider upgrading your existing internal hard drive (if possible), adding another internal hard drive (if possible), or adding an external hard drive.

Unpacking 101

"Mark, you're devoting an entire section to unpacking my Apple TV?" Yes, indeed, I am. Granted, this isn't a long section, but I wish I had a dime for every e-mail or phone call I've received from a computer owner who didn't save a cable, an installation CD, or even the box from a new piece of hardware (which turned out to be broken on arrival).

Here's a list of rules that everyone should follow when unpacking *any* computer hardware, including your new Apple TV unit:

- **Give the box a close inspection.** These days, shipping damage is far less likely than it was just a decade ago, but you can't take anything for granted. Before you open your box, check it thoroughly for punctures and crush marks.

- **Save your box and packing materials.** I always recommend that you keep the box and packing materials for at least a year. In fact, an Apple TV has a one-year hardware service warranty, so I definitely recommend keeping your box if you have the space. (Oh, and if you ever decide to sell your Apple TV, the magic phrase *original packaging and manuals* always looks good in your description!)

- **Check your parts list.** Make sure that your box contains what it should, either from a list in the user manual or from a description of the contents on the side of the box. (Paper packaging presents the perfect opportunity to hide small parts.) Luckily, there's not much to lose in your Apple TV box: a single power cable, the Apple Remote, a stash of documents, and the unit itself.

- **Stash your receipt as well as all unused items in the box.** After all, they originally came from there, and you'll know where they are if you need them.

- **Take the time to read the manual.** If you're wondering why you should read the Apple TV mini-manual — and this book — here's a very good explanation: Apple might update the manual with new instructions that supplants what I say at the time of this writing. Remember your training from Hollywood: Without documentation, you'll find out that you should have cut the blue wire *instead* of the red wire. (Ouch.)

Installing iTunes on Your PC

If you're using a Mac, you can probably skip this section with aplomb because every Mac computer that rolls out of Cupertino these days has iTunes installed already.

If you're using a PC, it's easy to download a copy of iTunes — note that QuickTime is also a required installation in order for iTunes to run. There's no cost, no cheesy advertisements, and I think you'll agree that iTunes is probably one of the best media players available these days, so it's a win-win situation!

Follow these steps to download iTunes:

1. **Open your Web browser and head to `www.apple.com/itunes/download`.**

2. **Click the Windows radio button, type your e-mail address, and then click Download iTunes.**

   Depending on your Windows security settings, you may see the dialog, as shown in Figure 2-1, requesting permission to run or save the program — click Run because you don't need to save the iTunes installer program after you're finished.

   After the download completes, you're prompted again for permission to run the installation software; click Run to continue.

   Figure 2-2 illustrates the opening screen of the iTunes Installation Wizard.

Figure 2-1:
Download-
ing iTunes
on a PC.

Figure 2-2:
A hearty
hello from
the iTunes
installation
program.

3. **Click Next and accept the terms of the licensing agreement — thank you, lawyers everywhere.**

   The Installer Options screen appears, as shown in Figure 2-3. The default settings are fine for virtually everyone (and I recommend that you keep them), but feel free to tweak as you find necessary. For example, your Apple TV works fine even if you decide not to make iTunes your default audio file player . . . but I bet that if you invested in an Apple TV unit, you probably want to use iTunes for all your listening and viewing needs.

4. Click Install to start the ball rolling.

After the software is installed, the screen shown in Figure 2-4 appears.

5. Click Finish to exit the installer program (and optionally, launch iTunes for the first time).

Figure 2-3: You can change a number of options while installing iTunes.

Figure 2-4: That was painless, wasn't it?

If you left the Install Desktop Shortcuts check box enabled on the Options screen, you notice that two new icons appear on your Windows desktop: the iTunes icon and the QuickTime Player icon.

If you allow the installer program to launch iTunes, you're presented with more legalese and then the iTunes Setup Assistant appears. Click Next, and you have the chance to

- ✔ **Search your Windows My Music folder for existing music in MP3, AAC, and WMA formats that can be added automatically to your iTunes library.** (Note that the original audio files remain in their original locations . . . iTunes is merely "makin' copies" for your iTunes Music library.)

- ✔ **Enable automatic organization of your iTunes Music folder.** By default, this is turned off because most folks don't like an application renaming and moving files by itself. Again, this behind-the-scenes organization occurs only in your iTunes Music folder . . . and I like a tidy and well-ordered music collection, so I turned on this option. (Go figure.)

- ✔ **Display the iTunes Store, where you can shop and buy audio and video content.** Alternately, you can open iTunes to view and enjoy your content collection. (I cover the iTunes Store in more detail in Chapter 11.)

Click Finish, and you're done. Congratulations, you've installed iTunes!

Picking Just the Right Spot

I'll be honest: Most audio/visual components don't require special placement instructions (other than reserving an AC power socket nearby). The Apple TV unit requires a prime piece of real estate, however, for two good reasons:

- ✔ **The wireless/wired Ethernet connection:** If you're using an 802.11g or 802.11n wireless connection to your Mac or PC, it's a good idea to place your Apple TV unit within about 75 to 100 feet of the broadcasting device (your computer, your router, or a wireless Ethernet access point). Note that different versions of wireless equipment may require shorter distances — for example, if you're using an older 802.11b wireless network, you may have to reduce the distance to get a solid signal. (If all that sounds like Mandarin Chinese to you, don't worry . . . I cover wireless networking like a blanket in Chapter 4 for Macs and Chapter 5 for Windows. I'm thorough that way.) Naturally, a wired connection has no signal strength concerns, but the Apple TV still needs to be within 20 feet or so of an Ethernet port.

If you're using a wireless connection, keep in mind that your attractive art-deco steel-and-aluminum entertainment shelving unit can reduce the signal strength of your connection — therefore, it's always a good idea to place the Apple TV unit on the top shelf or an open space. Don't bury your Apple TV unit beneath or behind your other home entertainment components!

Never stack anything on top of your Apple TV unit! 'Nuff said.

✔ **The Apple Remote:** Your Apple Remote needs a clear line of sight to the Apple TV unit to communicate with it. Also, the distance between the Apple Remote and the Apple TV should be about 30 feet or less. (Your mileage may vary, so feel free to experiment.)

As for heat: Don't worry about it. Your Apple TV unit generates far less heat than a computer.

Connecting Things Up — The Short Story

Making the connections between your Apple TV and your television or A/V receiver is a cinch! Although the basic ports and connections are covered in your Apple TV manual — and reviewed in detail in Chapter 7 — they can be summed up here in just a few paragraphs. To wit:

✔ **If you have an open HDMI connector on your TV or receiver:** Life is Truly Good. Connect an HDMI cable betwixt the HDMI port on the back of your Apple TV unit and your TV or receiver. (Note that your HDMI cable carries audio as well, so unless you're using an external speaker system, you don't need a separate audio connection.)

✔ **If you have component video connectors on your TV or receiver:** Connect the Red/Green/Blue cables between the component video jacks on the back of your Apple TV unit and your TV or receiver. You need a separate audio connection, either through an optical cable or the RCA stereo jacks.

✔ **If you have optical (or TOSLINK) connectors on your TV, receiver, or speaker system:** Using an external speaker system? Connect an optical cable between the optical audio port on the back of your Apple TV unit and your speaker system.

✔ **If you have RCA stereo jacks on your TV, receiver, or speaker system:** To use the left/right channel audio for standard stereo, connect the cables between the RCA stereo jacks on the back of your Apple TV unit and your speaker system.

Was That a Call for Help?

Before I close this chapter, I need to mention the stuff that I hope you don't have to read: That is, the technical support you can call in case something goes wrong with the installation of your Apple TV unit or its software.

At the time of this writing, Apple provides the following resources for Apple TV owners:

- ✔ **The User's Guide:** Apple provides a printed User's Guide in the box.

- ✔ **The Apple Web site Knowledge Base:** This searchable online database contains the answers to hundreds of questions — visit www.apple. com/support/appletv for all the goodness.

- ✔ **Telephone support:** You receive 90 days of complimentary telephone support with your Apple TV. To find the number for your area, visit www. apple.com/support/contact.

- ✔ **User support:** Helpful user discussion forums, which cover all sorts of common problems and solutions, are at www.apple.com/support/app.

Chapter 3

Configuring Your Apple TV

*T*he excitement is building . . . your Apple TV is out of the box, it's connected with all the right cables, and your wired or wireless Ethernet network is ready to serve up all those movies, photos, songs, podcasts, trailers, and who knows what else.

But first, you have to configure your Apple TV, so it can act as the link between your content and your home entertainment system — that means configuring your screen resolution and input signal, and adding your Apple TV to your network. Finally, you have to authorize your Apple TV so that it's recognized by iTunes on your computer.

All that may sound tough to handle, but with this chapter in hand, it's a walk in the park. Grab your Apple Remote and prepare for launch!

But First . . . Selecting Your TV's Input

Although this really isn't an issue with your Apple TV, you won't get far with your streaming superstar without selecting the proper input signal for your TV or A/V receiver. After you make the proper cable connection between your TV and your Apple TV unit, you also need to choose that incoming signal before your TV can display it.

Every TV and A/V receiver handles this chore a little differently — usually it's an onscreen menu that you display by using your TV's remote control. For example, my HDTV's onscreen input menu offers HDMI, Component, S-Video, and Cable/Air input selections. Because I use an HDMI cable connection between my Apple TV unit and my TV, I chose the HDMI input.

Make sure that you choose the input signal corresponding to the cable connection you make to your Apple TV, and you should have no problems.

Step 1: Configuring Your TV's Resolution

The first step you need to take to configure your Apple TV is to select the proper video resolution. The signal provided by your Apple TV must match your TV's high- or enhanced-definition resolution or else the picture appears distorted (or doesn't appear at all).

Make sure all is prepared:

1. Make all the cable connections.
2. Select the proper TV input signal.
3. Turn on both your Apple TV unit and your TV or A/V receiver.

In most cases, you're rewarded immediately with the Apple logo. Congratulations! This indicates that your home entertainment equipment can handle the current resolution just fine, and you can continue to the next section.

If, however, your TV doesn't recognize the incoming signal or the Apple logo looks distorted, use your Apple Remote to switch resolutions. Follow these steps:

1. **Press and hold both the Menu and the plus buttons on the Apple Remote for five or six seconds.**

   Your Apple TV cycles through the different video resolutions it supports.

2. **When the Apple logo and the line of text are displayed correctly, press the Play/Pause button to choose that resolution.**

You can switch resolutions from the Settings menu at any time — for example, if you upgrade your enhanced-definition TV to a high-definition TV in the future, you can switch to a true 1080i signal resolution.

Step 2: Configuring Your Apple TV's Network Settings

After your TV and your Apple TV unit are communicating loud and clear, it's time to get your Apple TV on your wired or wireless network so that the syncing and streaming can begin.

If you're using a wired Ethernet network connection to your Apple TV, you don't see the wireless configuration screens in this section — your Apple TV unit uses the wired network connection automatically.

Follow these steps to set up your Apple TV on your network:

1. **Select a language from the list that appears.**

   Use your Apple Remote to move up and down through the list of languages (as shown in Figure 3-1) — press plus to move up and minus to move down. After you highlight the proper language, press Play/Pause to accept it.

   You can usually move back a step in the process by pressing the Menu button.

   Your Apple TV displays the Wireless Networks screen, as shown in Figure 3-2.

Figure 3-1: Apple TV offers a world's worth of language support.

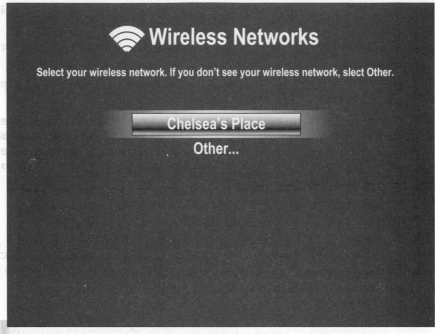

2. **Move the highlight cursor to your wireless connection and press the Play/Pause button to select it.**

   Your Apple TV displays the Wireless Security screen, where you can choose the type of wireless security you're using on your existing network (or the security you set up in Chapters 4 or 5).

   If you don't see your network listed, choose Other and read the sidebar, "Need to join a hidden network?," to find out why you don't see your network on this screen.

Need to join a hidden network?

If your wireless network doesn't automatically identify itself — by broadcasting the network name you assigned to it — it's a *hidden* network. In general, hiding your network from outsiders is a good thing, especially if you're living in a dorm or apartment building and you want to take an extra step to ensure that your data and your Internet connection remain private.

However, a hidden network also doesn't announce itself to your Apple TV, so it doesn't show up on the Wireless Networks screen. That's when you need to choose the Other . . . option from the menu and use your Apple Remote to enter the name of your hidden network. (Remember, the capitalization is important.) Choose Done, and you can continue with the security key entry.

3. **Move the highlight cursor to the security protocol you're using and press the Play/Pause button to select it.**

   No security key? If you've decided not to use encryption, your Apple TV networking configuration is finished.

   If your wireless network requires a security key for access, a password entry screen appears, as shown in Figure 3-3.

4. **Use the plus/minus/previous/next buttons on your Apple Remote to move the highlight cursor and then press the Play/Pause button to choose each letter in the password.** When you've entered the entire password, move the highlight cursor to DONE at the bottom of the screen and press Play/Pause to continue.

   Uppercase is different from lowercase!

5. **Your Apple TV unit connects to your wireless network.**

After you're connected, you see the mondo-cool Apple TV introductory video. Success! Now you can move to the next section, which links your Apple TV with your computer's copy of iTunes.

Figure 3-3: Entering a wireless security key.

Step 3: Configuring iTunes for Apple TV

Rejoice: Your Apple TV is now on your wired or wireless Ethernet network, ready to receive your content from your computer and your iTunes library! However, iTunes isn't just going to stream your valuable stuff to just any Apple TV it encounters — pretty wise, if you think about it — so it's time for you to authorize your Apple TV for use with your copy of iTunes.

Oh, and you get to name your Apple TV unit. I named mine *Otis,* but my oldest daughter keeps renaming it *Tenacious D* to mess with my head. Go figure.

1. **Run iTunes on your computer and click the Apple TV entry in the Devices section of the source list.**

   Figure 3-4 shows the passcode entry screen in iTunes.

2. **Type the passcode displayed by your Apple TV (see Figure 3-5) to authorize your copy of iTunes.**

   No need to press Enter or Return.

   With the correct passcode, you see the screen in Figure 3-6: It allows you to name your Apple TV unit. If you have multiple Apple TVs hanging around your domicile, this can become important . . . otherwise, feel free to choose something like *Otis.* (Or just leave it with the default name of Apple TV.)

Figure 3-4: iTunes demands that pesky passcode.

Connect to iTunes

To finish setup and sync your iTunes content to your Apple TV, open iTunes and select Apple TV from the Devices list. You will need to enter this passcode.

5 7 9 6 8

To use Apple TV for streaming only, press Menu and choose "Connect to iTunes" from the Sources menu.

Apple TV requires iTunes 7.1 or later

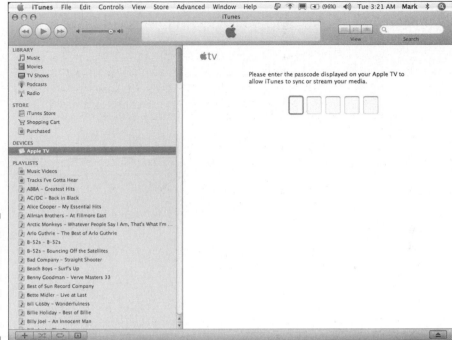

Figure 3-5:
Your Apple
TV displays
a passcode
for iTunes
autho-
rization.

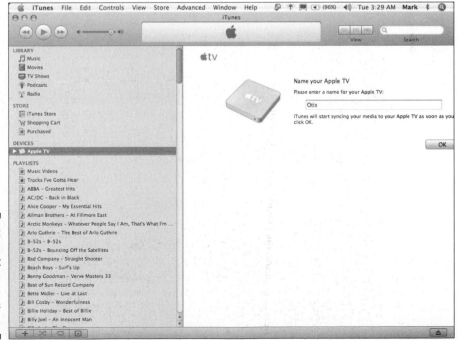

Figure 3-6:
And you
thought
choosing a
name for a
child was
hard . . . .

Do I really need to register?

In a word: *Yes. Do it.* Even if you don't normally register your hardware, anyone who's owned a Mac or an iPod can tell you that Apple can be pretty strict on providing support to customers who haven't registered. (That's not a bad thing, necessarily, it's just that you won't receive any help without that all-important registration.)

The Apple TV registration site is displayed within the iTunes window as soon as you finish naming your Apple TV unit. You don't have to provide an Apple customer ID to register, so you can still register even if you haven't created an iTunes Store account.

3. Type a name for your Apple TV unit and click OK.

Now sit back and relax while your Apple TV begins the syncing process with your iTunes library. If you want to monitor the syncing process, check out the iTunes track display, which shows you how much has been sent and displays the current item being transferred. *This* is why you bought your new toy!

Accessing the Settings Menu

You, good reader, are set! Stuff is syncing, and you can get down to the pure enjoyment contained in the rest of the book. But linger just one more section in this chapter because I want to introduce you to a menu that will become very, very familiar to you in a short period of time: the Apple TV Settings menu. Because I'm discussing configuration in this chapter, an introduction to the Settings menu is very apropos.

To display the Settings menu, press Menu on your Apple Remote until you're backed out all the way to the top-level Apple TV menu (as shown in Figure 3-7). Then move the selection cursor to the Settings menu and press Play/Pause to display the entries, as shown in Figure 3-8.

I refer to the Settings menu throughout the rest of the book, so take a look right now at the major headings it offers:

✔ **About:** This screen displays identifying information and statistics about your Apple TV, like the total capacity and how much space remains, the software version you're running, the connection and resolution you're using, and the signal strength of your wireless network connection.

Figure 3-7:
The top-
level menu
features the
cool Apple
TV logo.

✔ **TV Resolution:** Choose this Settings menu item to run the Resolution Selection Wizard, as I cover in the section, "Step 1: Configuring Your TV's Resolution," at the beginning of this chapter.

✔ **Network:** The items in this menu allow you to run the Wireless Configuration Wizard again, as well as to manually configure your TCP/IP settings. (In general, you shouldn't have to manually set your network configuration, but if an Apple technician or your office network administrator needs to tweak settings, you can do it here.)

✔ **Screen Saver:** Choose this Settings menu item to change and preview your screen saver setting, including the inactivity delay (in seconds) before the screen saver starts.

✔ **Repeat Music:** Turn this menu item on to repeat the current playlist until you exit with the Apple Remote.

✔ **Sound Check:** A favorite setting of mine: Turn Sound Check on, and your Apple TV makes sure that all the volume levels within each music track remain constant. (Think Air Supply followed by Black Sabbath.)

✔ **Sound Effects:** Choose this setting to mute all those subtle beeps, clicks, and boops while you're moving through the Apple TV menu system.

✔ **HDMI Brightness:** If your Apple TV has an HDMI connection to your TV, you can choose either a low or high brightness setting for your display.

✔ **Pair Remote:** This menu item allows you to pair your Apple Remote to your Apple TV, making sure that the commands you send with that remote are recognized only by your Apple TV. (I talk about this in detail in Chapter 9.)

✔ **Update Software:** Choose this menu item, and your Apple TV "phones home" to Apple to see if any software updates can be installed.

✔ **Language:** Choose this menu item to select the onscreen language, as I demonstrate in the section, "Step 2: Configuring Your Apple TV's Network Settings," earlier in this chapter.

✔ **Legal:** Oh, boy, this Settings menu item displays all the legalese and copyright information pertaining to your Apple TV. Great fun at parties.

✔ **Reset Settings:** If you're experiencing problems with your Apple TV unit, choose this menu item to restore all the settings on the Settings menu to their default values.

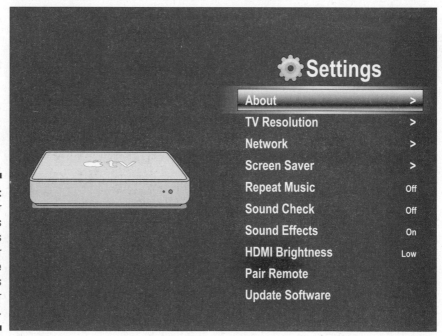

Figure 3-8:
Your
Settings
menu offers
control over
all the
features
of your
Apple TV.

Part II
Connecting Your Apple TV

The 5th Wave   By Rich Tennant

WARREN COULDN'T WAIT TO HOOK UP HIS NEW APPLE TV DEVICE TO HIS 52" FLAT PANEL HDTV DINNER

Dot's Veal Cutlet Peas and Yams

In this part . . .

Time to dive deeper into multimedia hardware and today's hottest home entertainment components! You find out how to set up a simple wireless network on the PC and Mac, and make the connection between your Apple TV and your TV set. You also find out all the details on today's high-definition TVs and state-of-the-art speaker systems.

Chapter 4

Creating an Apple Wireless Network

*Y*our Apple TV craves communication. Streaming and syncing content requires a constant flow of information between iTunes on your Mac and your Apple TV — therefore, in this chapter, I focus on the network connection of choice, an 802.11n wireless link between the two.

What's that? I just spoke French, and not particularly well? More like engineer-speak, or techno-gibberish! (I've heard it called both. And worse.) That's another aim of this chapter: to provide you with honest-to-goodness descriptions of today's wireless networking in everyday English. In just a few pages, I turn you into a network administrator, and you get your Mac connected to the wireless world. (Oh, and don't worry . . . you don't have to give up your *real* job. You can grow a beard if you like, though.)

Recognizing Wireless Standards in the Wild

Before setting up a connection, consider the wireless standards you're working with and whether your Mac's current wireless hardware (if any) is suited to the best performance with your Apple TV. Luckily, your Apple TV's wireless hardware is state-of-the-art, and it can connect to just about any wireless network on the planet . . . but some of the technologies I discuss in this section don't deliver content as fast as others.

(Feel free to photocopy this list and stick it on your fridge door.)

IEEE 802.11b

IEEE 802.11b has another name that you'll likely see on product advertisements, literature, or boxes in stores: *Wi-Fi,* or *Wireless Fidelity.* (Kinda like that cutting-edge Hi-Fi stereo from the '60s and '70s, where *Hi-Fi* stands for *High Fidelity.*) Most folks proclaim Wi-Fi as only 802.11b. Wi-Fi was the first version of wireless Ethernet. This version of wireless runs at speeds up to 11 million bits per second, or 11 Mbps. The reason why I say that it runs at speeds *up to* 11Mbps is because the actual speed that the data is transferred depends on things like signal strength and quality. When the conditions are such that your signal strength or quality is decreased — such as an inconvenient concrete wall between you and your Apple TV — you might find that your wireless connection slows to 5.5 Mbps, 2 Mbps, or even 1 Mbps.

Unfortunately, an 802.11b connection to your Apple TV results in some pretty doggone slow syncing and streaming — longer wait times before you can watch a movie or before your music selections are available for your listening pleasure. (Most things still work, just much slower than you might prefer. However, you can't stream movies and video over an 802.11b connection.) Therefore, I recommend that you avoid using an 802.11b connection unless you have no other choice — if possible, consider upgrading your network to at least the 802.11g standard, or 802.11n if possible. This might involve replacing your AirPort Base Station or adding a new USB 2.0 wireless network device to your Mac.

All older wireless Ethernet equipment, including Apple's older AirPort network cards and AirPort Base Station, used 802.11b. In fact, it's time for Mac owners to swell with pride yet again: Apple was the first computer company to ship 802.11b hardware. (Back then, in 1999, it was the original AirPort Base Station.) Now, of course, Apple has raised the bar with the 802.11n AirPort Extreme Base Station.

In general, Wi-Fi network cards can communicate with other Wi-Fi devices that are up to 1,000 feet away. Having said that, realize that 1,000 feet is a generous estimate when outdoors on a clear day with no wind blowing — you see what I'm getting at. In reality, when you set up your wireless network, things such as walls — especially concrete walls, like in basements — decrease the distance that you can cover. Plan on no more than 100 feet between your wireless Mac or base station and your Apple TV . . . as they say in the car ads, your mileage might vary.

Wireless Ethernet network bandwidth is shared between all computers using it . . . in English, that means that if you have a lot of people on your wireless network, the network can and does get noticeably slower.

One last thing about 802.11b networking: Wi-Fi uses the 2.4 GHz frequency range. It actually uses 11 different channels, but they're all around the 2.4 GHz range. I bring this up because if you're using a 2.4 GHz cordless phone or even a microwave, using either device can definitely interfere with or even shut down your wireless network. Keep this in mind when you buy your next phone or wonder why your streaming slows down when you're communing with Orville Redenbacher in the microwave.

802.11a

For years, I've wondered why *802.11a* was the *second* wireless Ethernet standard to arrive. No, I didn't get my letters mixed up. Thanks to my technical editor for this book, I've finally learned why 802.11b came out first, and 802.11a came out next: It turns out the working group for the 802.11a wireless standard got started before the 802.11b group, but they finished a couple of months after the 802.11b group! You learn something new every day in the world of computing. Anyway, 802.11a doesn't have a generally recognized handy nickname, like Wi-Fi, so just call it 802.11a.

802.11a isn't all that much different than Wi-Fi, but the few differences make a big impact. First off, 802.11a ran at speeds up to 54 Mbps — almost *five times* faster than Wi-Fi. This is because 802.11a used the 5 GHz frequency range instead of the cluttered 2.4 GHz range that Wi-Fi uses. The powers that be set aside the 5 GHz range just for wireless networking, so cordless phones and microwaves (or any other wireless devices, for that matter) can't interfere with the network. The downside to using the higher 5 GHz range, though, is that the distances that can be covered are even less than that of Wi-Fi — no more than about 60 feet to maintain the highest speeds.

Unfortunately, 802.11a equipment wasn't compatible with Wi-Fi, so it died a quick death in the marketplace and was speedily replaced by the more compatible 802.11g. 802.11a hardware can work with your Apple TV, but you might not be able to communicate with other computers that try to join your network. If possible, I recommend that you follow the wireless course charted by Apple, and use the 802.11g standard (which is backward-compatible with Wi-Fi) or the 802.11n standard (which is fastest, and best-suited to your Apple TV).

802.11g

Although some hardware manufacturers designed equipment that handles both Wi-Fi and 802.11a, Apple's release of the original AirPort Extreme wireless hardware provided both the speed of 802.11a and the compatibility with Wi-Fi. That's because it uses the *802.11g* standard, which operates at speeds up to 54 Mbps (like 802.11a) but also operates at the same frequency ranges and plays nicely with existing 802.11b equipment. (Notice that the naming conventions are now going in the right direction again. Go figure.)

Oh, and did I mention that Apple was once again the *first* company to offer 802.11g hardware as standard equipment? Feel free to enjoy the Superiority Dance yet again while you use AirPort Extreme.

Naturally, 802.11g has a downside: It returns to that pesky 2.4 GHz range, so your cordless phone and microwave can also wreak the same havoc that they did with your original AirPort equipment.

802.11g hardware is a good match for your Apple TV, and it's what I consider the minimum for best compatibility and streaming speed. If you're using a Mac that was manufactured within the last three years or so or you're using an Apple Extreme Base Station, you're covered. Breathe easier!

802.11n

The latest standard to appear is 802.11n, which is used in all current Mac models, the Apple TV, and the latest Apple Extreme Base Station. 802.11n offers the best speed (up to four times faster than 802.11g under real-world conditions) and the best compatibility with all the previous standards. In fact, 802.11n hardware can work with both 2.4 GHz and 5 GHz signals. It handles 'em all!

It's important to note, however, that 802.11n networks work at their top efficiency when *only* 802.11n hardware is in use — that's because your 802.11n hotrod hardware has to slow down (or even shift frequencies) to work with other standards. If you're using your Apple TV on a network with a new AirPort Extreme Base Station and a Mac of recent vintage, for example, you see significantly faster streaming times than you would with a mixed hodgepodge of 802.11b, 802.11g, and 802.11n hardware.

Is it worth upgrading from 802.11a or 802.11b to a full 802.11n network? *Definitely.* Upgrading from an 802.11g network is more problematic — you get significant speed gains across your whole network, but you should weigh the cost involved against the luxury of lightning-fast streaming and syncing with your Apple TV.

Here's a Mark's Maxim that you probably already guessed . . . but it bears stating anyway!

802.11n is the best on the block . . . and it's worth the upgrade from older stuff.

Do I Need to Buy Any Hardware?

I can answer this common question with another common question: What type of wireless network do you already have, if any? Depending on your answer, I explore the possibilities in this section.

I already have an existing wireless network set up

You should be able to use your existing hardware without any problem — however, if you're using an older 802.11b network, you may want to consider upgrading your base station and hardware (as I mention in the preceding section). I'm assuming that your wireless network is also supplying you with a broadband Internet connection so that you can download content and buy media from the iTunes Store.

Probably the most popular way to simultaneously create a network and share an Internet connection is to buy a hardware device that connects to your Internet connection, which then acts as the base station for your wireless network. These devices are *wireless cable/DSL routers.* The main downside to a hardware Internet connection-sharing device is that it costs more than a software solution.

Wireless cable/DSL routers are nice because they're easy to set up and configure. You can also leave them on, which means constant Internet access for those on your network (including your Apple TV). You don't have to worry about leaving your Mac turned on to connect to the Internet like you do with a software solution. Sounds like a good spot for a Mark's Maxim:

Hardware routers are the best choice for sharing your Internet connection, so if you can afford one, get one!

I have a Mac with wireless hardware

If your Mac has either internal 802.11g or 802.11n wireless hardware — which covers pretty much the entire Apple product line now and has for a year or two now — but you *don't* have a network with a wireless base station or Internet sharing device set up, you're not out of luck! You can use your Apple TV wirelessly by setting up an Internet sharing Ad Hoc network. I describe how to set up one later in the chapter.

I have a Mac without wireless hardware

You need to add a minimum of an AirPort Extreme wireless card to your Mac to connect to your Apple TV. Alternately, you could go the wired route and use an Ethernet cable to connect the two. (If you've set up an existing wired Ethernet network, you can simply run the cable from your Apple TV to an open Ethernet port on your switch or Internet router.)

For those looking to a wired connection, a simple 5, 10, or 25 feet Ethernet Cat5 cable — available at any Maze o' Wires electronic discount store — is all you need. The cable connects directly from your Mac to your Apple TV, and you can immediately head to iTunes and select your Apple TV in the Devices list.

Setting Up a Wireless Connection

An Internet sharing Ad Hoc network — also called a *computer-to-computer* network — is a fairly easy thing to accomplish in Mac OS X. Plus, you're not limited to just Macs: With an Ad Hoc network, you can also swap niceties with PCs and PDAs that have 802.11 network hardware, as well as your Apple TV. Besides your Apple TV connection, an Ad Hoc network is great for setting up an impromptu network in a classroom, exchanging recipes and pictures at a family reunion in a park, or blowing up your friend while gaming across the aisle of a Greyhound bus at 70 mph.

To set up an Internet sharing Ad Hoc network, you must create the computer-to-computer network on one of your Macs — in effect, turning it into a software-only, "virtual" base station. To create a computer-to-computer network for your Apple TV, follow these steps:

1. **Click the System Preferences icon on the Dock.**

2. **Click the Sharing icon.**

3. **Click the Internet tab of the Sharing dialog.**

   The settings shown in Figure 4-1 appear.

4. **Click the AirPort Options button.**

   Figure 4-2 shows the dialog that appears.

5. **Type a name into the Network Name box.**

6. **Click the Enable Encryption (Using WEP) check box to enable it.**

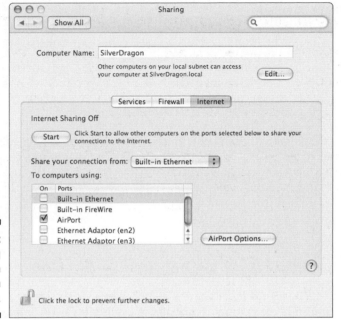

Figure 4-1:
The Sharing
pane in
System
Preferences.

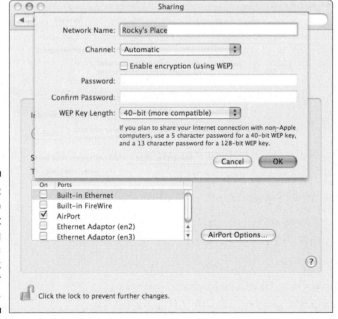

Figure 4-2:
Setting up
an Internet
sharing
Ad Hoc
network
for your
Apple TV.

7. **Click the WEP Key Length pop-up list box and choose the 40-bit key length setting.**

   Jot down the password you enter here for the configuration process in Chapter 3 — and yes, capitalization does count.

8. **Click OK.**

9. **Click the Share Your Connection From pop-up list and choose Built-in Ethernet.**

10. **Select the AirPort check box (in the To Computers Using list) to enable it.**

    After you do, you're issued a warning that enabling this could affect your ISP or violate your agreement with your ISP. In my experiences, this step has never caused any networking problems. However, if you have any doubts, contact your ISP and verify this.

11. **Click OK in the warning dialog to continue.**

    You go back to the Sharing dialog, which now has a Start button.

12. **Click Start to enable Internet sharing.**

    The Start button changes to a Stop button as shown in Figure 4-3 — but that's for your future use. When you close the System Preferences window, your network remains running (even after your Mac is rebooted or restarted).

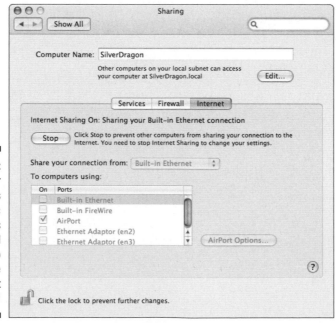

Figure 4-3:
Your wireless Ad Hoc network is online and ready to share the Internet love!

13. Click the Close button to close the System Preferences window.

If you haven't set Mac OS X to display your AirPort status in the Finder menu bar, open the Network pane in System Preferences, click the Show pop-up menu, and choose the AirPort entry. You see the Show AirPort Status in Menu Bar check box — click it to enable this feature, and then click Close to close System Preferences.

With your wireless network set up, you can proceed — in reverse — to Chapter 3, if you want to set up iTunes for your Apple TV streaming connection.

Chapter 5

Creating a Windows Wireless Network

. . . .

In This Chapter

▶ Mapping out the PC-to-Apple TV connection

▶ Checking for required hardware

▶ Configuring a wireless Ad Hoc network under Windows Vista and XP

. . . .

*I*n Chapter 4, I discuss the wireless communications network that you can set up to link a Mac to an Apple TV — and in this chapter, PC owners get their due! I demonstrate how to set up a wireless Ad Hoc network between a PC running Windows XP or Vista and an Apple TV.

Being the proud PC owner that you are, I bet that you probably skipped Chapter 4 like it was a minefield. However, I recommend you venture there before continuing with this chapter so that you can familiarize yourself with the descriptions of the different wireless standards I provide in Chapter 4. (That saves me repeating myself here.) You can stop reading when I start the step-by-step procedure for creating a wireless network on the Mac and then return here.

One warning: If you read all of Chapter 4, you realize just how much the Mac and the PC have in common. (A secret among us techno-wizards!)

Sharing Information the Windows Way

Done reading about 802.11b through 802.11n in Chapter 4? Good, because I skip right to the good stuff in this chapter.

All versions of Windows Vista can make use of an Ad Hoc network. The network allows your PC running iTunes to stream content to your Apple TV — and also allows other computers (both PCs and Macs) to connect and transfer files with your PC. Plus, you don't need several pounds of additional hardware that's required to build a full-scale Ethernet network (no Ethernet switch or router is necessary); just the network hardware for your PC.

Again, you have the option of choosing either a *wireless* network connection to your Apple TV (which is far more convenient, but slower) or a *wired* network connection (which entails the hassle of cabling, of course, but eliminates problems with distance and interference, and allows a significantly faster connection). As you can tell by the title of this chapter, I focus on a wireless connection, just like Apple does.

If you're currently using an Internet sharing device, an Ethernet switch, or an Ethernet router to provide broadband Internet to your PC, you actually already have a network in place, and your Apple TV can simply jump right in to the party.

If you do choose a wired connection, you need a single Cat5 Ethernet cable of the proper length to stretch between your PC (or switch/router/sharing device) and your Apple TV. If your PC is connected already to a wired network, plug the cable from your Apple TV to an open port on the switch, router, or sharing device.

By design (as you see in following chapters), iTunes works the same for both PC and Mac, so you don't need a separate set of instructions to follow to use your Apple TV.

What Hardware Is Required?

Your PC's current wireless hardware — and network, if you have one — provides the answer to this question. This section takes your options one at a time.

I already have an existing wireless network

Excellent! If you're using 802.11g or 802.11n hardware (a base station, switch, router, or Internet sharing device), you don't need to add anything else. (Folks still using older 802.11b hardware may want to invest in a new 802.11n network adapter, as well as a new base station or sharing device. You get much faster streaming if you use 802.11n hardware throughout your network, especially on those huge movie files you send betwixt your PC and your Apple TV unit.)

I have a PC with wireless hardware, but no network

Most PCs produced in the last couple of years have either internal 802.11g or 802.11n wireless hardware, which works perfectly with your Apple TV using an Ad Hoc network. (Step-by-step instructions on setting things up appear at the end of this chapter.)

My PC has no wireless hardware

If your PC doesn't come equipped with wireless hardware (and you'd rather use a wireless connection than a wired cable connection), you need to install a wireless Ethernet adapter card in your PC. (Make sure it's an 802.11n card, and you'll thank me vociferously later.)

If you're using a PC laptop and you can't add wireless hardware through your PC Card slots, consider a USB 2.0 external wireless adapter. For example, the N1 Wireless Adapter from Belkin (www.belkin.com), as shown in Figure 5-1, is a great example of an 802.11n external solution. This sells online for around $70 and provides your Apple TV with the content it craves at the fastest wireless speeds.

Figure 5-1: A typical external 802.11n wireless adapter that uses a USB 2.0 port.

Setting Up a Wireless Connection under Windows

If you're already using an existing wireless network under Windows XP or Vista, pat yourself on the back and go grab another soda: Your Apple TV connects like any other computer or network-ready device, so you're done.

If you aren't currently using a wireless network, don't despair — you'll be cele-brating soon enough! You can create an Ad Hoc (or *computer-to-computer* net-work) that allows direct communication between your PC and your Apple TV.

Other computers and wireless devices can join in on your Ad Hoc network, but I don't recommend it over the long haul. If you're going to create a perma-nent wireless network for more than just your Apple TV, you need to set up a full Ethernet network using a wireless base station, router, switch, or Internet sharing device. Why? Well, an Ad Hoc network isn't as efficient or as fast as an *infrastructure* network, where the base station handles the traffic between three or more devices. (The Ad Hoc network is more like a CB radio conver-sation, where anyone can jump in at once. Not very efficient, and speed sig-nificantly drops when everyone is talking at the same time.)

First, check to make sure that your PC's wireless adapter is set for Ad Hoc (not Infrastructure) mode. Your network adapter's software allows you to set this option, so check the documentation for your wireless adapter.

Creating the network under Windows Vista

Okay, is your wireless hardware ready? Then get to work. To set up an Ad Hoc network under Windows Vista, follow these steps on your PC:

1. **Choose Start⇨Connect To.**

   Vista displays the Connect to a Network dialog, as shown in Figure 5-2.

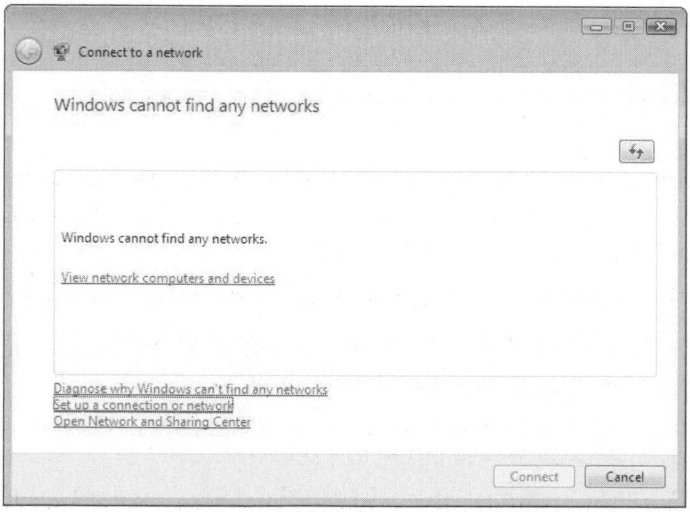

Connect to a network

Windows cannot find any networks

Windows cannot find any networks.

View network computers and devices

Diagnose why Windows can't find any networks
Set up a connection or network
Open Network and Sharing Center

Connect   Cancel

Figure 5-2:
Your PC
starts out
lonely.

2. **Click the Set Up a Connection or Network link.**

   The Connection Option dialog opens.

3. **Click the Set Up an Ad Hoc (Computer-to-Computer) Network and click Next.**

4. **Click Next on the information screen.**

   By the way, you may see a note on this screen stating that your Ad Hoc connection can reach only 30 feet. That's for Bluetooth networking, so you can grin quietly to yourself and ignore it. Also, your connection won't be temporary — you'll fix that.

5. **Type a name for your new network in the Network Name text box (see Figure 5-3).**

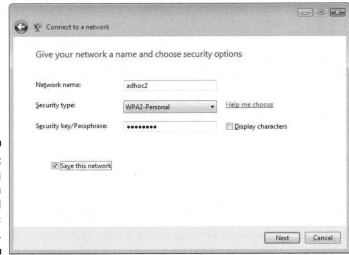

Figure 5-3:
Entering information for an Ad Hoc network.

6. **Click the Security Type pop-up menu and choose WPA2-Personal.**

   Your Apple TV doesn't work with other encryption standards, so *make sure* that you pick WPA2-Personal!

7. **Click in the Security Key/Passphrase text box and enter a password key.**

   Jot down this password key for your Apple TV setup.

8. **Click the Save This Network check box to enable it.**

   Again, this is a must-do — otherwise, your Ad Hoc network isn't available the next time you reboot your PC.

9. **Click Next to display the closing wizard screen and then click Close.**

Creating the network under Windows XP

If you haven't upgraded to Windows Vista, no need to panic: Your Apple TV is perfectly happy communicating with Windows XP (and sharing the Internet wirelessly) as well!

I assume you already have a broadband connection to the Internet set up on your PC — if you don't have a broadband connection yet, it's time to invest the time and money to locate an Internet Service Provider in your area who can hook you up with a fast connection. After your broadband service is up and running on your PC, you're ready to continue.

Follow these steps on your PC:

1. **Choose Start⇨Connect To, right-click the Internet connection that you want to share, and then choose Properties.**

   The Properties window appears.

2. **Click the Advanced tab.**

3. **Select the Allow Other Network Users to Connect through This Computer's Internet Connection check box to enable it.**

   If the Allow Other Network Users to Connect through This Computer's Internet Connection check box doesn't appear, don't lose heart! Most ISP technician gurus create a simple network during the installation of their Internet service — however, even if your installation didn't include the creation of a network, you can manually run the XP Network Setup Wizard to create an Ad Hoc network.

   a. *To run the wizard, choose Start⇨Connect To.*

   b. *Choose Show All Connections, and then click the Set Up a Home or Small Office Network link.*

   c. *Follow the prompts displayed by the wizard, and make sure that you enable the This Is a Computer-to-Computer (Ad Hoc) Network check box.*

4. **Click OK to save your changes and return to the XP desktop.**

   Windows XP indicates that a connection is shared by adding a friendly looking cupped hand under the connection icon.

If you haven't already, look at Chapter 3, where you can set up iTunes for your Apple TV streaming connection.

Chapter 6

Adding High-Definition and Super Sound

- -

- -

*F*ifteen years or so ago, everything was easy.

You had a TV — there was only one kind, with no silly acronyms to remember. You had a VCR, and it took one kind of tape. Your PC used two speakers, and you only needed to worry about one kind of monitor, too. (You probably couldn't afford a CD-ROM drive yet, but you were dreaming of one.)

These days, you might need a consultant at your local Maze O' Wires electronics store to help you figure out what connects to your Apple TV. Or, if you're lucky, you know someone in your family who has memorized all those cables, acronyms, and standards. Otherwise, you could spend hundreds of dollars on stuff that doesn't work well with your shiny new Content Connection.

We can't return to a simpler time, so this chapter provides you with the same information about high-definition TV and superior PC audio that an (honest) salesperson or your (knowledgeable) brother-in-law would give you while shopping.

High-Definition Explained

High-definition is all about three improvements that have been made to the standard broadcast, cable and satellite TV signal you've known and loved since your birth. Yep, there are only three real differences. (Refreshing to move aside all the techno-babble, isn't it?) Those improvements are

- ✔ **The picture is far higher in resolution.** An HDTV signal is far superior in *resolution* (the number of scan lines displayed by a TV or monitor). The higher the number of scan lines, the greater the amount of detail and the sharper the image. More on scan lines in a paragraph or two.

- ✔ **The picture can use a different aspect ratio.** HDTV signals are typically displayed in a *widescreen* format, or *16:9,* which indicates the stretched aspect ratio of length to height. The screens at most movie theaters are 16:9 aspect ratio as well. On the other hand, a standard TV uses a 4:3 ratio, so it's far closer to being square. (Unintentional pun, but it works.) Figure 6-1 shows the difference between these two aspect ratios.

- ✔ **HDTV is digital.** Virtually all HDTV signals are digital, so they're static-free and carry all sorts of additional goodies that a standard analog broadcast signal can't.

Figure 6-1:
A comparison between the two most common aspect ratios.

4:3 / 1.33:1 Standard TV and older movies	16:9 / 1.78:1 US Digital TV (HDTV)

As an acronym, the politically correct spelling is HDTV, without the dash. When the entire term is written out, it appears as *high-definition television*, with the dash. (You can promptly forget that because everyone recognizes what you're talking about, with or without dashes.)

Oh, and get this: Someone somewhere decided that standard analog TV needed a fancy-sounding acronym as well! (Probably a salesperson who wanted to leave you more confused.) Anyway, a standard interlaced TV signal is now also called *SDTV,* for *standard-definition TV.* It's also often referred to as an NTSC (National Television Standards Committee) analog signal in the United States. Sheesh.

Another format — *digital television,* or DTV — is broadcast digitally, and it offers the same 4:3 aspect ratio as analog SDTV and a 16:9 ratio as well. Naturally, digital TV images don't suffer from static or ghosting, but otherwise, the resolution is the same.

Oh, and don't forget EDTV, which is short for *enhanced-definition television.* The EDTV format is a subset of DTV signals, providing 480 or 576 lines in a progressive scan image, so you can consider it a good middle ground between SDTV and HDTV. (More on interlaced and progressive scan images in a moment.)

Your Apple TV unit requires a widescreen HDTV or EDTV unit for display.

Resolution in today's TVs is expressed as the vertical component of its resolution (that's the second number after the "x"), so a TV that can provide 1920 x 1080 resolution has a resolution of 1080.

Table 6-1 provides the scan lines for all four popular TV resolutions so that you can see the difference.

Table 6-1	TV Resolutions in a Nutshell			
Name	**Signal Type**	**Number of Scan Lines**	**Aspect Ratio**	**Resolution**
SDTV	Analog	480	4:3	720 x 480
EDTV	Digital	480 or 576	4:3 or 16:9	704 x 480 or 720 x 480
DTV	Digital	480 or 16:9	4:3	704 x 480 or 640 x 480
HDTV	Digital	1080i (interlaced) or 720p (progressive)	16:9	1920 x 1080i (interlaced) or 1280 x 720p (progressive)

Of course, an EDTV or HDTV television can also display good old analog signals, just like an SDTV set — as long as it has an NTSC/analog tuner. However, you don't get the better resolutions that I list in Table 6-1, which are reserved for digital signals.

"Wait a minute, Mark, what do *interlaced* and *progressive* mean?" Good question. You won't like the answer much, though, if you're already developing a headache because there are actually two types of HDTV sets:

- ✔ A **progressive** image is handled just like a computer monitor, resulting in a better quality picture although the resolution might actually be inferior to an interlaced signal. The image is built just like the text on this page, line by line, moving from the top of the screen to the bottom, as shown in Figure 6-2. A progressive-scan TV carries an appended *p* to the resolution figure.

- ✔ An **interlaced** image, on the other hand, is drawn in two sets of alternating rows — odd and even — across your screen. To avoid flickering, the image has to be refreshed many times a second (hence the term *refresh rate*). The faster the refresh rate for an interlaced system, the better it looks. An interlaced-scan TV is designated by an *i* following the resolution figure.

Figure 6-2:
A progressive-scan image.

If you've spent hours staring at a CRT PC monitor or a standard SDTV screen with a lower refresh rate, you've no doubt experienced the eyestrain associated with interlacing. (Some people can even distinguish the interlacing effect at lower refresh rates, especially under fluorescent lighting, and they'll get a smashing headache if they spend too much time looking at such a screen.)

The progressive versus interlaced question comes down to two points:

- ✔ **Most HDTV televisions and monitors use a progressive image.** *PC CRT monitors* (the old clunkers that look like TVs), *SDTV* (standard definition analog television) sets, and 1080i broadcast HDTV sets use interlaced-scan technology.

  All the high-tech technologies that appeal to PC and TV owners — think LCD, DLP, and plasma — are progressive-scan.

- ✔ **Progressive sets cost more.** This is why LCD, DLP, and plasma TVs are more expensive: They need extra hardware to de-interlace an interlaced HDTV broadcast signal. However, most viewers can tell a slight increase in detail (especially when there's movement onscreen) with a 720p progressive display, so progressive has the definite advantage.

If you need a refresher course in today's display technologies, Chapter 7 covers the different types of monitors and TV sets that'll cost you a king's ransom.

Talking about PAL and SECAM

"At least everyone around the world has the same signal standard, right, Mark? You mentioned it earlier. I think it was NTSC."

Oh, dear reader, if it was only that simple.

You see, NTSC is really the signal standard only within the United States, Japan, and part of South America. Australia, most of Europe, Africa, and the Far East use a signal standard called *PAL* (short for *Phase Alternation Line*), and the countries that were once part of the Soviet Union (as well as a handful of others) use a signal standard called *SECAM* (from the French term that translates to *Sequential Color with Memory*).

Your Apple TV supports NTSC and PAL sets.

And here's the kicker: These three signal formats are almost completely incompatible with each other. Because you may also hook up an entertainment PC to your TV, I need to warn you about SSI (short for Signal Standard Inconveniences).

The DVD problem

Have you ever noticed the signal mark on the back of a DVD case? If you buy the disc in the United States, it reads NTSC. However, if you buy an imported DVD movie through eBay or a Web store, it might have the PAL signal mark, indicating that it's meant to be played on PAL TV equipment.

Unfortunately, DVDs created for use on PAL equipment usually don't work on older NTSC DVD players sold within the United States. Because of this problem (and the furor it generated from DVD owners around the world), engineers got to work and took care of things. Most of the current crop of DVD players can actually handle both PAL and NTSC discs, but very few can handle SECAM.

If you have an older DVD player that doesn't accept PAL discs, keep your eye on the back cover of the disc box for the NTSC logo.

That's the scoop for DVD players. But what about your entertainment PC's DVD drive? On a PC, the signal compatibility of a DVD is handled by your region-code setting within Windows; most stand-alone DVD players are also region-code specific. For example, the United States is within Region 1, but Britain uses Region 2. (A DVD's region code is printed on the back of the DVD case.) A Region 0 (zero) disc can be played on any DVD player or PC DVD drive worldwide: They're effectively region-free.

You can certainly watch a Region 2 disc on your entertainment PC, using your DVD drive and a software DVD player. However, keep this dire warning in mind: *You can change DVD regions only a maximum of four times (on a PC) or five times (on a Mac), and that's it.* Each time you change the region, it remains that way until you change it again. This built-in limit is designed to prevent you from buying a large number of DVDs meant for other areas of the world. (Yep — it's a marketing thing.)

The imported video problem

So what's the other nasty problem that crops up with the NTSC versus PAL versus SECAM standoff? It has to do with folks who attempt to import or export incompatible video hardware.

It is indeed possible to use a PAL TV in your Massachusetts living room — provided that you spend additional money to convert the power supply, of course, and that you invest in a NTSC/PAL converter box.

Here's an even better idea: If you're planning on importing video hardware, it's always a good idea to check whether that PAL hardware supports an NTSC signal. (Many European and Asian manufacturers are adding NTSC support to their products, and you usually see this compatibility featured prominently on the box and in the product specifications.)

Does My Hardware Support High-Definition?

Part of the headache surrounding today's entertainment center is the problem of what connects to what device (including, of course, what you own already). Think about it this way: It's relatively easy to walk into your local electronics megastore and say, "Good salesperson, please show me all the high-definition sets that can accept an S-Video input from a standard camcorder." However, it's not quite as simple to stare at your Apple TV and figure out what works and what doesn't!

You can find an HD Ready label, shown in Figure 6-3, on many products. However, if a TV or monitor sports this label, it doesn't automatically mean that the unit has the built-in HDTV (also called *ATSC*) tuner that's required to pick up HDTV broadcasts — only that the TV or monitor can display the resolutions I mention earlier. If you connect your Apple TV unit to a set-top HDTV tuner, you're covered. But if not, I wouldn't want you buying a new fancy TV thinking that you can pick up HDTV broadcasts with your Apple TV, only to find out it doesn't have an HDTV tuner. Not good, and I've unfortunately had to break that news to many a reader recently.

Hence the following hardware HDTV compatibility list, which I might end up adding to the back of my business cards. This list tells you what types of *existing* hardware you have that will likely support HDTV, and what probably doesn't. Note that the table doesn't include LCD, DLP, and plasma screens, which Chapter 7 discusses in more detail. Most of the current crop of advanced televisions and monitors are already HD Ready.

Figure 6-3:
The HD
Ready label
helps a
shopper
keep things
straight.

This list isn't meant to be The Final Word because many manufacturers offer far more input connectors than others. Therefore, I recommend that you physically check and see what your hardware supports already. Sometimes, you might even have to resort to the device's user guide to tell what it can do.

With those caveats in mind, here's the hardware HDTV compatibility list:

- **Your existing CRT TV or computer monitor:** If your monitor or TV is tube-based, look for the HD Ready label, either on the case or in the user guide. If it's HD Ready, it needs at least HDMI input or component video jacks to work with your Apple TV. The display must be able to handle a signal at 480p (EDTV), 720p, or 1080i/1080p resolution (HDTV).

- **Your existing DVD player:** Look for a unit with HDMI output and HD upconversion (which provides a 1080i signal). However, the real stars of the HDTV show — when it comes to optical discs — are the new next-generation Blu-ray and HD-DVD formats, which provide a full range of high-definition signals (including the ultra-quality 1080p resolution). As you might imagine, cutting-edge Blu-ray/HD-DVD products are honking expensive right now (although the PlayStation 3 has lowered the bar a bit with its built-in Blu-ray drive) so if you want to continue using your standard DVD player, I completely understand. Your DVD player can still work with your high-definition display, of course, but the player doesn't produce a high-definition signal unless it's equipped with HD *upconversion* (which actually produces an HD signal from a standard DVD but without any extra detail or resolution that you'd get from Blu-ray or HD-DVD discs).

- **Your existing VCR:** No chance on getting a high-definition signal from your antique VCR, but you should be able to connect that VHS beastie to the composite input on your TV or your satellite/cable box.

- **Your existing satellite or cable TV box:** Most cable and satellite TV providers can hook you up with an HD connection. However, they'll likely have to exchange your current set-top box with another unit, and you'll probably be charged more.

Speaking of HD signals, here comes another of my patented segues!

Where Can I Get a High-Definition Signal?

Having a home entertainment Mac or PC, an Apple TV, and an HDTV or HD monitor of your dreams is one thing. Actually having high-definition content to *view* with all that expensive hardware is quite another. Sure, the duo of iTunes and Apple TV allows you to stream all your content from your Mac or PC, but what happens when you run out of your stuff and want more?

Luckily, at your disposal are a number of different methods of pulling in a high-definition signal to your new setup.

At the time of this writing, they include

- **A cable or satellite provider:** Typically, an HDTV signal from either type of connection costs you about $10 to $20 more a month (at the time of this writing). Cable connections are normally the most convenient. In fact, many HDTV sets now offer DCR (Digital Cable Ready) support that doesn't require a separate set-top box at all. However, if you have an existing satellite feed, you can probably get an upgraded HD satellite dish and a new HD receiver.

- **A DVD player or HD-DVD/Blu-ray player:** As I mention earlier, you can get a high-definition signal from a standard DVD player if it's equipped with HD upconversion — but limited to a 1080i interlaced signal. Only a Blu-ray or HD-DVD disc player (or a product like the PlayStation 3) can cover the entire spectrum of high-definition resolutions, both progressive and interlaced.

- **A broadcast HDTV signal:** As I mention earlier in the chapter, most TV stations in your area that broadcast in high-definition use the 1080i interlaced format. All you need to receive these high-def channels is a TV with an HDTV tuner (or a multimedia video card for your computer with a built-in HDTV tuner) and a good HD antenna. Check with your local TV stations for their offerings.

Different Flavors of Home Theater Sound

Okay, time to turn your attention to another set of standards: yep, your home entertainment audio system. If you're a regular at your local movie theater, you've probably seen a number of different sound systems advertised for moviegoers. Now, in fact, you can choose to add many of those same theater-quality sound standards to your home system.

The Dolby roundup

Here's the rundown on what's currently available for your home entertainment high-tech audio system:

- **Standard stereo:** The familiar two-speaker sound system that you've grown up with, *stereo* includes two channels, and you're likely to find stereo sound on just about every DVD in your collection as well as most cable and satellite broadcast channels. Nothing fancy here, but I wanted to start with something that everyone recognizes — it starts to get complex in a hurry.

You might also see a product advertised as a *stereo 2.1* speaker system. That's actually just a set of two stereo speakers with an additional subwoofer for extra bass.

✔ **Dolby Surround Sound:** Dolby Surround was the first major leap forward in sound technology after the introduction of stereo. This early standard required four channels (representing left, center, right, and a surround channel), but those four channels could be *encoded* (or carried) on the standard two stereo channels offered by videotapes and laserdiscs. You needed a Surround decoder, which most of us old-timers remember, to hear the improved sound. Later, this standard was improved to produce the Dolby Pro Logic encoding format.

✔ **Dolby Pro Logic II:** If you have a standard two-channel stereo audio signal, can you make it *sound* like a multiple-speaker surround-sound signal? Well, yes, if you're using Dolby Pro Logic (or its new and improved descendent, Pro Logic II). As you can imagine, simulated surround-sound isn't a big hit with dedicated audiophiles, so you're not likely to see it trumpeted on a PC audio card feature list or on the side of a high-tech speaker system, but Pro Logic II is often used by game programmers coding for video game consoles, like the Xbox 360 and the PlayStation 3, which play their audio through the stereo speakers on a standard TV set.

✔ **Dolby Digital:** Also commonly called *AC-3,* Dolby Digital is still the most common audio standard for today's DVDs and HDTV audio signals. You may see Dolby Digital advertised as Dolby Surround 5.1 because it requires five satellite speakers (right-front, center, left-front, right-rear, and left-rear) as well as a subwoofer to handle the sound.

Figure 6-4 shows a 5.1 channel surround-sound layout in a typical home theater.

✔ **Dolby Digital Plus:** Yep, you guessed it; this standard is a descendent of the original Dolby Digital. Currently, it's offered by some HDTV providers, and you find it on HD-DVD and Blu-ray discs. At the time of this writing, Dolby Digital Plus includes support for 7.1 speaker systems (adding an additional left and right speaker to the middle of the configuration).

✔ **Dolby Theater Sound:** Also called *Dolby DTS,* this standard is used in today's movie theaters, and it's likely that a film you've seen recently featured DTS sound. On the home front, DTS is typically offered with a 5.1 speaker system, using the same channel assignments as Dolby Digital. Because DTS audio takes up a nice chunk of space, it makes only a rare appearance on standard DVDs — usually on concert discs, for example — but it'll become far more widespread on Blu-ray and HD-DVD discs. To enjoy DTS audio, you need a DTS decoder, which is usually built in to DVD/Blu-ray/HD-DVD players. On the PC side, a DTS decoder can be implemented through software, so most software DVD players support DTS.

✔ **Dolby TrueHD:** You've reached the end of your Dolby journey with this new sound standard. TrueHD is required for HD-DVD discs and is optional for Blu-ray players, incorporating eight channels of the highest-quality 24-bit audio. Unlike earlier versions of Dolby audio, however, HDMI cables connect a TrueHD device to your AV receiver or entertainment PC sound card.

Your Apple TV unit offers both optical audio and analog stereo RCA audio jacks, as well as the HDMI connector's built-in audio support.

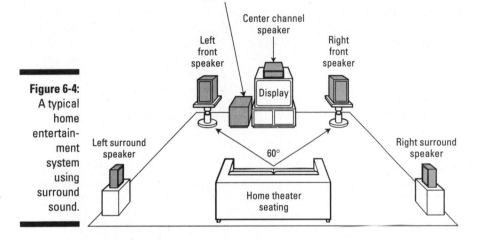

Figure 6-4:
A typical home entertainment system using surround sound.

Computer sound extras to consider

Today's high-end computer sound cards often provide more than one of these Dolby standards, and I know it's a temptation to simply shop for the card with either the highest price or the widest Dolby audio support. However, you should make other considerations when shopping for a new audio card besides "the Dolby factor."

For example, don't forget these features:

✔ **Top sound quality:** Today's top sound cards offer 24-bit audio. If you're interested in advanced theater sound, I wouldn't recommend that you settle for anything less.

✔ **Digital output:** Another must. The card you choose should have S/PDIF (Sony/Philips Digital Interface Format) output, allowing connections to most DVD players and A/V theater receivers.

✔ **Front-mounted connections:** PC owners either love or hate front-mounted connectors. If you appreciate them, consider a card that offers a faceplate that fits in one of your entertainment PC's 5¼-inch drive bays, presenting you with the input/output connections you crave.

✔ **EAX game audio:** Many PC games support EAX (Environmental Sound Standard) surround-sound audio, DirectSound3D, or Dolby Digital audio for immersive gameplay. (If your buddy takes a shot at you from your right in a game of *Quake 4,* that sound comes from your right as well. Gamers love this stuff.)

✔ **MIDI connections:** With a MIDI (Musical Instrument Digital Interface) instrument, a musician can play directly into a software sound editor, or the PC can "play" the instrument automatically. A sound card might require a special set of converter cables to connect a MIDI instrument, but if you're interested in using your entertainment PC as a home studio, MIDI is a must-have.

Do I need an A/V theater receiver?

If you're connecting your speaker system directly to your Apple TV's optical audio jack, no extra hardware is typically required. However, if you have plans for adding a Blu-ray or HD-DVD player in the future or if you prefer more versatility for your connection options, invest in an A/V home theater receiver.

With an A/V receiver as the hub of your audio system, your Apple TV becomes another input source. Then you can move that sound from the receiver to wherever you like. (Multiple speaker systems? You bet. I personally know two home theater owners with more than one set of speakers, which they switch between for different Dolby standards.)

Also, an A/V receiver provides the raw power that an Apple TV unit simply can't provide. For some folks, that's all the reason they need. (Just don't move in next door, please.)

Adding a New Speaker System

So which audio system is right for your entertainment PC? Well, as I mention in the previous section, a Dolby Digital 5.1 speaker system is currently the most common configuration for today's home theater installations. However, if you want to invest in the future and the highest-quality sound is important to you, a Dolby DTS or TrueHD system might be more attractive.

No matter which audio system you choose, keep these tips in mind when you're shopping for your new speakers and installing them in your home:

- **Is flat-panel right for you?** Flat-panel speakers take far less room, and they can often be mounted in locations where a standard speaker doesn't fit. However, they usually can't handle the same wattage, and some audiophiles feel that flat-panel speakers don't reproduce sound as well as a traditional speaker.

- **A secure mounting is a must.** No one likes a rattling speaker! Use a secure wall mount. Or, if you prefer a freestanding configuration, make sure that the pedestal or base you use is heavy enough to withstand the chopper flyby in *Blue Thunder*.

- **Where are the controls?** Minimalist speakers often place the volume and spatial controls on the subwoofer, which might or might not be your definition of convenience, depending on where everything is located. (If you're shopping for a speaker system, pass by any offerings that don't have onboard controls. Heck, some high-end speaker systems now have their own *remote* controls!)

- **THX-certified is A Good Thing.** If a speaker system is THX-certified, you can be assured that it meets stringent acoustic standards. (Like Dolby, *THX* is also a trade name for a theater sound standard — in fact, it was developed by Lucasfilm especially for the debut of *Return of the Jedi*.)

- **Shields up!** If you decide to place your speakers close to your Mac or PC, a CRT TV, or a CRT monitor, consider speakers that are magnetically shielded. Shielded speakers don't produce the video static and color mutations that occur with unshielded speakers parked close to a tube display.

Chapter 7

Introducing Your Apple TV to Your Television

*I*t's a funny thing: The salesperson at the electronics mega-discount-clearance store where you bought your new LCD monitor told you that it'd be a "cinch" to install. (I love that word.) Anyway, now you're home, and none of the cables from your Apple TV seem to fit, you can't get a signal from the HDTV antenna she sold you, or your display from your TV doesn't look anywhere near as good as what you saw in the store.

And the salesperson is nowhere to be seen.

Perhaps this chapter might be of service! I cover all sorts of connection and display conundrums that pop up as well as provide you with a comparison of which display technologies do what (and when, and to whom). And I lecture you about cables. (Oh, joy.)

Perhaps after perusing this chapter, you'll find your new monitor really is a "cinch" to install!

What's the Difference between a TV and a Monitor?

Begin your tour of connections and displays with Question Number One — experience has taught me that most folks ask about the difference between a TV and a monitor up front. No, Virginia, all displays are not the same!

In fact, a monitor has only one important difference from a standard TV, digital TV, or HDTV: Monitors do *not* have a built-in tuner for any of these signals. It doesn't matter whether a monitor is branded as a computer monitor or a home theater monitor, it still requires an external tuner.

If a monitor is listed as *Digital Cable Ready* (DCR), it should be able to display a signal from your cable box without any external help. However, if it's properly called a *monitor,* it can't display any type of over-the-air broadcast TV.

Does a monitor inherently give you a better-quality display than a TV? That's commonly thought as well, probably because of the superiority of the image provided by a computer monitor for so many years over a standard analog TV signal. I don't want to disappoint monitor owners. If the two units share these characteristics, they're essentially the same device:

- ✔ Display technology (such as LCD or CRT)
- ✔ Resolution
- ✔ Scanning technology (progressive or interlaced)

The TV can receive a broadcast signal of one type or another because it has a corresponding tuner built-in, but the monitor must rely on an outside tuner. Other than that, you'd be hard-pressed to tell the difference.

If you're not familiar with the terms *resolution, progressive scan,* or *interlaced scan,* Chapter 6 discusses them in detail as it regales you with high-resolution splendor.

Finally, one last common question: Can a TV be used with a computer *without* an Apple TV connection? Indeed it can, as long as one of the following is true:

- ✔ The video card used by the computer supports TV output.
- ✔ The TV can accept the analog or digital signal produced by the video card.
- ✔ The output from the computer can be converted by another device (often called a *scan converter*) into an input source that the TV can use.

To sum it all up, the once easy-to-recognize line that separated a TV set from a computer monitor is fast disappearing — and home theater owners, like you and me, benefit!

Technology Soup: CRT, LCD, Plasma, Projection

Boy, howdy. You'd think these super-intelligent engineers could make all this stuff simpler. (Actually, I have friends who are engineers, and they say that everything electronic always starts out easy to understand. Then they blame the marketing types for mucking things up.)

Well, in this section, I take on all these display technologies, explain them, and make them beg for mercy. Come along and enjoy the ride!

CRT displays

CRT stands for *cathode ray tube,* which is why these TVs and monitors are often called *tube* displays. The image is produced by a controlled stream of high-speed electrons that are "fired" at the inside front of the display tube through a vacuum, where they excite a phosphorescent layer that glows, producing the image. (Go figure.)

The original display technology used for both analog TV broadcasts and computer video for decades, CRT seems to have been left behind by more modern advances. Still, don't count this old warhorse dead yet, no matter what this month's home theater magazine tells you. In fact, a trip to your local electronics giga-store makes it quite clear that CRT technology is alive and well.

A CRT monitor or TV set is very bulky and quite deep from the front of the display to the back of the set because of the electron gun and dense glass tube. Older CRT displays had the distinctive curved glass that we all know and love, but most of today's models carry improved flat (or nearly flat) tubes, reducing the distortion at the edge of the image.

CRT displays provide superb color, and there's no problem with viewing in a well-lit room. You can sit anywhere and see the same image because there's no limitation to the viewing angle. On the downside, standard CRT displays have a size limitation of about 40 inches, and their image quality isn't as good as technologies like plasma or LCD. Plus, a CRT unit can display only one type of high-definition signal. CRT displays are the thickest front-to-back, and they weigh much more than an LCD or a plasma screen. (No hanging a CRT on the wall without a very sturdy bracket, and it doesn't sit flush, either.)

But did I mention that they're inexpensive? Yes, that's one of the main reasons for the continued lifespan of CRT TVs and monitors. This technology remains the least expensive on the market, even for sets that can display an HDTV signal.

LCD displays

Next up in the display technology beauty pageant is the LCD (liquid crystal display) flat-panel, which first appeared on laptop and notebook computers more than a decade ago. Each dot (or *pixel*) in an LCD display uses liquid crystal material that can display red, green, and blue; the pixels are controlled electronically to produce an image. The lighting for a typical home theater LCD TV or monitor is provided by a bright, white light located behind the LCD panel.

Many shoppers decide on LCD panels for their best-known features: They're remarkably thin (sometimes less than 2 inches thick), and they use far less power than a CRT display of the same size. Because LCD screens are so lightweight, you often see them attached to a wall or supported from the ceiling. Currently, most LCD flat-panel screens max out at about 52 inches.

LCD screens work fine in a well-lit room, but their color range is somewhat less than a CRT display, and they have a problem with viewing angles. The acceptable angle varies with the manufacturer and model, but you don't have quite the seating flexibility that you have with a CRT screen. Also, some screens based on older examples of LCD technology have problems with "ghosting" and blurring when displaying fast motion. LCD screens can suffer from dead pixels, just like an LCD computer monitor — but these generally appear at only a single pixel location, showing up when a certain color is displayed. Like most things in life, the more you spend, the less trouble you're likely to have. However, current LCD displays are far more affordable than plasma screens, so they fall in the medium price range.

If you're interested in the best possible image quality from an LCD display, make sure you invest in an *active matrix* screen, which offers far superior images than cheaper passive matrix models.

A typical LCD flat-panel display like the one shown in Figure 7-1 can handle more than one type of high-definition signal, dependent on the model and whether it has an onboard HDTV tuner.

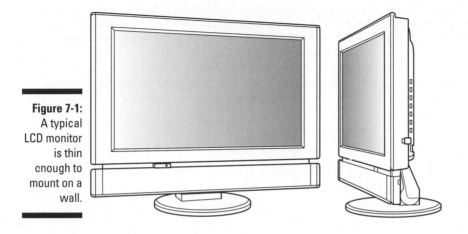

Figure 7-1:
A typical
LCD monitor
is thin
cnough to
mount on a
wall.

Plasma displays

Plasma. If you're a fan of cutting-edge technology, that word alone is enough to send your pulse racing. Perhaps it's because of all the references to plasma-based stuff in science fiction shows, like *Star Trek.* Anyway, I don't discuss warp engines or transporters . . . just home theater displays. (Too bad because I've always wanted a "phased plasma rifle" from *The Terminator.*)

Anyway, back to the real technology. A plasma display panel (PDP) produces an image by exciting a phosphorescent layer sandwiched between two pieces of glass. (If that sounds familiar, consider a CRT display, where you also have similar cxcitable phosphors.) Plasma screens, however, don't use an electron gun or a beam. Instead, each individual pixel is triggered by an electronic pulse, which causes a plasma discharge that reacts with the phosphorescent layer.

So what does all that engineer-speak mean? Well, like LCD flat-panel screens, plasma screens are only a few inches thick and are wall-mountable. They use more electricity than an LCD panel but still less than a CRT screen. Also, plasma screens can grow huge in the wild, up to about 70 inches for current models.

The advantages of a plasma display are manifold. A plasma display is bright, with deep blacks and a color range that rivals CRT displays. The viewing angle for a plasma screen is slightly better than an LCD flat-panel screen but still not as good as a CRT screen. Plus, the image quality and detail of a plasma screen is simply unbeatable in today's home theater market. It looks *awesome* and can handle HDTV programming at even the highest quality.

"Okay, Mark, hit me. What's the problem with plasma, then?" First and foremost, plasma screens are so honkin' expensive that you could literally buy two LCD flat-panel displays for the same price! Such technology doesn't come cheap.

Also, even the most expensive plasma screens are susceptible to four tribulations:

- ✔ **Burn-in:** Early plasma screens suffered from the same "ghosted" image you see on the screen at your ATM. This condition is called *burn-in,* and it's permanent. Today's plasma displays, however, use a number of different methods to combat burn-in, so this problem is less of a deal-breaker than it once was.

- ✔ **Special handling:** Plasma displays are much more fragile than other types of screens and must be handled *very* carefully during a move or shipment to avoid damage. (Kids and pets must watch their Ps and Qs.)

- ✔ **High-altitude sickness:** Because of the nature of the plasma inside the display, you're likely to hear a noticeable buzzing around an elevation of 6,000 feet or more above sea level.

- ✔ **Degradation:** The plasma gas in one of these displays actually degrades over a decade or so. The display starts to dim, eventually resulting in a screen that's hard to see. (Ah, but what a decade!)

Shopping for a plasma display? Ask the salesperson for the *plasma half-life* figures for the screens you're considering so that you can compare them. This figure is the amount of time it takes for a plasma screen to degrade to half its original brightness.

If you can afford to cough up the cash, you won't find a better image for your entertainment PC than a plasma display, but making the right choice between manufacturers and brands requires careful shopping and comparison.

Projection displays

The final home theater display category is the projection screen, and there are a number of them. All these technologies involve projecting an image onto either a sheet of glass or a separate screen, but how they achieve the projection differs.

A rear-projection unit is self-contained within a larger case, and a front-projection screen operates just like a theater movie projector or old-style slide projector.

The list includes

- ✔ **DLP rear-projection:** Short for *digital light processing,* DLP technology is literally done with mirrors — many thousands of them — all reflecting different hues of light onto the screen. Most DLP screens range in size from 40–60 inches, and they're priced a little higher for their image quality and size. Most can handle multiple HDTV resolutions.

- ✔ **CRT rear-projection:** Cheap, CRT rear-projection technology has been around since dinosaurs roamed the Earth, but it requires regular maintenance to adjust the convergence of the multiple cathode tubes. Also, CRT rear-projection screens are among the largest beasts on the planet, so if space is limited, you can move on. Again, 40–60 inches is the norm here, but these screens are usually limited to the lowest-quality HDTV signals.

- ✔ **LCOS rear-projection:** As a sister technology to LCD, you'd expect an LCOS (liquid crystal on silicon) projection display to offer a great image. In fact, it offers the best image quality and highest resolution of any rear-projection system on the market today, so these puppies are generally very pricey. An LCOS screen is likely to handle just about anything you throw at it, including the complete line of HDTV resolutions. They generally range from 50–60 inches.

- ✔ **Front projection:** Whatever you do, do not think "Uncle Milton's slide projector" when you see a home theater projector! Sure, it looks like the old self-contained slide projector, but these units are generally hung from the ceiling, and they can produce a whopping 200-inch image on a wall (although most folks opt for a fancy 100-inch 16:9 pull-down or fixed-frame screen). Most front-projection systems use DLP technology, and they're portable, just like their slide-show ancestors. Plus, they can project a wide range of high-definition signals, and they're usually cheaper than their rear-projection brethren.

It's time to be honest about projection systems. In general, these displays (no matter what technology they use) tend to have a narrow viewing angle, and they don't deliver the brightness required to look good in a well-lit room. With those considerations in mind, you won't find a bigger display size, and most of these monsters are still cheaper than a smaller plasma display.

Choosing your display

So which display is right for you? I was afraid you'd ask that because there's really no one right answer. You have to consider the space requirements, picture quality, and incoming signal types that your display must accept and try to wait out the rapidly decreasing prices while the high-definition support improves. However, I can give you one Mark's Maxim that's guaranteed to apply to every human eye and every shopper:

It's critically important to view each type of display technology *in person* before making a buying decision.

That's right. Even if you're planning on eventually buying from an online store, spend the time and do the footwork at your local electronics and home theater stores. Your eyes are the only judge of quality that matters in the end. In fact, that LCD display might look sharper to your eye than the plasma screen right next to it that sells for thousands more.

Make sure you do your shopping at a major electronics store or home theater store. They have the high-definition programming available for demonstrations, allowing you to truly compare one screen against the other, and they have the widest range of display technologies on hand.

Naturally, you probably save a considerable amount by shopping online, but don't forget that the sheer bulk of some sets (like a rear-projection screen) or the careful handling required by some displays (like plasma screens) likely result in expensive shipping costs. Unless, of course, you're a very smart shopper and look for free shipping bargains!

Table 7-1 might qualify for the most information-packed table I've ever created. You'll also find it on the Cheat Sheet (at the front of this book) for maximum portability.

Table 7-1	All Those Display Technologies Compared			
Technology	**Relative Cost**	**Typical Maximum Size**	**Pros**	**Cons**
CRT	Very inexpensive	40 inches	Great color quality; no viewing angle problems; can display 1080i* HDTV	Bulky; mediocre image detail
LCD	Average to high	52 inches	Thin; lightweight; low power; good image detail; handles most HDTV signals	Mediocre color quality; limited viewing angle; blurring or ghosting on cheaper sets

Technology	Relative Cost	Typical Maximum Size	Pros	Cons
Plasma	Very expensive	70 inches	Thin; lightweight; great image detail; great color quality; handles all HDTV signals	Fragile; slight chance of burn-in; brightness degradation; sensitive to high altitudes; limited viewing angle
Rear-projection	Average to high	60 inches	Good to great image detail; good to great color quality; handles most HDTV signals	Bulky; might require adjustment and maintenance; limited viewing angle; requires a dark room
Front-projection	Average	200 inches	Good color quality; handles most HDTV signals	Requires a separate wall or screen; mediocre image quality; requires a dark room

Read more about 1080i in Chapter 6.

Spotting Video Connectors in the Wild

Part Two of the video connection safari revolves around the little connectors you use to get all these fancy devices talking to your Apple TV or A/V receiver — and just how *irritating* those connectors can be, if not properly explained. Heck, half of them look like the other half, and it takes a degree in Advanced Thakamology just to find the right plug.

Good reader, after you finish this section, pilgrims will travel thousands of miles just to hear your cable advice! (Or at least, you'll be a hero to your family and friends.)

A cavalcade of shiny gold things

Some of the connectors in this list are specifically designed for your PC, and others have appeared as part of the home theater revolution of the last five years. Don't forget: Your Apple TV accepts only some of these connectors. (I tell you which are Jobs-approved, of course.)

VGA: The old classic

Most PC owners are quite familiar with a standard VGA connector, as shown in Figure 7-2. For many years, the VGA connector was practically the only way to connect a monitor to your computer. This 15-pin, D-sub video port originally appeared with the IBM Video Graphics Array (VGA) specification.

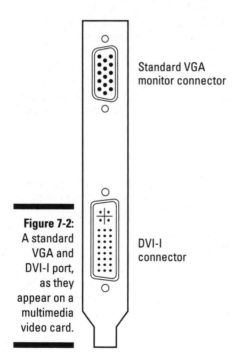

Standard VGA monitor connector

DVI-I connector

Figure 7-2: A standard VGA and DVI-I port, as they appear on a multimedia video card.

However, the glory days of the VGA connector are past because most PC owners now turn to flat-panel LCD monitors as their first display choice. You'll still likely find a VGA connector on the back of CRT monitors and more expensive LCD flat-panel monitors, but the days when this standard applied to larger home theater CRT televisions has passed.

Your Apple TV unit doesn't support the standard VGA connector and would probably scamper away if you approached with a VGA cable in your hand.

DVI-I: Modern PC digital goodness

The new standard on the block for computer-to-monitor connections is the 29-pin DVI-I (Digital Video Interface-Integrated) connector, which is used to connect practically everything else in the digital display world to your Mac or PC. This includes LCD flat-panel monitors, plasma screens, front projection units, and many rear-projection TVs as well. Your DVD player might have a DVI-I connector.

DVI-I carries both analog and digital video signals, making it somewhat of a Jack-of-all-trades in the computer world. This dual personality allows it to carry

 ✔ The high-definition digital traffic between an entertainment PC and a high-end display

 ✔ A clunky analog connection between a PC and a CRT monitor (with an adapter)

A DVI-**D** connector, however, carries only a digital signal, so when you hear someone talking about a DVI cable, it's perfectly correct to ask, "To which flavor of the *Digital Visual Interface* do you refer?" (Can you tell how much fun I am at parties?) Anyway, it's likely they're referring to the far more common DVI-**I** connection.

The multitalented Figure 7-2 also shows off a DVI-I connector.

Now, for the word you've been waiting for: The DVI-I connector does *not* work as-is with your Apple TV. However, relatively inexpensive DVI-to-HDMI cables are available that can handle this task. (What's HDMI? I'm glad you asked . . . .)

HDMI: The home entertainment superstar

Ah, here's the cable you've gotta know if you're building a home theater. The *High-Definition Multimedia Interface* is aptly named because it can carry both a high-definition video signal and the multichannel audio you crave! The HDMI cable is the connector of choice on your Apple TV. (Too bad they're so doggone expensive. Sigh. Such is life.)

HDMI cables come in two species:

 ✔ **The Type A cable:** This 19-pin connector is far more common and is designed for current high-def signals — this is the species used by your Apple TV unit. Figure 7-3 shows it off.

 ✔ **The Type B cable:** Although it's not currently used much, the 29-pin Type B cable will become much more important in the future, when super-high-definition signals above 1080p become available.

Figure 7-3:
The svelte
lines of an
HDMI
Type A
connector.

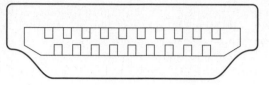

HDMI can connect monitors and TV sets to your Apple TV, a computer multi-media video card, or to an A/V receiver as well as DVD players and speaker systems. HDMI is also a requirement for a Blu-ray or HD-DVD player.

TOSLINK: Digital audio at work

Although this acronym is absolutely ridiculous (it's short for *TOShiba-Link*, from the company that created it), the TOSLINK connector is a welcome sight for audiophiles who want top-quality sound from an entertainment computer. (I know, I know, this is supposed to be a section on video connections, but TOSLINK is A Big Connector for components used in home theater systems, so I include it here.)

Figure 7-4 illustrates a fiber optic TOSLINK connector used to carry Dolby Digital and Dolby DTS signals. Your Apple TV includes a TOSLINK port.

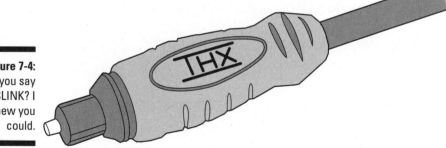

Figure 7-4:
Can you say
TOSLINK? I
knew you
could.

If you don't have an A/V receiver or speaker system with a TOSLINK port, never fear! Your Apple TV also includes the standard circular RCA stereo jacks for analog audio (which date all the way back to when rocks were brand-new). The left- and right-channel jacks are compatible with virtually all stereo and speaker systems.

Component: The unsung video hero

Of all the different connectors in this section, the ubiquitous red, green, and blue of component video is probably the most familiar (next to the VGA port, that is). Even the most high-end display usually still includes these three RCA jacks (see Figure 7-5), and they're included on the back of your Apple TV. Component video has been a standard for a decade now, and these cables provide the best analog connection to older devices that don't support DVI-I or HDMI.

Component video is considered an acceptable connection for 1080i (interlaced) high-definition signals, and it's also a favorite for VCRs and DVD players. If you install a multimedia video card with a built-in tuner in your PC or Mac, you're virtually guaranteed a component output.

If you happen upon the term *YPrPb* in your travels, do the technology dance because you now know that it's another term for the color coding used with a component video connection.

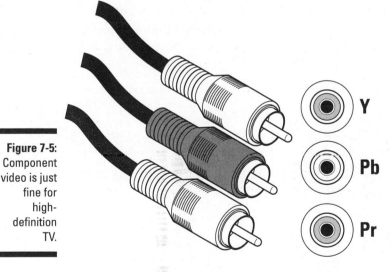

Figure 7-5: Component video is just fine for high-definition TV.

Do not get component video confused with composite video! Whereas component video is carried over three cables (one for luminance, and two for chrominance), *composite* video requires only one cable. It's usually yellow, which I always joke about. ("Yellow means *stay away!*") Anyway, composite video is crunched and compressed to fit over that one cable, and the color quality and detail of a composite signal is downright horrible. Avoid any equipment that requires a composite video connection unless you're into old 8-bit computers and video games, like the Atari 800, Commodore 64, and Colecovision! (Yes, this type of connection really is that old.)

Let's talk converters

With the huge list of common connectors (and the thousands of different electronic devices available today), you can usually find a converter that can take the signal from one type of port — for example, an HDMI connector — to another port, like a DVI connector. In fact, just about anything can be connected to anything these days, if you have the money. So why the treatise on different connectors in this chapter?

One big reason: *A converted signal usually loses something.* Rarely does a signal arrive at its destination through a converter without a drop in quality or a loss of one type of data or another. (In this example, several types of hardware control data can't be sent from HDMI to DVI.) Also, some converters have to be adjusted to provide the best possible signal.

The only way you can be absolutely sure that your signal remains clean and unchanged is to push data out of one connector through a good-quality cable *to the same type of connector* on the destination device! HDMI to HDMI, DVI to DVI, VGA to VGA, and so on.

S-Video: An old-timer connector for older equipment

An S-Video cable used to be a welcome sight in the 1980s and '90s for those interested in high-end video, but these days, this connector is better known for its compatibility with older hardware.

S-Video carries only an analog video signal, and it's a step up from the original composite video connections common in the 1970s. However, the quality of an S-Video connection suffers when compared with the color quality and detail of a component video connection, so use a component connection instead of S-Video whenever possible.

Your Apple TV doesn't include an S-Video connector (and if that's the only connector available on your TV, it's time to go shopping).

And they shall be connected with cables

Cables aren't created equally, as you might expect by the prices you'll pay. Why pay more for a DVI-I or HDMI cable that costs twice as much as one that works exactly the same?

That's a tough one to answer especially because many home theater owners simply can't tell a difference between the image delivered by the highest-quality cable and the generic example. I'll be honest: Many people can't distinguish those differences because their eyes aren't as trained or as experienced in The Ways of High-Definition. Other folks simply don't have vision that can discriminate between the two signals.

However, I do know a number of hi-tech video enthusiasts who actually *can* tell those two signals apart (just like I can tell the difference between a 192 Kbps MP3 audio file and a lower-quality 128 Kbps version of the same song on certain speaker systems). Therefore, here are the features to look for if you want the very best in digital data transfer between your entertainment PC and your display:

- **Shielding:** The best cables have at least two layers of magnetic and electrical shielding, typically using foil separators.

- **High-quality copper:** Look for cables that feature high-density, braided, pure copper conductors.

- **Strong strain relief:** Your expensive cable lasts longer, and you're much less likely to weaken a cable or end up with an intermittent short. (And take my word for it, you *don't* want that.)

- **24K gold-plated connectors:** Not just for the bling, either. Any audiophile can tell you that a gold connector is longer lasting and provides better signal quality.

Pulling the signal from satellite or digital cable

Your existing cable or satellite TV feed should work fine in concert with your Apple TV, but that feed doesn't plug directly into the unit — remember, the audio and video ports on your Apple TV are *output* ports, not input ports. Therefore, depending on the set-top box you're using, you'll probably connect DVI, HDMI, coaxial cable, or component video output from your cable or satellite box to the input connectors on your entertainment computer's video card, a home theater switchbox, or an A/V receiver.

If you want HDTV, there's a catch. Both cable and satellite TV providers require upgraded receivers to provide an HDTV signal, and your satellite provider might require you to upgrade your dish as well. Check up front about what connectors your upgraded receiver needs and make sure that your hardware can accept that cable. (Otherwise, it's converter time. Sigh.) Contact your provider's customer support or the company's Web site to find out what connectors are provided.

As an extra added attraction, though, your upgraded receiver might allow you to pull in over-the-air broadcast HDTV as well — that is, after you install a separate broadcast HDTV antenna.

You got pets? So do I. I love my cats and my dog, but their teeth can shred an expensive $100 HDMI cable in seconds. If you have indoor pets, make sure that your cabling is hidden within PVC plastic pipe, under plastic runners or a wooden floor, or suspended from the ceiling. Keep those animals away from your entertainment PC!

One final query: "Mark, what about the other connectors on the back of my Apple TV?" Good question — but I won't answer it in this chapter, because those ports and jacks aren't audio and video connectors. Instead, you're talking about the wired Ethernet port, the USB 2.0 connector, and the AC power connector, each of which I cover elsewhere in the book.

Part III
Exploring Your Apple TV

The 5th Wave   By Rich Tennant

"I was syncing iTunes with my Apple TV over several wireless protocols and I'm pretty sure it started streaming bits of my subconscious, so just keep the tinfoil hat on until I'm finished."

In this part . . .

Time to dig deeper into every aspect of your Apple TV! You find out more about how to program your iTunes-to-Apple TV connection for automated synchronization and how to use your spiffy new Apple Remote. You enjoy photo slideshows on your widescreen TV, create playlists to arrange your content, and I even introduce you to the mushrooming world of streaming Internet media!

Chapter 8

Syncing and Streaming Apple TV with iTunes

"*N*o Apple TV is an island." (I'm sure someone famous said that.)

It's true, though. Your Apple TV has no internal DVD-ROM drive — gasp — and it has to receive all your content from your computer. Without the Content Connection to iTunes, your Apple TV unit is an expensive plastic doorstop. Therefore, syncing and streaming your media is an important topic (and worth a chapter to itself).

In this chapter, you find out how to set up your automatic syncing rules that govern what's shared between your Apple TV and your iTunes library — in fact, I show you how to stream content from multiple computers! Oh, and I explain the difference between syncing and streaming . . . which will make you the center attraction at your next dinner party.

Syncing the Automatic Way

Ah, fully automatic — in my opinion, it's the way things were meant to be. You can set up your Apple TV to automatically sync all your content, even when you're not watching or listening (a real advantage for those folks using 802.11b networks, or anyone with a large selection of movies and videos).

In fact, iTunes acts as a traffic cop, sending media over in a predetermined order. (Video goes across the Content Connection first because it takes the longest.) Here's the order that the different types of media follow during the synchronization process:

- ✔ Movies
- ✔ TV programs and music videos
- ✔ Music and audiobooks
- ✔ Podcasts
- ✔ Photos

With automatic syncing, adding new content pushes older content off your Apple TV's hard drive, removing it from the unit. (Of course, the content that's deleted from your Apple TV isn't removed from your iTunes library, so you don't actually lose anything — you can always resync something later or stream it instead. More on this later in the chapter.)

Now, here's an important thing about that order: Stuff is removed in *reverse order* (photos and podcasts first) if you add a new movie or video to your collection and your Apple TV hard drive is already filled to the brim. Of course, if your unit's hard drive has remaining space, you don't see anything removed from your Apple TV.

Unlike your other types of media, photos aren't configured for automatic syncing by default. In order to set up photos with automatic syncing, flip to Chapter 12 to select the source for your images. After you specify where your photos are coming from, iTunes can automatically sync them with the rest of your media library.

In the rest of this section, I cover how to specify syncing rules for your movies, TV shows, music, and podcasts.

Syncing movies

By default, all movies in your iTunes library are synchronized. To set up a sync rule for movies, follow these steps:

1. **Launch iTunes on your computer.**

2. **Click the Apple TV item under Devices in the source list.**

3. **Click the Movies tab.**

   You see the pane shown in Figure 8-1.

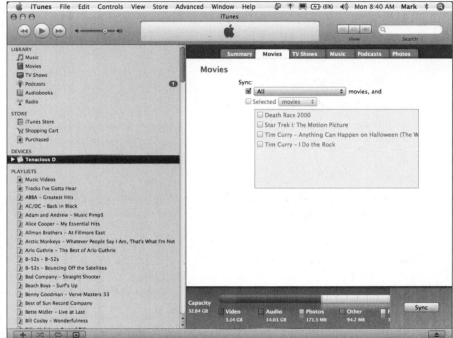

Figure 8-1:
Setting up
automatic
syncing
rules for my
movies.

4. **Choose which movies to sync:**

   - *To sync all your movies:* Click the Sync check box and choose All from the Sync pop-up menu.

   - *To limit the movies:* Click the Sync pop-up menu. Choose the most recently added movies to your iTunes library or the movies you haven't watched.

   - *To sync only certain movies:* Click the Selected check box and click the Movies pop-up menu to choose from either movies or playlists. Enable the check boxes next to the movies or playlists you want to sync.

5. **Click Sync.**

Syncing TV shows

The default syncing rule for TV shows is to transfer all of them from your computer. You can select individual shows or playlists to sync by following these steps:

1. **Launch iTunes on your computer.**

2. **Click the Apple TV item under Devices in the source list.**

3. **Click the TV Shows tab (see Figure 8-2).**

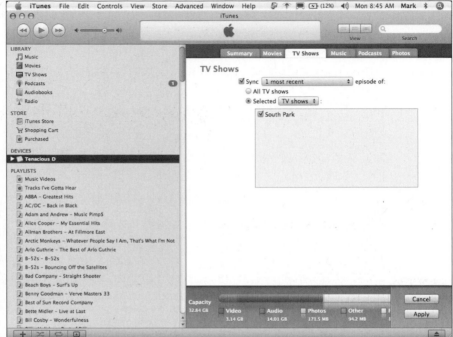

Figure 8-2:
Limiting the number of episodes of *South Park* on my Apple TV.

4. **Choose which TV shows to sync:**

   • *To select all TV shows in your collection:* Click the Sync check box to enable it and click the All TV Shows radio button.

   • *To limit the TV shows synchronized*: Click the Sync pop-up menu. Choose the episodes most recently added to your iTunes library or the episodes you haven't watched.

   • *To sync only certain shows*: Click the Selected check box to enable it and click the TV Shows pop-up menu to choose from either complete series or playlists. Enable the check boxes next to the shows or playlists you want to sync.

5. **Click Sync.**

Syncing music and music videos

Your Apple TV is set to sync all songs, playlists, and music videos when you connect to it with iTunes. To restrict what is synced, follow these steps:

1. **Start iTunes on your computer.**

2. **Click the Apple TV item under Devices in the source list.**

3. **Click the Music tab.**

   You see the pane shown in Figure 8-3.

Figure 8-3:
Music video
syncing can
be enabled
or disabled
from the
Music pane.

4. **Select which songs to sync:**

   • *To select all your music in your collection (including audiobooks):*
   Click the Sync Music check box to enable it and click the All Songs
   and Playlists radio button.

   • *To sync only certain playlists*: Click the Selected playlists radio
   button. Enable the check boxes next to the playlists you want to
   sync.

5. **Click the Include Music Videos check box to enable or disable the
   syncing of all music videos in your library.**

6. **Click Sync.**

Syncing podcasts

Podcasts aren't just limited to your iPod! In fact, I personally prefer listening to podcasts on my Apple TV . . . the voices are often easier to understand with my speaker system, and I'm not dodging pedestrians and dogs while trying to concentrate on the topic.

By default, all episodes of your podcast collection are synced. To select certain podcasts or episodes, follow these steps:

1. **Launch iTunes on your computer.**

2. **Click the Apple TV item under Devices in the source list.**

3. **Click the Podcasts tab.**

4. **Choose which podcasts to sync:**

   • *To select all the podcasts you've added to your library*: Click the Sync check box to enable it and click the All Podcasts radio button.

   • *To limit the episodes:* Click the Sync pop-up menu. Choose the episodes most recently added to your collection or the episodes you haven't heard.

   • *To sync only certain podcasts*: Click the Selected Podcasts radio button. Enable the check boxes next to the podcasts you want to sync.

5. **Click Sync.**

For complete details on setting up your photo syncing rules, visit Chapter 12.

Syncing versus Streaming: What Gives?

Although synchronization and streaming involve the same process — sending your content from your iTunes library on your PC or Mac to your Apple TV — there are important differences. I aim to sort things out in this very section, pardner.

The Tao of syncing

So far in this book, I concentrate on *syncing* — the content your Apple TV receives from iTunes is actually stored on your Apple TV's local hard drive. After the files (including photos) are saved to the hard drive, they can be instantly played or viewed, with no initial waiting, buffering, or assorted inconveniences. A syncing feature or connection is indicated in the Apple TV menu by a chain of two links (flip ahead to Figure 8-6).

Your computer doesn't even have to be on while you're enjoying content from your Apple TV. Because the media files are stored locally on the unit's hard drive, your daughter can take that laptop to the library and you won't lose your evening's entertainment.

However (and this is a *big* however), you can only sync files from one iTunes library at a time, even if two or three other computers in your home or office have gigantic iTunes libraries full of stuff you want to see and hear. Figure 8-4 illustrates the syncing process.

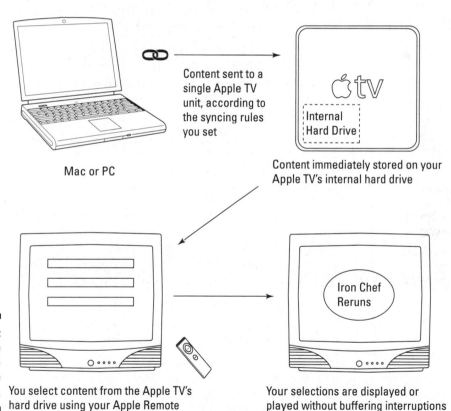

Figure 8-4: If you're synchronizing, you're saving.

Mac or PC

Content sent to a single Apple TV unit, according to the syncing rules you set

Internal Hard Drive

Content immediately stored on your Apple TV's internal hard drive

You select content from the Apple TV's hard drive using your Apple Remote

Iron Chef Reruns

Your selections are displayed or played without buffering interruptions

By the way, I show you how to switch to a new iTunes library for syncing in Chapter 16.

Also, as I mention earlier in this chapter, your Apple TV's hard drive is a finite beast; therefore, you can synchronize only about 32GB of data; the rest of the drive is taken up by Mac OS X (the operating system) and various and sundry system files. At that 32GB ceiling, your Apple TV starts automatically removing stuff from the hard drive to make room for anything new you send.

Because you'll most likely concentrate on a single iTunes library, syncing makes sense, providing the best performance and the least amount of data transfers.

The streaming solution

On the other hand, the content that you stream to your Apple TV isn't saved to the unit's hard drive — you watch, listen, or display stuff and then it's gone, as shown in Figure 8-5. For example, if you want to watch a movie twice in the same day over a streaming connection, the movie file has to be transferred again. (Nowhere near as efficient as saving a local copy to your Apple TV's hard drive.) A streaming feature or connection is indicated in the Apple TV menu by an ellipses and a right-facing arrow (look ahead to Figure 8-6).

Photos can't be streamed to your Apple TV, so the Photos menu item doesn't even appear in the Apple TV menu system while you're streaming content.

Bad news for older network hardware: Video streaming is disabled if you're using a slower 802.11b network. In other words, you can only watch video on a syncing connection over an 802.11b network.

You may still encounter the occasional pause in a movie or a music playlist if you're using 802.11g because your Apple TV must share your network bandwidth with other computers and devices (resulting in slower network transfer speeds). Playback may stop entirely for a few seconds while your Apple TV waits for the rest of the file to transfer. I admit it's pretty distracting when it happens. As long as you're streaming instead of syncing, the possibility for a buffering delay exists — even on a "pure" 802.11n wireless network or a wired Ethernet connection.

Oh, and the streaming computer you've chosen has to remain turned on and connected to your local network (which makes sense because it has to continuously feed the media you select to your Apple TV). If your son borrows your PC for a gaming session across town, you can't stream any content from that machine. Note that if the streaming computer is set to automatically sleep or hibernate, the streaming stops.

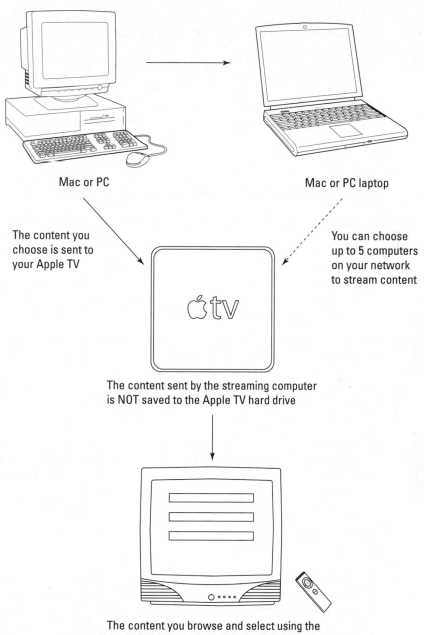

Mac or PC

Mac or PC laptop

The content you choose is sent to your Apple TV

You can choose up to 5 computers on your network to stream content

The content sent by the streaming computer is NOT saved to the Apple TV hard drive

Figure 8-5:
If you're streaming, you're pulling in content temporarily.

The content you browse and select using the Apple Remote is displayed on your TV, but as soon as the computer is turned off or leaves the network, streaming stops

Choosing between syncing and streaming

"So, Mark, why would I choose to stream at all?" Good question, good reader, and here's the payoff:

- ✔ **You can stream content from up to *five* iTunes libraries on your local wired or wireless network!** (That's in addition to the one you've selected to sync with.)
- ✔ **You can browse *all* the content in an iTunes library, not just 32GB worth.**

In other words, it's a question of access and amount: Syncing provides the best performance and doesn't require continuous access to your computer, but you're limited to one library and 32GB. Streaming provides only fair performance and requires that your PC or Mac be on and connected, but you can access and enjoy more stuff from more than one library.

Table 8-1 — which my editors and I are particularly proud of — sums everything up and may very well be sold separately in the future. (You get yours included free with this book!)

Table 8-1		The Big Matchup: Syncing Versus Streaming					
Method Pauses	Library	Stored on Apple TV Hard Drive	802.11b Support	Computer Must Stay On	Photo Features	Buffering	Capacity
Syncing	1	Yes	All media	No	Yes	No	32GB maximum
Streaming	Up to 5	No	No video	Yes	No	Yes	Unlimited browsing

Wait — can I use both syncing and streaming?

(Pause for dramatic effect . . . .)

Doggone right you can! Steve and the men and women of Cupertino wouldn't have things any other way. In fact, you've hit on the Absolute Nirvana of Apple TV: You choose one iTunes library to sync with, but you stream content from other computers on the network. Just remember that you can't sync and stream at the same time . . . in fact, while you're streaming, the Apple TV icon disappears from iTunes on the computer you've set up for syncing.

Because I've already shown you how to sync your stuff in this chapter, it's time to demonstrate how to set up a streaming connection.

Doing the Streaming Thing

To set up a streaming connection with a PC or Mac on your network running iTunes, follow these steps:

1. **Launch iTunes on the computer you want to stream from.**
2. **Select the Sources menu item on your top-level Apple TV menu.**

    You see the screen shown in Figure 8-6.

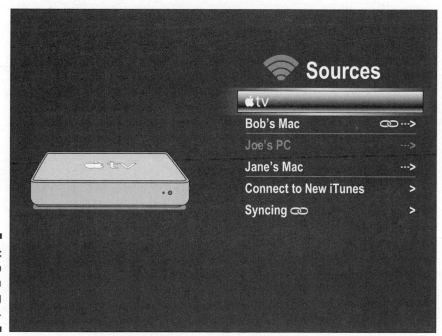

Figure 8-6: Preparing to authorize a streaming computer.

3. **Select the Connect to New iTunes menu item.**

   Your Apple TV displays yet another of those funky passcodes.

4. **Within iTunes, click the Apple TV icon that appears.**

   The icon is marked with the (somewhat) obvious line "Click to set up."

5. **Enter the passcode that Apple TV provides in Step 3.**

   Again, Apple wants your content to remain yours, and only an authorized copy of iTunes can sync or stream with your Apple TV.

Feel free to repeat these steps right now for up to five other computers on
your network running iTunes. It's a streaming free-for-all!

If you've already set up an iTunes library as your syncing source, it's automatically set up for streaming as well. Just another perk from your friendly
Apple TV.

You can now use your Apple Remote to browse and select media over the
streaming connection. To switch between streaming libraries, return to your
old friend the Apple TV Sources menu. (It's rather like switching inputs on
your widescreen TV.) You also use the Sources menu to switch between syncing and streaming modes.

After you authorize a copy of iTunes for syncing or streaming, it remains
authorized and appears on the Sources menu. Note in Figure 8-6 that the
copy of iTunes on Bob's Mac can be used for both syncing *and* streaming —
the Absolute Nirvana status I mention earlier — whereas Jane's Mac is available for streaming.

Chapter 9

Great, Another Remote Control

*N*o, stay with me! There's never been a simpler remote to use, and it looks completely different from any other remote control on your coffee table. (Unless, of course, you already own an iMac, Mac mini, or MacBook laptop . . . in which case you could conceivably get things mixed up because those computers come with the same Apple Remote. Don't worry, I show you how to keep track of which is which.)

Sit back and relax because this chapter requires only your thumb. I show you how you can control features and configure settings with your Apple Remote. You can speed through movies and pause your music with aplomb.

Heck, I even provide step-by-step instructions on what to do when the battery needs changing — because sooner or later, even a Lilliputian remote that uses a watch battery needs more juice.

Introducing the Apple Remote

Ladies and gentlemen, children of all ages: Allow me to introduce you to that first-generation iPod Shuffle look-alike, that superstar no thicker than a pack of chewing gum. In Figure 9-1, I give you the Apple TV's Apple Remote! (No need for applause, the Apple Remote has garnered enough in the press already.)

If you're already a Mac owner who's used the Front Row application, you know that the Apple Remote has been shipping with all sorts of Macs for a couple of years now. Front Row is essentially a menu system for displaying multimedia from iTunes and iPhoto on your Mac's screen, and for remotely controlling your Mac's DVD player. (Sound familiar? Yep, it's the computer-based ancestor of Apple TV!)

Your Apple Remote has a maximum range of about 30 to 40 feet — but that mileage varies in the real world, of course. To determine the maximum distance in your living room, pick up the remote and pause and restart a song or movie while you slowly walk backward. When the indicator light on your Apple TV no longer flashes white and there's no response from your Apple TV unit, you've reached the end of the line.

The Apple Remote has detent buttons — in other words, they click — so it's easy to tell when you've made a choice. With that in mind, here's a Mark's Maxim that I follow religiously:

Don't mash the buttons on your Apple Remote. Treat it with kindness, and it'll last.

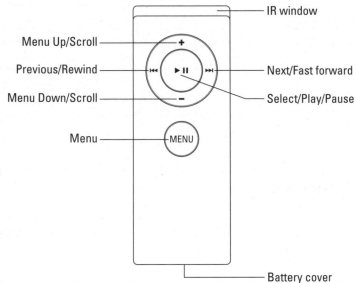

Figure 9-1:
The svelte lines of the coolest remote in computing.

Using the Menu System

Although your Apple Remote is simple and elegant in design, it actually has multiple uses within all the different Apple TV functions. For example, one moment your remote is navigating menus, the next moment it's working magic while you're watching a movie or listening to an audiobook.

In this section, I detail everything that your Apple Remote can do with a series of informative tables . . . truly, the stuff of classic literature.

Navigating menus

First up on the review of Apple Remote functions is the most basic set of controls, as shown in Table 9-1: navigating the Apple TV menus and selecting submenus, features, and settings.

Table 9-1	Apple TV Menu Functions
Button	*Action*
Menu	Press once to return to the previous menu, press and hold to return to the top-level (Main) menu.
Menu down/scroll	Navigate down through menu options.
Menu up/scroll	Navigate up through menu options.
Play/Pause	Select the highlighted menu item or toggle the highlighted setting.

The plus and minus buttons on your Apple Remote *do not* control the volume of your media. In order to increase or decrease the volume, use the remote for your TV or external speaker system.

Playing movies

While playing video, your Apple TV remote makes you the director — use it to adjust, pause, and move through your favorite films and music videos. Table 9-2 provides all the details.

Table 9-2	Apple TV Video Functions
Button	*Action*
Play/Pause	Play the video (press again to Pause).
Next/Fast forward	Press once to skip to the next chapter, or press and hold to fast-forward (press again to increase speed).
Previous/Rewind	Press once to return to the previous chapter, or press and hold to rewind (press again to increase speed).

There are also two "combo" button sequences for video. Press Play/Pause to pause a video, and then you can press and hold Next/Fast forward or Previous/Rewind to play the video in slow-motion. Also, press Play/Pause to pause the video, and then press Next/Fast forward or Previous/Rewind (*without* holding down the button) to advance or back up in ten-second increments. *Sweet!*

Watching a video podcast? If the podcast has embedded chapter markers, you can press Next/Fast forward or Previous/Rewind to move through the chapters, just like a movie.

Playing audio of all sorts

Next, I get to the music — and audiobooks, and audio podcasts. While listening to audio, your Apple Remote shoulders the responsibilities shown in Table 9-3.

Table 9-3	Apple TV Audio Functions
Button	*Action*
Play/Pause	Play the audio (press again to Pause).
Next/Fast forward	Press once to skip to the next track, or press and hold to fast-forward the current audio.
Previous/Rewind	Press once to return to the beginning of the current track, press twice to return to the previous track, or press and hold to rewind the current track.

Watching a photo slideshow

A slideshow is probably static, right? Not with your Apple TV! Table 9-4 lists the controls available from the Apple Remote while you're watching a slideshow.

Table 9-4	Apple TV Slideshow Functions
Button	*Action*
Play/Pause	Play the slideshow (press again to Pause).
Next/Fast forward	Press to skip to the next image.
Previous/Rewind	Press once to return to the previous image.

Special functions

Finally, I come to the button combinations that you can use to control your Apple TV hardware itself. They include

✔ **Reset your Apple TV:** Press and hold the Menu and minus buttons together for six seconds to reset your Apple TV. (More about the reset function in Chapter 18.)

✔ **Put your Apple TV in standby mode:** Done watching and listening to your content? You can put your Apple TV in standby mode, which minimizes the electricity it uses and reduces the heat it produces. Press and hold Play/Pause for six seconds to enter standby mode — press Play/Pause again to wake up your Apple TV unit.

✔ **Pair your remote:** Press and hold Menu and Next/Fast forward for six seconds to pair the Apple Remote you're using and your Apple TV. (More on pairing your remote later in this chapter in the section, "Pairing Your Apple Remote.")

Changing the Battery

Sooner or later, it happens: You press buttons on your Apple Remote, and nothing happens. Moving closer to your Apple TV unit doesn't work, and the status indicator on the front of the box doesn't flash white or amber when you press a button. You probably need a new battery for your Apple Remote — you'll know for sure when your Apple TV displays a picture of your Apple Remote and a low battery warning!

To change the battery, follow these steps:

1. **Use a small Phillips screwdriver or the point of a pencil to press the button on the bottom of your Apple Remote.**

2. **Slide the battery holder outside the body of the remote.**

3. **Remove the old battery.**

4. **Insert a new battery, with the positive terminal facing up.**

   Your Apple Remote uses a standard CR2032 watch battery.

5. **Slide the battery holder back into the body of the remote.**

6. **Press until the cover clicks shut.**

Pairing Your Apple Remote

At the beginning of the chapter, I promised to solve that age-old question that bothers every Mac owner with two Apple Remotes: How do you make sure that the Apple Remote you're holding is the one that controls your Apple TV?

The answer is simple . . . put a sticker on the bottom of your Apple TV's remote. (I know, my handy home entertainment tips leave something to be desired, but it works.) Oh, and one more thing . . . you can pair that Apple Remote with your Apple TV!

A word of explanation: *Pairing* your Apple Remote ensures that your Apple TV responds only to the buttons you're pressing on that specific remote. If you use another Apple Remote to control your Mac desktop or laptop, that remote no longer wreaks havoc with your Apple TV. (Instead, using an unpaired remote causes the Apple TV status light to flash amber each time you press a button.)

To pair an Apple Remote with your Apple TV, follow these steps:

1. **On the top-level (main) Apple TV menu, highlight the Settings menu item and press Play/Pause.**

2. **Move the highlight cursor to the Pair Remote Control menu item and press Play/Pause.**

   You see a flashing indicator showing your Apple Remote and the Sync (chain) icon. Your remote is now paired with your Apple TV.

3. **Press Menu to return to the top-level Apple TV menu.**

   Pressing a button on your paired Apple Remote causes the status indicator light on the front of your Apple TV to flash white.

To pair your remote directly from the Apple Remote itself, press and hold the Menu and Next/Fast forward buttons for six seconds. (This is the only way to pair a new Apple Remote to your Apple TV if the original breaks or is lost.)

If you need to unpair your Apple Remote, return to the Settings menu and choose Unpair Remote.

Chapter 10

Working with Internet Media

*W*hat do you see in your mind's eye when you imagine the Internet? Some kind of huge, hulking single computer that secretly works to control the world? Or perhaps some sort of ethereal cloud of knowledge, data, and opinion that everyone reaches through a modem of some sort?

More than ten years ago, when I first started writing about the Internet, those indeed were the common conceptions. Now, though, just about everyone knows that the Internet is actually your PC and mine, along with literally millions of others of all shapes and sizes.

And my point? Well, right about now, you *should* be saying to yourself, "Self, there has to be music, movies, and pictures that folks want to share with me on all those computers! Not just the stuff I create myself, and the stuff I've bought on the iTunes Store, but content that I've downloaded to my Mac from other sources."

In this chapter, I introduce you to all the media available via the Internet as well as how you can view and play all that content with both your computer and your Apple TV.

Do I Need a Broadband Connection?

When asking yourself whether you need a broadband connection, the short answer is *yes*. You need a broadband connection to truly enjoy the different types of media that the Internet offers: cable, DSL, or satellite — any works fine. You can enjoy every type of streaming media currently available on planet Earth.

The long answer is *almost always.* With a (somewhat sharp) poke in my ribs from my editor's elbow, I suppose I can grudgingly admit that it is possible to get some types of media from the Internet over a dialup modem connection. For example, you can indeed download things like

- ✔ Digital images
- ✔ Movie clips
- ✔ MP3 songs

However, if you do decide to use a dialup connection to retrieve the good stuff, I must warn you of two very big problems:

- ✔ **Internet streaming media is a no-no.** Dialup speeds just aren't fast enough to allow your Mac or PC to receive and play *streaming* (real-time) content, such as Internet radio stations. If you're scratching your head at the word *streaming,* don't worry: All will become clear in the next section.

- ✔ **Downloading media of any quality takes forever.** I'm talking hours here instead of minutes. Remember, a broadband connection is many times faster than even a (theoretically) perfect 56 Kbps dialup modem connection. Most folks I know just don't have that sort of patience, including yours truly.

To sum up everything, consider this pithy Mark's Maxim:

If you're considering tapping into everything multimedia that the Internet has to offer, make sure you have a broadband connection for the best possible experience.

Boy, howdy, that sounds like marketing. I need a Diet Coke.

Understanding the Whole Streaming Thing

I've read that early adopters of radio just couldn't seem to get a handle on precisely where the music and voices were coming from. Owners of these newfangled music boxes would literally walk around the set, scratching their heads, wondering where the instruments were stashed!

Eventually, of course, radio sets became commonplace, and folks came to understand how broadcasting worked: Someone generated radio and TV signals through the air. Surprisingly, that's essentially how streaming video and music works over the Internet as well.

"So is Internet streaming like the content streaming I can use on my Apple TV?" They are indeed similar. As you can see in Figure 10-1, a *streaming media server* resides on a computer on the Internet, and it waits for another computer elsewhere on the Internet to request a connection. After the connection is made by the media server (or *host*), the visiting computer (or *client*) receives the music or video.

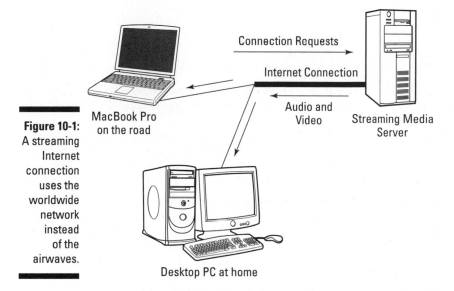

Connection Requests

Internet Connection

Audio and Video

MacBook Pro on the road

Streaming Media Server

Desktop PC at home

Figure 10-1: A streaming Internet connection uses the worldwide network instead of the airwaves.

Some media servers provide a constant flow of data. (Check out the sidebar, "Hey, do you remember the '70s?" for my favorite example.) Other servers handle only a single request. For instance, if you click a link to a video clip and the clip is streamed to your computer in real time, that video lasts only for a set time and then the connection is reset.

Getting a Handle on Internet Media Formats

Confusing and downright cryptic, *formats* are all-important when it comes to playing and recording audio, video, and images with your computer. If a program doesn't recognize the format of a media file that you download from the Internet or rip from a CD or DVD, you might as well try to watch that movie or listen to that tune with Windows Calculator or Leopard's Disk Utility!

That's my job: to familiarize you with the media formats that you find on the Internet as well as which organ(s) of your body you use to enjoy them. (Before you start getting nervous, you need only eyes and ears. There's no ODR files that you *smell*. Not this week, anyway.)

In the PC world, the snazzy three- or four-character names (extensions) that I list here follow after the period in a filename, like this:

```
BOC_godzilla.mp3
```

If I know my song names, that's likely the Blue Oyster Cult rock classic *Godzilla.* Whatever it is, it's in MP3 format, which means it's definitely audio.

Naturally, there are exceptions to this naming rule, and both PC and Mac owners might not see these file extensions, but the formats remain constant and immutable!

Audio formats

Looking for a little Ella Fitzgerald or Bill Monroe that you can play in iTunes? The six common audio formats for digital music on the Internet are

- ✔ **MP3:** This is the most popular audio format on the Internet — the mover and shaker you've heard so much about over the last few years. MP3 files produce excellent quality at a small size, but a discerning ear can hear the effects of the compression used to shrink an MP3 file. MP3 files aren't copy-protected.

- ✔ **WMA:** Microsoft's Windows Media Audio format offers better compression than MP3, so your song files are smaller and sound better. However, WMA files are almost always copy-protected, so they can't be easily shared among devices or multiple PCs.

- ✔ **AAC:** AAC is the standard for compressed audio on the Mac, offering smaller file sizes with better sound than MP3 audio. Oh, and don't forget the big selling point: The music you buy and download from the Apple iTunes Store is in AAC format. The filename extensions on an AAC file are .m4a (for the files you ripped yourself) and .m4p (for the audio you've bought from the iTunes Store).

- ✔ **WAV:** Microsoft's original uncompressed Windows audio format provides the highest quality possible, but they're so honking huge that WAV files are used these days by only the most discerning audiophiles (and you can bet those folks aren't using an iPod because they'd likely run out of space with a dozen songs)!

- ✔ **AIFF:** The original uncompressed Mac audio format, which like WAV supplies the highest audio quality possible but results in whopping file sizes. Again, AIFF is used only by those with terabytes of hard drive space and a real devotion to their music.

✔ **Apple Lossless:** Considered a step up from AAC, Apple Lossless format provides smaller file sizes than uncompressed formats, like WAV and AIFF, but the files aren't as small as music compressed with MP3 or AAC. Ah, but here's the payoff: With *lossless* compression there's never a loss in audio quality! Therefore, you often find audiophiles and audio professionals choose Apple Lossless to rip and store their audio within iTunes, and Apple Lossless is the format of choice for iPod owners who don't mind using up the additional space for the best possible portable audio quality. (Oh, and the filename extension for Apple Lossless is again .m4a. Go figure.)

Video formats

Video clips that you find on the Internet run the gamut from dancing babies to proof of extraterrestrial visits to serious tutorials on how to use Photoshop. Therefore, consider these four common video formats before you download that ABBA concert clip:

✔ **MPG/MPEG:** Nope, not miles per gallon. Rather, this is an MPEG movie. MPEG is the video format used for both DVD movies and broadcast digital television. You'll often find MPEG clips for downloading on the Internet — however, some may use alternate versions of the MPEG format, so you may not be able to play them on your Apple TV.

The acronym letters stand for *Moving Pictures Experts Group,* a gaggle of about 350 august persons around the world who decide on standards for video. The name sounds a bit lofty, but these folks are indeed smart.

✔ **AVI:** Another favorite from Microsoft, AVI format is the standard format for video clips in Windows. AVI files are average quality and average size, so it's not likely that you'll watch an entire feature-length movie in AVI format. However, Windows Movie Maker uses the AVI format, and it's a popular format for clips cast about the Internet.

✔ **WMV:** This is the latest Microsoft video format, used exclusively with Windows Media Player versions 9, 10, and 11. WMV is rapidly becoming a favorite because of the format's excellent quality and relatively small files.

✔ **MOV:** Apple's MOV format is the native video format for QuickTime under both Windows and Mac OS X.

✔ **H.264/AVC:** A high-quality video format that offers superior compression (meaning smaller file sizes) than the MPEG video used for DVD movies. The videos and movies offered on the iTunes Store use H.264, and it's the video format of choice for your Apple TV.

✔ **DivX:** The DivX format offers a great combination of small file sizes and impressive quality but hasn't quite reached the mainstream yet like MPEG or H.264. If your DVD player, computer video player, or video-editing application supports DivX, it's a good choice for downloading content (as well as burning content to a recordable DVD disc).

Image formats

Last, but certainly not least, I cover the common picture formats for sharing images on the Internet. You're probably already familiar with JPEG images, which are by far the most popular format: JPEG is the format used by most digital cameras to store photographs and is also the ruling format for putting pictures on Web pages. JPEG images offer a good cross between compression (meaning smaller file sizes) and quality.

However, here are a number of other formats that you might encounter during your cybernetic travels:

- **PNG:** A relative newcomer, the PNG format is essentially an improved JPEG format, with even better compression. PNG is becoming more popular with mainstream Web designers, having been a hit with Linux users for years now.

- **GIF:** Ah, a format dating back to *before* the Good Old Days of the Web! The GIF format was once the standard for virtually all digital photographs, offering smaller file sizes that were easily displayed by most browsers . . . but JPEG and PNG offer far better image quality, so GIF has been relegated to the bench. You're more likely to encounter a Ford Pinto these days than a GIF image.

- **TIF/TIFF:** A great cross-platform choice, TIFF images are popular among Windows, Macintosh, and Linux graphics professionals who need archival quality. JPEG images compress better than TIFF, but TIFF images are higher in quality.

- **BMP:** Ah, old-timer PC owners will easily recognize the familiar Windows Bitmap format, which is still the standard Windows image format. Bitmap images offer the highest quality possible, so they're great for archiving source images to CD or DVD, but boy, howdy — a bitmap image is *huge*. (That's because they're not compressed at all.) Don't even think about putting a bitmap image on your Web site unless you're a photographer offering superior images for downloading.

- **PDF:** Hmm . . . is it an image format, or a document format? Actually Adobe's PDF format is both! The free Adobe Acrobat Reader application (available at www.adobe.com) can display or print a document in its original appearance across all sorts of platforms, including computing stalwarts like UNIX and mobile PDAs like the Palm. Graphics professionals use PDF to ensure that their projects look and print the same no matter what type of computer receives them.

Formats Supported by Apple TV

In the last section, I cover the most popular formats for audio, video, and photographs on the Internet, and you can play most of the audio and video formats I mention on your Mac or PC through iTunes. (Of course, other third-party applications for both computers can play all sorts of proprietary formats as well, like DivX.)

However, your Apple TV is a bit more finicky when it comes to the content it can use, so the list of supported formats is much shorter. At the time of this writing, here are the formats you can stream from iTunes to your Apple TV:

- **Audio:** Your Apple TV supports AAC, Apple Lossless, AIFF, WAV, and MP3 files.

- **Video:** You can watch video in H.264 and standard MPEG-4 formats (not including formats that require special codecs, like DivX).

- **Photos:** Apple TV can handle pictures in JPEG, BMP, TIFF, GIF, and PNG formats.

"But Mark, what happens if I want to watch an AVI video using my Apple TV?" Unfortunately, dear reader, you have to *convert* (a fancy word for change) that AVI video to a supported format, like MPEG-4, before you can stream it to your TV by using iTunes and Apple TV. A number of third-party solutions convert formats, and you can even use QuickTime Pro to take care of many conversions. Appendix A includes more information on converting file formats.

Oh, and that's yet another reason to keep your Apple TV unit updated with the latest firmware — Apple might add more support for other formats in the future. (Keep your fingers crossed, like I do.)

Listening to Downloaded Music

Okay, you've located a number of great yodeling classics in MP3 format on a Web site, and you've downloaded them to your computer with the greatest of ease. You'll be happy to know that adding those hits to your iTunes library is just as simple!

In this section, I show you how to add music that you've downloaded to your collection, and make it available to iTunes and your Apple TV.

Where can I get music?

First, you have to consider the various sources of digital music on the Internet. You can grab stuff from the following:

- ✔ **Band Web sites:** Many bands distribute tracks from their albums in MP3 format, free for the downloading.

- ✔ **Amazon.com:** Amazon always has a surprising selection of free music online.

- ✔ **MP3 Web sites:** Favorite sites, like Download.com and mp3.com, are great choices for pulling down free music from practically every genre. Again, a trip to Google.com and a quick search are all you need to uncover dozens of free MP3 sites.

- ✔ **Apple's iTunes Store:** A featured free song is always on the Apple iTunes Store, but you'll also be attracted to the large selection of ultra-cheap tracks. (At 99 cents a pop, you can easily create a great mix CD for your next road trip.)

You might have noticed that the preceding list doesn't include the tracks that you can rip from your audio CD collection. No surprise there because I don't count your CD/DVD drive as an Internet source. Remember, you're not downloading anything when you rip music from an audio CD, and you don't even have to be connected to the Internet.

You can find all sorts of illegal pirated music available from sharing networks and Usenet newsgroups. Note the word *illegal*. I don't discuss these sources in this book. The quality of these pirated files isn't guaranteed, so you might end up with incomplete or choppy music. (Oh, and before you spend your time downloading music from these bandits, remember that you're usually being tracked.)

Adding and listening to your hits with iTunes

Ready to add your favorite Slim Whitman classics to your iTunes library? You can use a number of different methods to add one or more songs in iTunes:

- ✔ Drag the song file icons from the Leopard Finder to the iTunes track list.

- ✔ Drag the song file icons from Windows Explorer to the iTunes track list.

- ✔ Choose File⇨Add to Library to display a standard File Open dialog. Navigate to the songs you want, select them, and then click Choose.

- ✔ Press Ctrl+O on a PC or ⌘+O on a Mac.

To add an entire folder of songs, choose File➪Add to Library again, but this time select the folder that contains the Sum Total of All Songs that Frank Zappa Ever Performed. Click OK to add the songs to your library. (Better have a huge amount of free space on your drive to hold the contents of *that* folder!) Alternately, drag the folder to the iTunes source list and drop it on the Playlists header, and iTunes creates a new playlist with the same name as the folder and automatically imports the songs. That, friends, is the very definition of *sassy*!

To play a song, double-click the song name in the track list. iTunes displays the track name and progress slider in the Track/Status display. (Try clicking and dragging the diamond in the progress slider, and you'll discover an easy way of moving through your music.)

For more information on organizing your music into playlists, check out Chapter 11. It's a good chapter, I guarantee!

Buying media on the iTunes Music Store

As I mention earlier, you can spend a little pocket change to get primo media. For example, the iTunes Store is ready to serve your needs, with well over a million tracks for you to choose from! Most single tracks cost only 99 cents each, and most full albums cost ten bucks at the time of this writing. Recently, that Jobs fellow added music videos, full-length movies, and TV shows as well, so you can pick up video to watch at the same time. *Sassy!*

After you create an account, browsing or buying is easy. Click the iTunes Store entry in the source list. After a moment or two, you see the entrance to the Store (as shown in Figure 10-2). To browse, simply

- Click an album cover from the entrance page.
- Click a link to one of the day's top songs, albums, movies, or videos.
- Click a link in the iTunes STORE section to start browsing.
- Click the Power Search link to perform an advanced search for just that one artist or album.

While you drill deeper into your favorite media, notice the back and forward arrows and the Home icon right under the iTunes track display. These controls work just like a Web browser, moving you to previous and next pages or returning you to the top-level entrance page (respectively).

Figure 10-2:
Nothing but
media at
the Apple
iTunes
Store!

Have you noticed those little arrows next to the album and artist names in the iTunes track list? If you already clicked one to experiment, you know that they automatically take you to the iTunes Store so that you can purchase more media by the same (or similar) artists.

To buy an item, just click the corresponding Add button next to the item in the list. The tracks that you marked are saved in the Shopping Cart subentry (under the Store entry in your iTunes source list). After you finish shopping, click the Shopping Cart entry and click the Buy Now button. iTunes immediately begins downloading your new media. Enjoy!

Listening to Internet Radio

Looking for music without downloading? As long as you have a broadband Internet connection, you can enjoy streaming Internet radio without buying or downloading a single tune! The streaming audio iTunes receives with a broadband Internet connection sounds just like an FM radio broadcast, without static (and usually without commercials, either).

With iTunes open, select the Radio icon in the source list. Figure 10-3 illustrates the station list, categorized by genre. Click a right-facing triangle to *expand* or *collapse* a category (tech-speak for displaying or hiding, respectively, the entries that it contains).

To enter a station's Web address directly into iTunes, choose Advanced⇨ Open Stream from the menu. iTunes displays a text box in which you can type or paste the station's Web address. Click OK and sit back.

After you decide what you want to hear, double-click a station entry to start playing the music.

The higher the bit rate, the better the sound. A bit rate of 128 Kbps gives you CD-quality sound, but it takes a high-speed Internet connection (such as a DSL or cable modem connection) to move all that data fast enough to provide uninterrupted music. (You'll know that you've chosen a station with too high of a bit rate if iTunes keeps pausing during play so that it can catch up to the station's data.)

You can also use Windows Media Player to listen to streaming Internet music. Click the Radio tab to display the list you see in Figure 10-4 and then click the plus or minus signs to expand or collapse the categories. Again, a double-click of any station entry is all that's required to start the music.

Figure 10-3: Lots of classical music on demand.

Hey, do you remember the '70s?

Do you remember Farrah Fawcett, disco balls, and the AMC Javelin? Do you yearn for the incomparable music that dates from 1970 to 1979? Then, my friend, do I have an Internet radio station for you! It's *MLC Radio Online* (I bet you saw that coming, didn't you?), and it features the absolute best from the Decade That Shall Never Come Again. Rock, folk, disco, R&B, soul, and even the beginnings of New Wave and Alternative. (And yes, it does include *Kung Fu Fighting* by Carl Douglas. After all, the song was *hot.*)

MLC Radio Online requires a high-speed connection (DSL, cable modem, or satellite) because all those hits are 128 Kbps, CD quality! It isn't in iTune's default list — are you listening, Mr. Jobs? — but the station address is on my Web site, MLC Books Online, at `www.mlcbooks.com`. See you there, *Starsky & Hutch* fans!

Figure 10-4:
This is how Mr. Gates listens to Internet radio.

Locating Video on the Internet

I'm not talking about the postage stamp–sized video clips you get in e-mail from Aunt Harriet. (They are *hugely* funny, aren't they? The dog and the bowl of spaghetti — a true laugh riot. Woo-hoo.)

No, I mean *streaming* video clips (of decent dimensions) that document current events — or even entire TV shows. Like free music on the Internet, free video clips are all over cyberspace!

You can use the tried-and-true Google method of searching for free clips, but I have a number of favorite sources that I want to share. They include

- **News Web sites:** Sites, like CNN.com and *The New York Times* (at `nytimes.com`), have an exceptionally good selection of video clips.

- **Apple's Movie Trailers site:** Check out Apple's QuickTime Movie Trailers site at `www.apple.com/trailers` to see a huge selection of the latest high-quality movie trailers. In fact, many are even in high definition!

   These clips are in MOV format, so you need QuickTime to see them. The iTunes installation program also installs the QuickTime player (see Figure 10-5).

- **ABC:** Visit `www.abc.com` for the network's free video clips, including previews and prime time TV episodes.

- **iTunes Store:** Yep, you can often find free episodes of TV shows on the TV Episodes section of the Store. *w00t!*

- **Microsoft Windows Media Player music videos:** Crank up Windows Media Player and click the Video tab to display a collection of music videos.

Figure 10-5:
The elegant lines of Apple's QuickTime player for clips in MOV format.

Watching Streaming Internet Video

How you watch a streaming video clip over the Internet couldn't be easier: Just click a link to a video clip on a Web site. However, what happens next depends on the format of the file. You might see one of the following appear:

✔ **A custom Web video player:** The site might have a custom-made video player that uses Java or Adobe Flash to display the clip within your browser. Figure 10-6 illustrates the Web video player used by Microsoft on the MSN Music site.

✔ **The QuickTime player:** As I mention earlier, you see the QuickTime player window if you're watching trailers on the Apple Web site or if the clip you're receiving is in MOV format.

✔ **The Windows Media Player:** If a streaming video is in AVI or WMV format, the incoming signal might automatically run Windows Media Player to display the clip.

To watch a QuickTime video within iTunes, just drag the file's icon to the iTunes window.

Figure 10-6:
A custom streaming video player can run automatically from a Web site.

Chapter 11

Enjoying Music and Video on Apple TV

In This Chapter

▶ Using playlists to arrange your content

▶ Shuffling music

▶ Watching all types of video

▶ Enjoying podcasts and audiobooks

▶ Buying new content from the iTunes Store

▶ Downloading free streaming content from Apple.com

*1*t's just plain *deceptive*. That's what it is.

I'm talking about The Apple TV menu system. It looks so doggone simple, most folks don't give it a second glance. In fact, I'll bet that many Apple TV owners have never even considered digging much deeper because it's so easy to dive right in to their movies and music.

Don't be fooled, dear reader! Look past those mirrored surfaces, muted sounds, and attractive icons and see the power and flexibility under the surface of your Apple TV's menu system. In this chapter, I demonstrate how you can take advantage of the built-in filtering features, and you find out more about how you can create playlists under iTunes to fit your every mood. I also show you how to access each type of content (even those that are located where you might not expect them, like music videos).

Finally, I delve into the iTunes Store — where I've spent just a little cash on a huge chunk of content already — and I demonstrate just how cool it is to stream music videos and movie trailers from Apple!

Just remember: Looks *can* be deceiving when it comes to menus!

Working with Playlists

If you've already accumulated thousands of songs and dozens of videos and films, you know the hard truth about your content: Your iTunes Library can quickly become a fearsomely huge beastie. For example, your library can store thousands upon thousands of songs, and if it grows anywhere near that large, finding a good selection of music for your next square dance party on your Apple TV is *not* going to be a fun task.

Here's the kicker: In order to organize (or "divide and conquer") your content on your Apple TV, it's essential to turn to your iTunes application on your computer! You can do this by using playlists.

A definition first: A *playlist* is a collection of some of your files from the Library that you want to group together. You can create as many playlists as you want, and each playlist can contain any number of

✔ Songs

✔ Videos and movies

✔ Podcasts

✔ Audiobooks

✔ Music videos

Whereas the Library sections list all available content, a playlist displays only the media that you add to it. Further, any changes that you make to a playlist affect only that playlist, leaving the Library intact.

To create a playlist, you can do any of the following:

✔ **Choose File⇨New Playlist.**

✔ **Press ⌘+N on the Mac, or Ctrl-N on the PC.**

✔ **Choose File⇨New Playlist from Selection.** This creates a new playlist and automatically adds any tracks that are currently selected. (Remember, to select a track, click it. To select multiple tracks, hold the ⌘ key on the Mac or the Ctrl key on the PC while clicking.)

✔ **Click the New Playlist button in the iTunes window** (the plus sign button in the lower-left corner, as shown in Figure 11-1). You get a newly created empty playlist (the toe-tappin' *untitled playlist*).

All playlists appear in the source list. To load a playlist, select it in the source list; iTunes displays the contents.

Figure 11-1:
Figure 11-1:
Add a new
playlist
using this
button in
iTunes.

New Playlist

To help organize your playlists, it's a good idea to ... well ... *name* them. (Aren't you glad now that you have this book?) For example, suppose that you want to plan a party for your polka-loving friends, and you want to show off your Apple TV. Instead of running to your Apple Remote after each song to change the music, you could create a polka-only playlist. Select and start the playlist at the beginning of the party, and you won't have to worry about changing the music or video the whole night. (You can concentrate on the accordion.)

Oh, and it gets better: The same song or video can appear in any number of playlists because the items in a playlist are simply pointers to the actual content in your Library — not the files themselves. Add and remove them from any playlist at will, secure in the knowledge that your stuff remains safe in the Library. Removing a playlist is simple: Select the playlist in the source list and then press Delete on the Mac, or Backspace on the PC.

Removing a playlist doesn't actually delete all those items from your Library.

You can also create a *smart playlist,* which can automatically fill the contents of a playlist by using rules that you set. (I discuss smart playlists in Chapter 17.)

It's easy to sync your Apple TV according to individual playlists that you select (reducing the size of your content on your Apple TV hard drive, speeding up the syncing process, and eliminating content you don't want to sync). You find more on limiting your synced content by playlist in Chapter 8.

Filtering Audio by Artist, Album, and Other Stuff

"Okay, Mark, playlists are cool, but is there any way to organize my content using the Apple TV itself?" You bet! You can sort and filter your music and music videos from the comfort of your couch, using your Apple Remote. Note that these filters work whether you're syncing or streaming content, so you always see the corresponding submenu items.

To view the categories available for filtering music, choose the Music menu item from the Apple TV main menu. Besides the playlists I discuss in the previous section, the Music menu items include

- ✔ **Music videos:** Display just your collection of music videos. Fun for the entire family! (Especially if you have everything that Weird Al has ever done, like I have.)
- ✔ **Artists:** Sort your content by the Artist tag.
- ✔ **Albums:** Choose music and music videos by the album where they appeared.
- ✔ **Songs:** Sort your music by song name.
- ✔ **Genres:** As I mention elsewhere in the book, I'm not a particularly huge fan of genre classification from other people — of course, I've assign the genre tags to my music, so filtering by genre works like a charm.
- ✔ **Composers:** No, it's not all about just classical music — soundtracks also benefit from the Composer filter. (Heck, more than half of my music collection has a composer assigned, including rock and alternative stuff.)
- ✔ **Audiobooks:** I discuss audiobooks later in this chapter.

Here's yet another good reason to take the time to "detail" your content: Completing the tag information in iTunes for your music allows you to take full advantage of these filtering criteria. If a song's tag information doesn't include a genre or album name, take the time to enter that data so that you have more complete control over your music when it arrives on your Apple TV!

To back out of a sort or filter submenu, just press the Menu button on your Apple Remote — this allows you to divide and conquer your music collection from another angle.

Shuffling Songs 101

One of the most popular features of Apple's iPod personal music players has been its *Shuffle* feature: Turn Shuffle on, and your iPod randomly plays selections from your entire music library. iTunes also has a Shuffle mode, as does your Apple TV.

You can turn Shuffle mode on from the Music menu. When your Apple TV is in Shuffle mode, the Shuffle icon appears above the progress bar while you're listening to your music. (It looks like two parallel arrows crossing each other.)

You can use the Next/Fast forward button on your Apple Remote to move to the next song. Press Previous/Rewind once to restart the current song at the beginning. Press the Previous/Rewind button twice in quick succession to return to the previous song.

Your Apple TV also offers a *Party Shuffle* feature, which also provides a random selection of songs taken from your iTunes Library. Unlike regular Shuffle mode, however, in Party Shuffle mode your Apple TV displays the list of songs that are coming up, and you can jump directly to a song by selecting it from the menu and pressing Play/Pause. From within the Apple TV Playlist menu, choose the Party Shuffle menu item. Enjoy!

Watching All Sorts of Video

You have all sorts of video on your Apple TV, right? Your stuff can include

- ✔ Your own video clips that you've created with iMovie HD, Final Cut, Final Cut Express, or any other application that creates video
- ✔ Short videos that you've downloaded from Web sites
- ✔ Full-length movies and music videos that you've bought from the iTunes Store
- ✔ TV show episodes that you've bought from the iTunes Store
- ✔ Video podcasts

You'll note that I didn't include movie trailers, top TV shows, top films, and top music videos offered by Apple in that list — that's because those are free streaming offerings from the Apple Web site, and I cover them later in this chapter.

In this section, I cover each class of video and how you access them on your Apple TV.

Viewing your films and videos

You can sync or stream your full-length movies and your own video to your Apple TV hard drive, as I demonstrate in Chapter 8. To choose what to watch, select Movies from the top-level Apple TV menu and press Play/Pause. You see your collection of films and clips listed. Films that you've purchased from the iTunes Store include a short description as well as

- Major actors
- The film's director and producer
- The genre
- The total length in hours:minutes:seconds format

Videos that you've downloaded or created on your computer won't have this information, of course, but Apple TV displays a frame from the video to help you keep track of the subject and the total length of the video.

If you've purchased audio or video content from the iTunes Store and the item displays the [Explicit] label in the description, you'll hear or see adult material. Keep this in mind when children are close by!

While you're watching your video, you can press Play/Pause to display the progress bar, which indicates your current point in the video.

If you press Menu to back out of a movie or video while it's playing and you return to that movie or video later, Apple TV displays a prompt asking if you want to return to the action at the point where you left off, or if you'd rather start at the beginning again. Use your Apple Remote's plus and minus buttons to make your selection and then press Play/Pause.

Watching TV on . . . well . . . your TV

Apple has a huge number of television shows available on the iTunes Store these days. To choose a show, choose TV Shows from the top-level Apple TV menu and press Play/Pause.

Note that you can choose between displaying your episodes by the date you downloaded them (Date) or by their title (Show). To toggle the display mode, press the Next/Fast forward and Previous/Rewind.

Like films you buy from the iTunes Store, TV show episodes have a description, and you also see

- ✔ The original air date
- ✔ The episode number
- ✔ The season number (if the iTunes Store offers multiple seasons of the show)
- ✔ The total length in hours:minutes:seconds format

Enjoying music videos

Although you and I might consider music videos to fit more in the Movies category, Apple places them on the Music menu (and also includes them in the Music syncing rules, as I cover in Chapter 8). Therefore, to watch a music video from your collection, choose Music from the top-level Apple TV menu, press Play/Pause, and then select Music Videos and press Play/Pause again.

Music videos are grouped into submenus by the artist, just as if you'd chosen the Artist category from the Music menu. Selecting an artist displays a list of all the music videos performed by that artist. To see a complete listing of all your music videos, select the All submenu.

Each music video thumbnail includes

- ✔ The artist
- ✔ The genre
- ✔ The total length in hours:minutes:seconds format

Watching video podcasts

Unlike the original audio-only podcasts, video podcasts include still images and video clips along with the audio. Your Apple TV includes video podcasts under the Podcasts menu — from the top-level Apple TV menu, choose the Podcast menu item and press Play/Pause. The podcasts available from iTunes appear grouped by the show name.

If the podcast you select includes multiple episodes, you can choose a specific episode from the submenu that appears.

Each video podcast includes a short description, as well as

- ✔ The artists
- ✔ The original air date
- ✔ The total length in hours:minutes:seconds format

Listening to Audio Podcasts and Audiobooks

Still think podcasts and audiobooks are meant only for folks with an iPod? Your Apple TV can open up the world of podcasting just as easily, and you can sync just the most recent or unplayed podcast episodes to help conserve space on your Apple TV's hard drive (as I explain in Chapter 8).

Like albums and music videos, audiobooks are sold on the iTunes Store. However, virtually all podcasts are free to download from the Store — you won't even need an iTunes Store account to subscribe and download to podcasts. After you subscribe to a podcast using iTunes, the application keeps track of updated episodes and can download them automatically for you.

To access your collection of podcasts, select the Podcasts menu item from the top-level Apple TV menu. If you've synced multiple episodes for a show you select, you can choose a specific episode from the submenu that appears.

While playing, your Apple TV can display any still images that are included with a podcast episode. Other information displayed includes

- ✔ The artists
- ✔ The original air date
- ✔ The total length in hours:minutes:seconds format

Apple TV treats your audiobooks as music, so you find the Audiobooks submenu under the Music menu. The audiobook information displayed includes

- ✔ The artists
- ✔ The original air date
- ✔ The genre
- ✔ The number of tracks
- ✔ The total length in hours:minutes:seconds format

Buying Stuff from the iTunes Store

I know I've been jabbering away about the iTunes Store for this entire chapter, I have a good reason for my enthusiasm: The Store is the hottest spot on the Internet for buying music and video, and you can reach it from the cozy confines of iTunes. (That is, as long as you have an Internet connection.)

The iTunes Store creates an account for you based on your e-mail address, and it also keeps secure track of your credit card information for future purchases. After you use the iTunes Store once, you never have to log in or retype your credit card information again for that account.

Figure 11-2 illustrates the lobby of this online audio/video store. Click the iTunes Store item in the source list, and after a few moments, you're presented with the latest offerings. Click a link in the store list to browse according to media type, or click the Power Search link to search by song title, artist, album, or composer. The Back/Forward buttons at the top of the iTunes Store window operate much like those in Safari or Internet Explorer, moving you backward or forward in sequence through pages that you've already seen. Clicking the Home button (which, through no great coincidence, looks like a miniature house) takes you back to the Store's main page.

Figure 11-2: Hmmm . . . now where's that Liberace section?

Interested in browsing? You can subscribe to podcasts, peruse audiobooks, and sample TV shows to your heart's content, but if you're searching for something specific, click in the Search iTunes Store text box at the upper-right corner of the iTunes window.

To display the details on a specific album or track, just click it. If you're interested in buying just certain items (for that perfect party mix), you get to listen or watch 30 seconds of any media — for free, no less, and at full sound quality. To add an item to your iTunes Store shopping cart, click the Add Song/Movie/Album/Video/Podcast button (sheesh!).

When you're ready to buy, click the Shopping Cart item in the source list and then click the Buy Now button, as shown in Figure 11-3. (At the time of this writing, tracks are 99 cents or $1.39 a pop, depending on whether the file has a limit on duplication, and an entire album is typically $9.99 . . . what a bargain!) The $1.39 tracks are also higher quality.

The tracks and files that you download are saved to a separate Purchased playlist. After the download is finished, you can play them, move them to other playlists, burn them to CD or DVD, share 'em over your network, or ship them to your iPod, just like any other item in your iTunes Library.

Figure 11-3:
Preparing to add to my already huge selection of Bing Crosby.

If you've selected to sync all items in your iTunes Library — as I discuss in Chapter 8 — any media you buy and any playlists you create are automatically sent to your Apple TV hard drive. However, if you decide to select only certain playlists and items, the stuff you buy might not be automatically synced, and you might have to manually update your syncing rules.

Remember all those skeptics who claimed that buying digital audio and video could never work over the Internet because of piracy issues and high costs? Well, bunkie, hats off to Apple: Once again, our favorite technology leader has done something the *right* way!

Streaming Content from Apple.com and YouTube.com

Before moving on to photos in Chapter 12, I'd be remiss if I didn't close this one with the details I promise earlier on streaming content. Your Apple TV can display short audio and video clips that are automatically downloaded directly from the Apple and YouTube Web sites — all you need is the broadband Internet connection on your wired or wireless network that I mention as a minimum requirement in Chapter 2.

Each time you select a streaming content feature, the selection is automatically updated, so you find a continuously changing smorgasbord of music and video clips every time you visit!

You can access these streaming snippets o' content through the following menu items (look for the "streaming arrow" icon):

- **iTunes Top Movies:** Select Movies from the top-level Apple TV menu, and you can sample the theatrical trailers of top-selling movies from the iTunes Store.

- **YouTube video clips:** At the time of this writing, Apple has announced that YouTube video clips will be available from the Apple TV menu system. Like the content from Apple.com, the YouTube.com content will be free, and the clips you view are downloaded immediately from the site.

- **Theatrical Trailers:** Also available from the Movies menu, this is one of my favorite features within Apple TV . . . you can see the current crop of trailers for the latest movies on your TV, in high-resolution! (Sure to be a hit demonstration for your friends and family.)

✔ **iTunes Top TV Episodes:** Available from the TV Shows menu — peruse the bestselling TV shows from the iTunes Store.

✔ **iTunes Top Songs:** Select Music from the top-level Apple TV menu for the most popular songs from the iTunes Store.

✔ **iTunes Top Music Videos:** Choose Music from the Apple TV main menu to watch a sampling of the best music videos from the iTunes Store.

Don't forget, the streaming content I've mentioned here is absolutely free, and you can return as often as you like to check for new offerings. Truly *sassy!*

Chapter 12

Apple TV as a Photo Album

• •

In This Chapter

▶ Sending images from iPhoto and Aperture to your Apple TV

▶ Using photos from a folder on your computer's hard drive

▶ Syncing pictures from Photoshop Elements or Album

▶ Setting up your slideshow

▶ Controlling your slideshow with the Apple Remote

• •

*W*hen you bought your Apple TV, you probably didn't think of your widescreen TV as a huge electronic photo album. That's because most of us picture music and video as media before . . . well . . . *pictures!* Leave it to Apple to provide the connection between your iPhoto collection of digital photographs and the convenience of Apple TV.

In this chapter, I show you how to sync your favorite images, how to select just the right music, and how to set up a slideshow that leaves your family smiling, giddy, reminiscent, and — most of all — very impressed.

Choosing Images 101

It may seem a little strange to be selecting albums and film rolls from within iTunes instead of iPhoto, but in fact, you can sync photos to your Apple TV from several different sources:

🖜 Your iPhoto library

🖜 Your Aperture library

🖜 A location on your computer's hard drive

🖜 Adobe Photoshop Album (version 2 or later)

🖜 Photoshop Elements (version 3 or later)

After you sync your photos to your Apple TV, your widescreen TV becomes one of those "digital photo picture frames" — only much, *much* bigger, and with music, and animation. 'Nuff said.

Syncing images from iPhoto or Aperture

To select images from iPhoto or Aperture on a Mac, follow these steps:

1. **Launch iTunes on your Mac.**
2. **Click the Apple TV item under Devices in the source list.**
3. **Click the Photos tab.**

   The pane, as shown in Figure 12-1, appears.

4. **Click the Sync Photos From check box to enable it and choose iPhoto or Aperture from the pop-up menu.**
5. **Choose which photos to sync:**

   - *To sync all photos in your iPhoto library:* Click the All Photos and Albums radio button.

   - *To sync only certain albums and film rolls:* Click the Selected Albums radio button and enable the check boxes next to the desired albums and film rolls.

6. **Click Sync.**

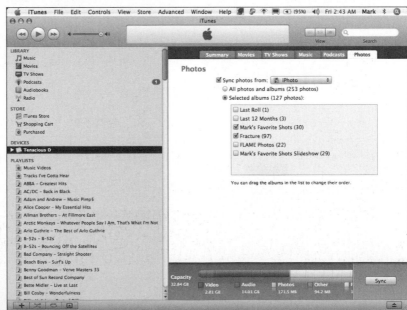

Figure 12-1: Selecting the images from my iPhoto library to sync — within iTunes!

Syncing images from a folder

To select images from a folder on your Mac's or PC's hard drive, follow these steps:

1. **Launch iTunes on your computer.**

2. **Click the Apple TV item under Devices in the source list.**

3. **Click the Photos tab.**

4. **Click the Sync Photos From check box to enable it and click Choose Folder from the pop-up menu. Select the folder that contains your photos in File/Folder Selection dialog.**

5. **Choose which photos to sync:**

   • *To sync all photos in the selected folder (and all subfolders):* Click the All Photos radio button (see Figure 12-2).

   • *To sync only certain subfolders*: Click the Selected Folders radio button and enable the check boxes next to the desired folders.

6. **Click Sync.**

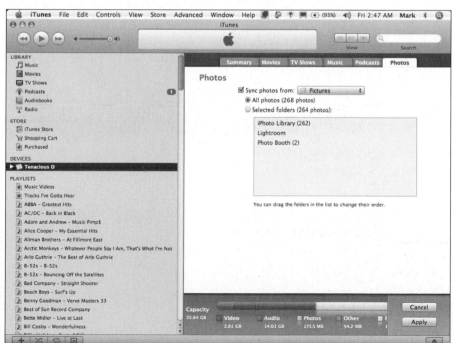

Figure 12-2:
Pulling images in from a folder is no problem.

Your Apple TV can use the following image formats:

- JPEG
- Bitmap (BMP)
- TIFF
- GIF
- PNG

Syncing images from Photoshop Album or Elements

To select images from Adobe Photoshop Album or Elements on a Mac or PC, follow these steps:

1. **Start iTunes on your computer.**

2. **Click the Apple TV item under Devices in the source list.**

3. **Click the Photos tab.**

4. **Click the Sync Photos From check box to enable it and choose Photoshop Album or Photoshop Elements from the pop-up menu.**

5. **Choose which photo to sync from:**

   - *To sync all photos in the application's library:* Click the All Photos and Albums radio button.

   - *To sync only certain albums:* Click the Selected Albums radio button and enable the check boxes next to the desired albums.

6. **Click Sync.**

Configuring Your Slideshow Settings

After you sync your images from your computer to your Apple TV, you can configure the Photo slideshow feature. The images are displayed in a slideshow, as professionally as any famous PBS documentary series, with the music you choose from your Apple TV music selections. In a word, it's *awesome*.

To set up your slideshow, follow these steps:

1. **From the top-level Apple TV menu, move the highlight cursor to the Photos item and press Play/Pause.**

   Figure 12-3 illustrates the Photo menu.

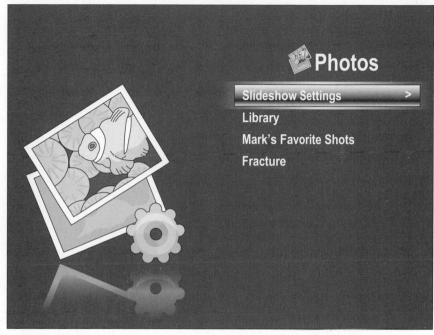

2. **Move the highlight cursor to the Slideshow Settings item and press Play/Pause.**

   Figure 12-4 illustrates the Slideshow Settings menu.

3. **Move the highlight cursor to the Time Per Slide item and press Play/Pause.**

4. **Choose how long to display your images.**

   You can choose to display each image for 2, 3, 5, 10, or 20 seconds.

5. **Press Menu to back up to the previous menu.**

6. **Move the highlight cursor to the Music item and press Play/Pause.**

7. **Choose the music you want to play with the slideshow.**

   By default, your Apple TV chooses a tune at random from your music collection (the Library setting). Unfortunately, this doesn't always fly with the mood you want to project, so feel free to choose another playlist and press the Play/Pause button to lock in your perfect music.

   Go silent by choosing the Off option.

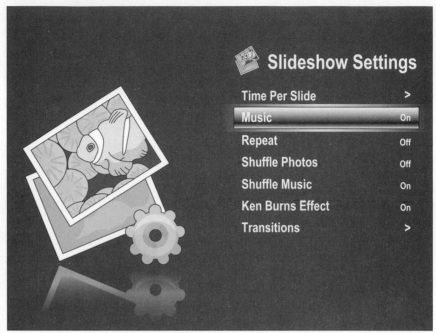

Slideshow Settings

Time Per Slide   >

Music   On

Repeat   Off

Shuffle Photos   Off

Shuffle Music   On

Ken Burns Effect   On

Transitions   >

Figure 12-4:
Setting up
a super
Apple TV
slideshow.

8. **Press Menu to back up to the previous menu.**

9. **Move the highlight cursor to the Repeat item and press Play/Pause to toggle it off or on.**

   If Repeat is on, the slideshow cycles continuously.

10. **Move the highlight cursor to the Shuffle Photos item and press Play/Pause to toggle it off or on.**

    Turning Shuffle on randomly displays the images — if it's off, the images appear in order as they appear in the library or album.

11. **Move the highlight cursor to the Shuffle Music item and press Play/Pause to toggle it off or on.**

    If Shuffle Music is on, the background music changes after each track is complete. If this option is off, the songs are played in the order they appear in the playlist you select in Step 7.

12. **Move the highlight cursor to the Ken Burns Effect item and press Play/Pause to toggle it off or on.**

    Trust me, you want this on! With Ken Burns Effect toggled on, the camera slowly pans across the image automatically to provide a mesmerizing animation effect. If you must have a static display, however, you can turn this off.

13. **Move the highlight cursor to the Transitions item and press Play/Pause.**

    Okay, some folks find transitions distracting, while others get a kick out of randomizing them. You can select a single type of transition between images or choose Random to throw caution completely to the wind. If you're looking for a more staid presentation for a public kiosk or office presentation, feel free to choose Off.

14. **Press Menu to back up to the previous menu.**

You're ready to choose the images for your slideshow and start the ball rolling.

Controlling Your Slideshow

To start your slideshow, return to the Photos menu (refer to Figure 12-3) and choose either Library (for all the pictures you've synced to your Apple TV) or one of the albums that you specified in iTunes. The slideshow begins immediately.

You can control the slideshow while it's running by using your Apple Remote:

 ✔ Press **Play/Pause** to pause and restart the show.

 ✔ Press **Menu** to exit and return to the Photos menu.

 ✔ Press **Next** to jump to the next photo.

 ✔ Press **Previous** to return to the previous photo.

Part IV
Creating Your Own Media

The 5th Wave · By Rich Tennant

"Ronny found a way to apply the 'shuffle' option from iTunes to movie content on Apple TV. Right now he's watching 'The Queen,' with scenes from 'SpongeBob SquarePants,' and 'Godzilla.'"

In this part . . .

So you're ready for the creative techno-wizard stuff? This part covers a range of applications that you can use to create your *own* Apple TV content, including the Big Three: video, audio, and images, using iMovie, iPhoto, and iTunes!

Chapter 13

Creating a Photo Library Using iPhoto

....

In This Chapter

▶ Exploring the iPhoto window

▶ Importing, organizing, and editing photos

▶ Publishing a custom photo book

▶ Creating a slideshow on your Mac

▶ Photocasting your images to friends and family

....

*B*aseball fans, take note: Apple hit the ball out of the park with *iPhoto,* a photography tool for the home user that can help you organize, edit, and even publish your photographs. (iPhoto sports more features than a handful of Swiss Army knives.) After you shoot your photos with a digital camera or receive a Picture CD from a film developer, you can import them into iPhoto, edit them, publish them, and access them wirelessly from your Apple TV unit. You're not limited to photos that you take yourself, either; you can work with all kinds of digital image files. You can even create a photo album and use the iPhoto interface to order a handsome hardbound copy shipped to you — for those moments that your family is watching something other than Apple TV.

In this chapter, I walk you through an overview of what iPhoto can do. After that, I give you a brief tour of the controls within iPhoto so you can see what features are available to you, including features for managing, printing, and sharing your photos.

Introducing the iPhoto Window

In Figure 13-1, you can see most of the major controls offered in iPhoto. (Other controls appear automagically when you enter different modes — I cover them in upcoming sections of this chapter.)

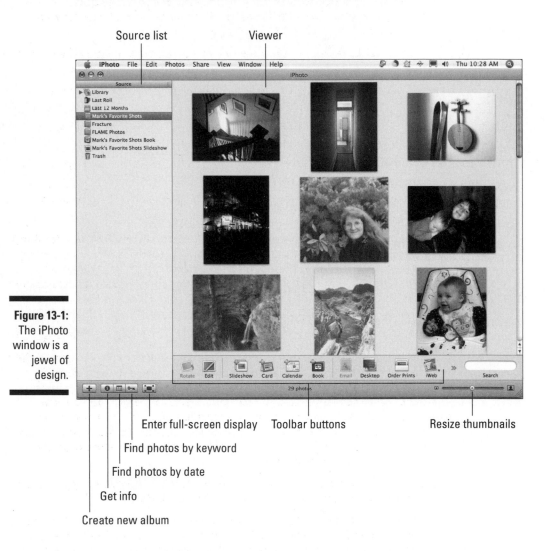

Figure 13-1: The iPhoto window is a jewel of design.

Although these controls and sections of the window are covered in more detail in the following sections, here's a quick rundown of what you're looking at:

✔ **Source list:** This list of image locations determines which photos iPhoto displays.

 • You can choose to display either your entire image library or just the last "roll" of digital images that you downloaded from your camera.

 • You can create new albums of your own that appear in the source list; albums make it much easier to organize your photos.

✔ **Viewer:** This pane displays the images from the currently selected photo source.

 You can drag or click to select photos in the viewer for further tricks, such as assigning keywords and image editing.

✔ **Create New Album button:** Click this button to add a new blank album, book, or slideshow to your source list.

✔ **Get Info button:** Click this button to display information on the currently selected photos.

✔ **Find Photos by Date button:** Click this button to view photos added in a specific month or date. While you're viewing the calendar, click the tiny Date toggle button at the top-left of the calendar display to switch between month and date displays. (A month or date that appears in bold contains at least one image.)

✔ **Find Photos by Keyword button:** Click this button to view photos that you mark with one or more keywords. (More on this later in the chapter.)

✔ **Enter Full Screen button:** Click this button to switch to a full-screen display of your photos. In full-screen mode, the images in the selected album appear in a film strip across the top of the screen, and you can click one to view that image using your monitor's entire screen real estate. You can also use the same controls that I discuss later in this chapter for editing and adjusting images — just move the mouse cursor to the top edge of the full-screen display to show the menu, or to the bottom edge to show the toolbar.

✔ **Toolbar buttons:** This group of buttons selects an operation you want to perform on the images you've selected in the viewer.

✔ **Thumbnail Resize slider:** Drag this slider to the left to reduce the size of the thumbnails in the viewer. This allows you to see more thumbnails at once, which is a great boon for quick visual searches. Drag the slider to the right to expand the size of the thumbnails, which makes it easier to differentiate details between similar photos in the viewer.

Working with Your Photo Library

Even a superbly designed image display and editing application like iPhoto would look overwhelming if everything were jammed into one window. Thus, Apple's developers provide different operation modes (such as editing and book creation) that you can use in the one iPhoto window. Each mode allows you to perform different tasks, and you can switch modes at just about any time by clicking the corresponding toolbar button.

In this section, I discuss three of these modes — import, organize, and edit — and what you can do when you're in them.

Importing images from your camera

In *import* mode, you're ready to download images directly from your digital camera — as long as your specific camera model is supported in iPhoto. You can find out which cameras are supported by visiting the Apple iPhoto support page at `www.apple.com/macosx/upgrade/cameras.html`.

Follow these steps to import images:

1. **Connect your digital camera to your Mac.**

   Plug one end of the USB cable into your camera and the other end into your Mac's USB port, and prepare your camera to download images.

2. **Launch iPhoto by clicking its icon in the dock (or in your Applications folder).**

   The first time that you launch iPhoto, you have the option of setting its auto-launch feature — I recommend this feature, which starts iPhoto automatically whenever you connect a camera to your Mac.

3. **Type a roll name for the imported photos.**

4. **Type a description for the roll.**

   If you don't expect to download these images again to another computer or device, you can select the Delete Items from Camera after Importing check box to enable it. iPhoto automatically deletes all the images after they're downloaded from the camera. This saves you a step and helps eliminate the guilt that can crop up when you nix your pix. (Sorry, I couldn't resist.) Of course, you can also leave the check box disabled and take care of deleting images manually, using the camera's menu system.

5. Click the Import button to import your photographs from the camera.

The images are added to your Photo Library, where you can organize them into individual albums as well as in a separate "virtual" film roll in the source list.

"What's that about a roll, Mark? I thought I was finally getting away from that!" Well, you are — at least a physical roll of film — but after you download the contents of your digital camera, those contents count as a virtual roll of film in iPhoto. You can always display those images by clicking Last Roll or by choosing a specific roll (both are in the source list). Think about that . . . it's pretty tough to arrange old-fashioned film prints by the roll in which they originally appeared, but iPhoto makes it easy for you to see just which photos were part of the same download group!

Organizing photos (without a shoebox)

In the days of film prints, you could always stuff another shoebox with your latest photos or buy another sticky album to expand your library. Your digital camera, though, stores images as files instead, and many folks don't print their digital photographs. Instead, you can keep your entire collection of digital photographs and scanned images well ordered and easily retrieved by using iPhoto's *organize* mode. Then you can display them as a slideshow, print them to your system printer, use them as desktop backgrounds, or burn them to an archive disc.

Importing images from your hard drive

If you have a folder of images that you've collected already on your hard drive, a CD, a DVD, an external drive, or a USB Flash drive, adding them to your library is easy. Just drag the folder from a Finder window and drop it into the source list in the iPhoto window. iPhoto automatically creates a new album with the folder name, and you can sit back while the images are imported into that new album. iPhoto recognizes images in several formats: JPEG, GIF, RAW, PNG, PICT, and TIFF. (*Remember:* Apple TV only supports five of those formats —

images in RAW format are not available from Apple TV.)

If you have individual images, you can drag them as well. Select the images in a Finder window and drag them into the desired album in the source list. To add them to the album currently displayed in the viewer, drag the selected photos and drop them in the viewer instead.

If you'd rather import images by using a standard Mac Open dialog, choose File⇨Import to Library. Simplicity strikes again!

A new kind of photo album

The key to organizing images in iPhoto is the *album*. Each album can represent any division you like, be it a year, a vacation, your daughter, or your daughter's ex-boyfriends. Follow these steps:

1. **Create a new album.**

   You can either choose File⇨New Album or click the plus (+) button at the bottom of the source list. The New Album sheet appears, as shown in Figure 13-2.

Figure 13-2: iPhoto uses albums to organize your images.

2. **Type the name for your new photo album.**

3. **Click OK.**

iPhoto also offers a special type of album — a *Smart Album* — which you can create from the File menu. A Smart Album contains only photos that match certain criteria that you choose, using the keywords and ratings that you assign your images. Other criteria include recent film rolls, text in the photo filenames, dates the images are added to iPhoto, and any comments you add. Now here's the really nifty angle: iPhoto *automatically* builds and maintains Smart Albums for you, adding new photos that match the criteria (and deleting those that you remove from your Photo Library, or those with criteria that you change)! Smart Albums carry a gear icon in the source list.

You can display information about the currently selected item in the information panel under the source list — just click the Show Information button at the bottom of the iPhoto window, which sports the familiar "*i*-in-a-circle" logo. You can also type a short note or description in the comment box. For more in-depth information, select the desired item and then press ⌘+I.

You can rename an image by selecting it in the viewer — you'll notice that the Title and Date fields below the source list turn into text edit boxes, so you can simply click in either box to type a new name or alter the photo's date-stamp. The same method works when you select a photo album in the source list — you can change the album name from the Album text box.

You can drag images from the viewer into any album you choose. For example, you can move an image to another album by dragging it from the viewer to the desired album in the source list.

To remove a photo that's fallen out of favor, follow these steps:

1. **In the source list, select the desired album.**
2. **In the viewer, select the photo (click it) that you want to remove.**
3. **Press Delete.**

When you remove a photo from an album, you *don't* remove the photo from your collection (which is represented by the Library entry in the source list). That's because an *album* is just a group of links to the images in your collection. To completely remove the offending photo, click the Library entry to display your entire collection of images and delete the picture there.

To remove an entire album from the source list, just click it in the source list to select it — in the viewer, you can see the images that it contains — and then press Delete.

Change your mind? Daughter's ex is back in the picture, so to speak? iPhoto comes complete with a handy-dandy Undo feature. Just press ⌘+Z, and it's like your last action never happened. (A great trick for those moments when you realize you just deleted your only image of your first car from your Library.)

Organizing with keywords

"Okay, Mark, iPhoto albums are a great idea, but do you really expect me to look through 20 albums just to locate pictures with specific functions?" Never fear, good Mac owner. You can also assign descriptive *keywords* to images to help you organize your collection and locate certain pictures fast. iPhoto comes with a number of standard keywords, and you can create your own as well.

To illustrate, suppose you want to identify your images according to special events in your family. Birthday photos should have their own keyword, and anniversaries deserve another. By assigning keywords, you can search for Elsie's sixth birthday or your silver wedding anniversary, and all related photos with those keywords appear like magic! (Well, *almost* like magic. You need to choose View➪Keywords, which toggles the Keyword display on and off in the viewer.)

iPhoto includes a number of keywords that are already available:

✔ Favorite

✔ Family

✔ Kids

✔ Vacation

✔ Birthday

✔ Grayscale

✔ Widescreen

✔ Checkmark

What's Checkmark all about, you ask? It's a special case — adding this keyword displays a tiny check mark icon in the bottom-right corner of the image. The Checkmark keyword comes in handy for temporarily identifying specific images because you can search for just your check-marked photos.

To assign keywords to images (or remove keywords that have been assigned already), select one or more photos in the viewer. Choose Photos➪Get Info and then click the Keywords tab to display the Keywords pane.

Click the check box next to the keywords that you want to attach to the selected images to mark them. Or, click the marked check boxes next to the keywords that you want to remove from the selected images to disable them.

Digging through your library with keywords

Behold the power of keywords! To sift through your entire collection of images by using keywords, click the Find Photos by Keyword button at the bottom of the iPhoto window. iPhoto displays the Keywords panel, and you can click one or more keyword buttons to display just the photos that carry those keywords.

The images that remain in the viewer after a search must have *all* the keywords that you specify. If an image is identified, for example, by only three of the four keywords you chose, it isn't a match and doesn't appear in the viewer.

You're gonna need your own keywords

I bet you take photos of other things besides just kids and vacations — and that's why iPhoto allows you to create your own keywords. Display the iPhoto Preferences dialog by pressing ⌘+, (comma), click the Keywords button in the toolbar, and then click Add (the button with the plus sign). iPhoto adds a new unnamed keyword to the list as an edit box, ready for you to type its name.

You can rename an existing keyword from this same dialog, too. Click a keyword to select it and then click Rename. ***Remember.*** Renaming a keyword affects *all the images that are tagged with that keyword.* That might be confusing when, for example, photos originally tagged as Family suddenly appear with the keyword Foodstuffs. To remove an existing keyword from the list, click the keyword to select it and then click Delete.

Playing favorites by assigning ratings

Be your own critic! iPhoto allows you to assign any photo a rating of anywhere from zero to five stars. I use this system to help me keep track of the images that I feel are the best in my library. Select one (or more) images and then assign a rating using one of the following methods:

- Choose Photos⇨My Rating and then choose the desired rating from the pop-up submenu.
- Press ⌘+0 through ⌘+5.

Sorting your images just so

The View menu provides an easy way to arrange your images in the viewer by a number of different criteria. Choose View⇨Arrange Photos and then click the desired sort criteria from the submenu. You can arrange the display by film roll, date, title, or rating. If you select an album in the source list, you can also choose to arrange photos manually, which means that you can drag and drop thumbnails in the viewer to place them in the precise order you want them.

Naturally, iPhoto allows you to print selected images, but you can also publish photos on your .Mac Web site. Click the HomePage button in the toolbar, and iPhoto automatically uploads the selected images and leads you through the process of creating a new Web page using the HomePage online wizard.

Editing images with aplomb

Not every digital image is perfect — just look at my collection if you need proof. For those shots that need a pixel massage, iPhoto includes a number of editing tools that you can use to correct common problems.

The first step in any editing job is to select the image you want to fix in the viewer. Then click the Edit button on the iPhoto toolbar to switch to the Edit panel controls, as shown in Figure 13-3. Now you're ready to fix problems, using the tools that I discuss in the rest of this section.

Figure 13-3:
iPhoto switches to edit mode to handle photo tweaks.

While you're editing, click Next and Previous buttons to move to the next image in the current album or back to the previous image.

Rotating tipped-over shots

If an image is in the wrong orientation and needs to be turned to display correctly, click the Rotate button to turn it once in a counterclockwise direction. Hold down the Option key while you click the Rotate button to rotate in a clockwise direction.

Crop 'til you drop

Does that photo have an intruder hovering around the edges of the subject? You can remove some of the border by *cropping* an image, just as folks once did with film prints and a pair of scissors. (We've come a long way.) With iPhoto, you can remove unwanted portions of an image — it's a great way to get Uncle Milton's stray head (complete with toupee) out of an otherwise perfect holiday snapshot.

Follow these steps to crop an image:

1. **Select the portion of the image that you want to keep.**

   In the viewer, click and drag the part that you want. When you drag, a semi-opaque rectangle appears to help you keep track of what you're claiming. (Check it out in Figure 13-4.) Remember, whatever's outside this rectangle disappears after the crop is completed.

Figure 13-4: Drag a selection box to choose what you want to keep.

2. **(Optional) Choose a preset aspect ratio.**

   If you want to force your cropped selection to a specific size — such as 4 x 3 for an iDVD project — select that size from the Constrain pop-up menu (to the left of the Crop button).

3. **Click the Crop button in the Edit panel.**

   Oh, and don't forget that you can use iPhoto's Undo feature if you mess up and need to try again — just press ⌘+Z.

iPhoto features multiple Undo levels, so you can press ⌘+Z several times to travel back through your last several changes.

Enhancing images to add pizzazz

If a photo looks washed-out, click the Enhance button to increase (or decrease) the color saturation and improve the contrast. Enhance is automatic, so you don't have to set anything, but keep in mind that Enhance isn't available if any part of the image is selected. (If the selection rectangle appears in the viewer, click anywhere outside the selected area to banish the rectangle before you click Enhance.)

To compare the enhanced version with the original photo, press Control to display the original image. When you release the Control key, the enhanced image returns. (This way, if you aren't satisfied, you can press ⌘+Z and undo the enhancement immediately.)

Removing rampant red-eye

Unfortunately, today's digital cameras can still produce the same "zombies with red eyeballs" as traditional film cameras. *Red-eye* is caused by a camera's flash reflecting off the retinas of a subject's eyes, and it can occur with both humans and pets.

iPhoto can remove that red-eye and turn frightening zombies back into your family and friends! Click the Red-Eye button and then select a demonized eyeball by clicking in the center of it. To complete the process, click the X in the button that appears in the image.

Retouching like the stars

iPhoto's Retouch feature is perfect for removing minor flecks or lines in an image (especially those you've scanned from prints). Click Retouch, and you'll notice that the mouse cursor turns into a crosshair — just drag the cursor across the imperfection. Like the Enhance feature, you can compare the retouched and the original versions of the image by holding down and releasing the Control key.

Switching to black-and-white or sepia

Ever wonder whether a particular photo in your library would look better as a black-and-white (or *grayscale*) print? Or perhaps an old-fashioned *sepia* tone in shades of copper and brown? Just click the Effects button to convert an image from color to shades of gray or shades of brown, respectively.

Adjusting brightness and contrast manually

Click Adjust to perform manual adjustments on brightness and contrast (the light levels in your image). To adjust the brightness and contrast, make sure that nothing's selected in the image and then drag the Brightness/Contrast sliders until the image looks the way that you want.

Producing Your Own Coffee-Table Masterpiece

Okay, here's the scenario: You're showing off your photos on your television using Apple TV, and a friend of yours is smitten with a particular set of images. You could conceivably print those images from within iPhoto. . . but wouldn't it be great to present that lucky friend with a *book*?

Book mode unleashes what I think is probably the coolest feature of iPhoto: the chance to design and print a high-quality bound photo book! After you complete an album — all the images have been edited just the way you want, and the album contains all the photos you want to include in your book — iPhoto can send your images as data over the Internet to a company that can print and bind your finished book for you. (No, they don't publish *For Dummies* titles, but then again, I don't get high-resolution color plates in most of my books, either.)

At the time of this writing, you can order many different sizes and bindings, including a hardbound 8.5-by-11-inch keepsake album with ten double-sided pages for about $30 (shipping included). Extra pages can be added at $1.49 a pop, respectively.

iPhoto 6 can also produce and automatically order calendars and greeting cards, using a process similar to the one I describe in this section for producing a book. Who needs that stationery store in the mall anymore?

If you're going to create a photo book, make sure that the images have the highest quality and highest resolution. The higher the resolution, the better the photos look in the finished book. I personally always try to use images of over 1,000 pixels in both the vertical and horizontal dimensions.

To create a photo book, follow these steps:

1. **Click the desired album in the source list to select it.**

2. **Click the Book toolbar button.**

3. **Select the size of the book and a theme.**

   Your choices determine the number of pages and layout scheme, as well as the background graphics for each page.

4. **Click Choose Theme.**

   iPhoto displays a dialog asking whether you want to lay out your photos manually or allow iPhoto to do everything automatically. Automatic mode is fine, but I'm a thorough guy, so I choose to lay out this book manually.

I really need a slideshow

Of course, Apple TV provides you a built-in slideshow mode — but what if you want to create a slideshow separately, using iPhoto on your Mac, and burn that show to a DVD? Rest easy! Just click the album you want to display and then click the Slideshow button in the toolbar; you'll notice that iPhoto adds a Slideshow item in the source list. The same scrolling thumbnail strip appears at the top of the viewer — this time displaying the images in the album. Click and drag the thumbnails so that they appear in the desired order.

To choose background music for your slideshow, click the Music button in the Slideshow toolbar to display the tracks from your iTunes library. Drag the individual songs you want to the song list at the bottom of the sheet — you can drag them to rearrange their order in the list as well. Click OK to accept your song list.

To configure your slideshow, click the Settings button in the Slideshow toolbar. In the sheet that appears, you can specify the amount of time that each slide remains onscreen, as well as an optional title and rating displays. I can recommend the Automatic Ken Burns Effect — yep, the same one in iMovie — which lends an animated movement to each image. Widescreen laptop owners can appreciate the Slideshow Format pop-up menu, which allows you to choose a 16:9 widescreen display for your slideshow.

Click the Adjust button to modify the settings for a specific slide (useful for keeping a slide onscreen for a longer period of time or for setting a different transition than the default transition you choose from the Slideshow toolbar).

To display a preview of a single slide and its transitions, click the desired slide and then click Preview; this is a handy way of determining whether your delay and transition settings are really what you want for a particular slide. When you're ready to play your slideshow, click the Play button and iPhoto switches to full-screen mode. You can share your completed slideshow by clicking Share in the iPhoto menu, where you can send the slideshow to iDVD (for later burning onto a DVD), export it as a QuickTime movie, or send it through e-mail.

5. **Click Manually.**

   In Book mode, the viewer changes in subtle ways. It displays the current page at the bottom of the display and adds a scrolling row of thumbnail images above it (often called a *lightbox* view, like the default view in Apple's Aperture application). This row of images represents the remaining images from the selected album that you can add to your book. You can drag any image thumbnail into one of the photo placeholders to add it to the page. You can also click the Page button at the left of the thumbnail strip — it looks like a page with a turned-down corner — to display thumbnails of each page in your book. (To return to the album image strip, click the Photos button under the Page button.)

6. **Rearrange the page order to suit you by dragging the thumbnail of any page from one location to another in the strip.**

7. **In the Book toolbar below the page view, you can adjust a variety of settings for the final book, including the book's theme, page numbers, and comments.**

   At this point, you can also add captions and short descriptions to the pages of your photo album. Click any one of the text boxes in the page display and begin typing to add text to that page.

8. **When you're ready to publish your book, click the Buy Book button.**

9. **In a series of dialog that appear, iPhoto guides you through the final steps to order a bound book.**

   Note that you're asked for credit card information.

I wouldn't attempt to order a book using a dialup modem connection. The images are likely far too large to be sent successfully. If possible, use a broadband or network connection to the Internet while you're ordering. If your only connection to the Internet is through a dialup modem, I recommend saving your book in PDF format and having it printed at a copy shop or printing service instead. (Choose File⇨Print and then click the Save as PDF button.)

Sharing Images through Photocasting

While displaying your images on your television, has anyone ever remarked, "I'd love to see those photos on my computer at home."? Again, you could do things the hard way and burn a disc with the images. . . but why not let iPhoto do the work?

It's simple! iPhoto 6 introduces a photocasting feature that does for images what podcasting does for audio: You can share your photos with friends, family, business clients, and anyone else with an Internet connection! (Your adoring public doesn't even require a Mac; they can use That Other Kind of Computer, and an Apple TV isn't required.) However, you *must* be a .Mac subscriber to photocast albums to others — if you haven't heard the news on Apple's .Mac service yet, see www.apple.com/dotmac/ for the details.

Here's how photocasting works: You designate an album to share by selecting it in the source list and then clicking the Photocast button in the iPhoto toolbar. (If the Photocast button doesn't appear in your toolbar, it's because there's not enough room at your current screen resolution! Click the double-right arrow >> button to display the remaining toolbar buttons.) iPhoto displays the Publish a Photocast sheet, as shown in Figure 13-5.

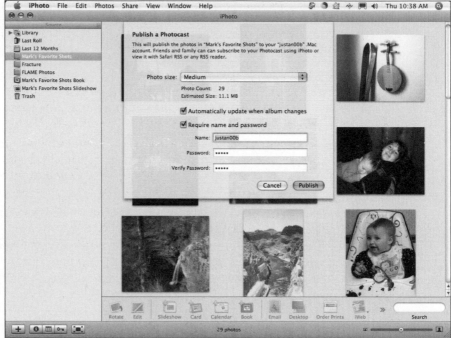

Figure 13-5:
Treat others
to your
soccer
photos,
auto-
matically!

Specify the size of the images you want to offer (full size is highest quality, natch, but also takes the longest time to upload and download). By default, any changes you make to the contents of this album are updated automatically on your .Mac account, and in turn are updated automatically to everyone who receives your images. You can turn off this feature, however, if you have a large number of images and you update often (which can result in your sister's computer downloading a lot of data).

Prefer a little security for those images? In that case, you can require that your photocast audience enter a login name and password before they can receive your photos.

Click Publish and you'll see that iPhoto indicates your images are being uploaded with a cool twirling progress icon to the right of the album in the source list. When the process is complete, iPhoto indicates that the album is being photocasted with a special networky-looking icon to the right of the album. You're on the air!

Now for the other side of the coin: By clicking Announce Album in the iPhoto toolbar, iPhoto automatically prepares an e-mail message in Apple Mail that announces your new photocast! Just add the recipient names and click Send. This spiffy message includes complete photocast subscription instructions for

- ✓ **Folks using iPhoto 6 on a Mac:** As you can imagine, this is the easiest receive option to configure. After these folks are subscribed, they get an automatically updated album of the same name that appears in their source list, and they can use those images in their own iPhoto projects!

- ✓ **Folks using Windows or an older version of iPhoto:** These subscribers can use any Web browser with RSS support (like the Safari browser that comes with Mac OS X) or any RSS reader. (In effect, your photocast becomes an RSS feed for those without iPhoto 6.)

Chapter 14

Mastering Moviemaking with iMovie HD

*W*elcome to the exciting world of moviemaking on your Mac, where *you* call the shots. With iMovie HD, you can try your hand at all aspects of the movie-creating process, including editing and special effects. Built with ease-of-use in mind, iMovie lets you perform full-blown movie production on your Macintosh with a minimum of effort.

Don't let iMovie HD's fancy buttons and flashing lights fool you: This application is a feature-packed tool for any amateur filmmaker. The iMovie HD controls work the same as many top-notch, movie-editing tools that professionals use. From basic editing to audio and video effects, iMovie HD has everything that you need to get started creating high-quality movies — which you can then send right to your TV with your Apple TV unit!

Shaking Hands with the iMovie HD Window

If you've ever tried a professional-level video editing application, you probably felt like you were suddenly dropped in the cockpit of a jumbo jet. In iMovie HD, though, all the controls you need are easy to use and logically placed.

Video editing takes up quite a bit of desktop space. In fact, you can't run iMovie HD at resolutions less than 1024 x 768, nor would you want to.

To launch iMovie HD, click the iMovie HD icon on the dock. (The icon looks like a director's clapboard.) You can also click the Application folder in any Finder window sidebar and then double-click the iMovie HD icon.

When you first launch iMovie HD, the application displays a top-level dialog, as shown in Figure 14-1. From here, you can create a new iMovie HD project, open an existing project, or let iMovie HD do things automatically through Magic iMovie. (I cover Magic iMovie later in the section, "Automating Your Filmmaking with Magic iMovie.")

Figure 14-1:
The top-level menu you see in iMovie HD.

To follow the examples I show you here, follow these strenuous steps:

1. **Click the Create a New Project button.**

2. **When iMovie HD prompts you to type a name for your project, do so.**

3. **Click Create.**

   You're on your way! Check out Figure 14-2: This is the whole enchilada, in one window.

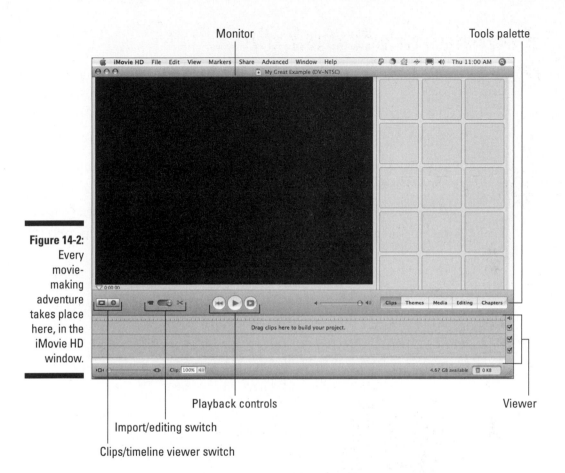

Monitor

Tools palette

Figure 14-2:
Every
movie-
making
adventure
takes place
here, in the
iMovie HD
window.

Playback controls

Viewer

Import/editing switch

Clips/timeline viewer switch

The controls and displays that you use most often follow:

✔ **Monitor:** Think of this just like your TV or computer monitor. Your video clips, still images, and finished movie play here.

✔ **Tools palette:** This row of buttons allows you to switch between your available media clips (video clips, photos, and audio) and the various tools that you use to make your film. For example, Figure 14-2 illustrates the Clips pane, which appears when you click the Clips button (go figure).

All the video clips that you use to create your movie are stored in the Clips pane. I show you what each of the panes in the Tools palette looks like as you tackle different tasks in this chapter.

✔ **Clips/timeline viewer:** iMovie HD switches between two views — the clips viewer and the timeline viewer — and I cover 'em both later in this chapter. The buttons that you use to toggle between the two views are labeled in Figure 14-2, and the clips viewer is shown.

✔ **Playhead:** The vertical line that you see in the viewer is the *playhead,* which indicates the current editing point while you're creating your movie. When you're playing your movie, the playhead moves to follow your progress through the movie.

✔ **Scrubber bar:** This bar makes it easy to crop, trim, or split a selected clip. The entire length of a clip that you select is covered by the scrubber bar, so you can drag the playback handle at the top of the bar to quickly move through the clip.

✔ **Playback controls:** If these look familiar, it's no accident: These controls are used to play your movie (in window and full-screen mode) and to return the playhead to the beginning of the movie. A different set of controls appears when you import digital video from your DV camcorder.

✔ **Import/editing switch:** Click this switch to toggle between importing DV clips from your DV camcorder and editing your movie.

Those are the major highlights of the iMovie HD window. A director's chair and megaphone are optional, of course, but they do add to the mood.

What, You've Never Assembled a Movie?

I don't want to box in your creative skills here — after all, you can attack the moviemaking process from a number of angles. (Pun unfortunately intended.) However, I've found that my movies turn out the best when I follow a linear process, so before I dive into specifics, allow me to provide you with an overview of moviemaking with iMovie HD.

Here's my take on the process, reduced to seven steps:

1. **Import your video clips either directly from your DV camcorder or from your hard drive.**

2. **Drag your new selection of clips from the Clips pane to the viewer and arrange them in the desired order.**

3. **Import or record audio clips (from iTunes, GarageBand, or external sources such as audio CDs or audio files you've recorded yourself) and add them to your movie.**

4. **Import your photos (directly from iPhoto or from your hard drive) and place them where needed in your movie.**

5. **Add professional niceties, such as audio, transitions, effects, and text to the project.**

6. **Preview your film and edit it further if necessary.**

7. **Share your finished film with others through your Apple TV, the Web, e-mail, or a DVD that you create and burn with iDVD 6.**

That's the first step-by-step procedure in this chapter. I doubt that you'll even need to refer to it, however, because you'll soon see just how easy it is to use iMovie HD.

Importing Video, Photos, and Audio — the iMovie HD Way

Sure, you need video clips to create a movie of your own, but don't panic if you have but a short supply. You can certainly turn to the other iLife applications for additional raw material.

Along with video clips you import from your DV camcorder, your Mac's iSight camera, and your hard drive, you can also call on iPhoto for still images (think credits) and iTunes for background audio and effects. In this section, I show you how.

Importing video clips

Your Mac is probably already equipped with the two extras that come in handy for video editing: namely, a large hard drive and a FireWire port. Because virtually all DV camcorders today use a FireWire connection to transfer clips, you're all set. (And even if your snazzy new DV camcorder uses a USB 2.0 connection, you're still in the zone!) Here's the drill if your clips are on your DV camcorder:

1. **Plug the proper cable into your Mac.**

2. **Set the DV camcorder to VTR (or VCR) mode.**

   Some camcorders call this Play mode.

3. **Slide the import/editing switch (labeled in Figure 14-2) to the left.**

   The playback controls under the monitor change subtly, now mirroring the controls on your DV camcorder. This allows you to control the unit from iMovie HD. *Keen!* You also get an Import button as a bonus.

4. **Locate the section of video that you want to import by using the playback controls.**

5. **Click Stop and then rewind to a spot a few seconds before the good stuff.**

6. **Click the Play button again (this may not be necessary on all cameras).**

7. **Click the Import button at the bottom of the monitor.**

   iMovie HD begins transferring the footage to your Mac's hard drive.

8. **When the desired footage is over, click the Import button again to stop the transfer.**

   iMovie HD automatically adds the imported clip to your Clips pane.

9. **Click Stop to end the playback and admire your handiwork.**

If your clips are already on your hard drive, rest assured that iMovie HD can import them, including those in *high-definition video* (HDV) format. iMovie HD also recognizes a number of other video formats, as shown in Table 14-1.

Table 14-1	Video Formats Supported by iMovie HD
File Type	**Description**
DV	Standard digital video
iSight	Live video from your Mac's iSight camera
HDV	High-definition (popularly called *widescreen*) digital video
MPEG-4	A popular format for streaming Internet and wireless digital video

To import a video file, follow this bouncing ball:

1. **Click the Clips button on the Tools palette to display the Clips pane.**

2. **Choose File⇨Import.**

3. **Double-click the clip to add it to the Clips pane.**

   Alternatively, you can also drag a video clip from a Finder window and drop it in the Clips pane.

Putting photos in your movie

Still images come in handy as impressive-looking titles or as ending credits to your movie. (Make sure you list a gaffer and a best boy to be truly professional.) However, you can use still images also to introduce scenes or to separate clips according to your whim. For example, I use stills when delineating the days of a vacation within a movie or different Christmas celebrations over time.

Here are two methods of adding stills to your movie:

✔ **Adding images from iPhoto:** Click the Media button on the Tools palette and then click the Photos button, and you'll experience the thrill that is your iPhoto library, right from iMovie HD (as shown in Figure 14-3). You can elect to display your entire iPhoto library or more selective picks, like specific albums or film rolls. When you find the image you want to add, just drag it to the right spot in the viewer.

✔ **Importing images from your hard drive:** Choose File⇨Import to add images in any format supported by iPhoto. These images show up in the Clips pane, and you can drag them to the viewer just as if they're video clips. If you're a member of the International Drag-and-Drop society, you can drag images directly from a Finder window and drop them into the viewer as well.

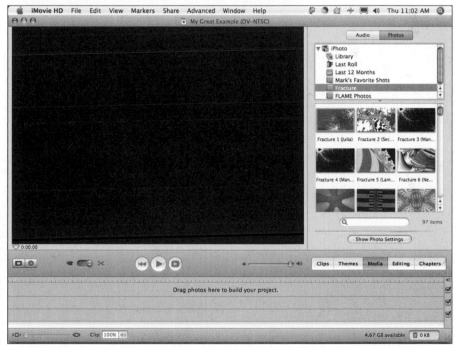

Figure 14-3:
Your iPhoto library is always available within iMovie HD.

Adding audio to your masterpiece

You can pull in everything from Wagner to Weezer as both background music and sound effects for your movie. In this section, I focus on how to get those notes into iMovie HD and then how to add them to your movie by dragging them to the timeline viewer.

You can add audio from a number of sources:

- ✔ **Adding songs from iTunes:** Click the Audio button at the top of the Media pane to display the contents of your iTunes library. Click the desired playlist in the scrolling list box, like the Dinah Washington playlist I select in Figure 14-4. (If you've exported any original music you've composed in GarageBand to your iTunes Library, you can use those songs in your own movie!) You can add a track at the current location of the playhead in the timeline viewer by clicking the song to select it and then clicking the Place at Playhead button.

- ✔ **Adding sound effects:** Yep, if you need the sound of a horse galloping for your Rocky Mountain vacation clips, click either Standard Sound Effects or Skywalker Sound Effects in the scrolling list box. iMovie HD includes a number of top-shelf audio effects from Skywalker Studios that you can use in the second audio track on the timeline viewer. This way, you can add sound effects even when you've already added a background song. Again, to add a sound effect at the current location of the playhead in the timeline viewer, click the effect to select it and then click Place at Playhead.

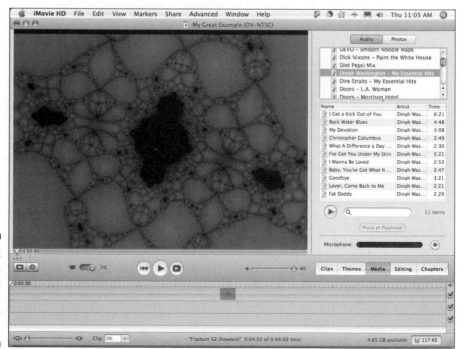

Figure 14-4:
Importing background music directly from iTunes.

If you have several gigabytes of music in your iTunes library, it might be more of a challenge to locate "Me and Bobby McGee" by Janis Joplin, especially if she's included in a compilation. Let your Mac do the digging for you! Click in the Search box below the track list and begin typing a song name. iMovie HD narrows down the song titles displayed to those that match the characters you type. To reset the search box and display all your songs in the library or selected playlist, click the X icon that appears to the right of the box.

✔ **Ripping songs from an audio CD:** Load an audio CD and then choose Audio CD from the scrolling list box. iMovie HD displays the tracks from the CD, and you can add them at the current playhead position the same way as iTunes songs.

✔ **Recording directly from a microphone:** Yep, if you're thinking voice-over narration, you've hit the nail on the head.

✔ **Importing audio from your hard drive:** Choose File⇨Import to import digital audio in any format recognized by QuickTime. The big players are MP3, AAC, Apple Lossless, WAV, and AIFF. The audio you import is inserted in the viewer at the current playhead location. Of course, you're also welcome to drag audio files from a Finder window and drop them into the viewer.

iMovie HD displays all the audio for your movie in two tracks in the timeline viewer, so you don't see your audio in the clips viewer.

With iMovie HD, you can fine-tune the audio that you add to your project. With the desired audio track selected, click the Editing button on the Tools palette and then click the Audio FX button. You see an array of audio controls that allow you to reduce the ambient noise in an audio track, apply the reverb effect you'd expect in a cathedral or an arena, and even apply precise changes with a graphic equalizer! To hear what the audio sounds like with the effect applied, click Preview — if you like what you hear, click Apply.

Mixing Your Media Together

Time to dive in and add the building blocks to create your movie. Along with video clips, audio tracks, and still images, you can add Hollywood-quality transitions, optical effects, and animated text titles. In this section, I demonstrate how to elevate your collection of video clips into a real-life furshlugginer *movie*.

Adding clips to your movie

You can add clips to your movie using the clip viewer or the timeline viewer. The Dynamic Duo work like this:

- **Clip viewer:** This displays your clips and still images. Each clip that you add occupies the same space. This is a great view for rearranging the clips and still images in your movie.

- **Timeline viewer:** This displays clips with relative sizes. The length of each clip in the timeline viewer is relative to the duration of the scene. (In plain English, a 60-second clip that you add to the timeline viewer appears half the length of a 120-second clip.)

To add a clip to your movie

1. **Click the Clips button on the Tools palette to display the Clips pane.**

2. **Drag the desired clip from the Clips pane to the spot where it belongs in either viewer.**

Do this several times, and you have a movie, just like the editors of old used to do with actual film clips. This is a good point to mention a moviemaking Mark's Maxim:

Preview your work — and do it often.

Use the View Fullscreen playback button under the monitor to watch your project while you add content. If you've ever watched directors at work on today's movie sets, they're constantly watching a monitor to see what things look like for the audience. You have the same option in iMovie HD!

Removing clips from your movie

Don't like a clip? Bah. To banish a clip from your movie

1. **Click the clip in the viewer to select it.**

2. **Press Delete.**

   The clip disappears, and iMovie HD automatically rearranges the remaining clips and still images in your movie.

If you remove the wrong clip, don't panic. Instead, use iMovie HD's Undo feature (press ⌘+Z) to restore it.

Deleting clips for good

iMovie HD has its own separate trash system (separate from Mac OS X trash) located at the bottom of the application window. If you decide that you don't need a clip or still image and you want to delete it from your iMovie HD project completely, drag the media item from either the Clips pane or from either viewer and drop it on top of the Trash icon. (Note that deleting a clip or still image from iMovie HD doesn't delete it from your hard drive.)

To delete the contents of the iMovie HD trash, choose File➪Empty Trash. To display the contents of the iMovie HD trash, click the Trash icon; to retrieve an item that you suddenly decide you still need, drag the item back into the viewer.

Reordering clips in your movie

If Day One of your vacation appears after Day Two, you can easily reorder your clips and stills by dragging them to the proper space in the clip viewer. When you release the mouse, iMovie HD automatically moves the rest of your movie aside with a minimum of fuss and bother.

Editing clips in iMovie HD

If a clip has extra seconds of footage at the beginning or end, you don't want that superfluous stuff in your masterpiece. Our favorite video editor gives you the following functions:

- ✔ **Crop:** Deletes everything from the clip except a selected region
- ✔ **Split:** Breaks a single clip into multiple clips
- ✔ **Trim:** Deletes a selected region from the clip

Before you can edit, however, you have to select a section of a clip:

1. **Click a clip in the Clips pane to display it in the monitor.**

2. **Drag the playback head on the *scrubber bar* (that blue bar below the monitor) to the beginning of the section that you want to select.**

3. **Shift-click anywhere on the scrubber bar to the right of the starting point.**

   The selected region turns yellow when you select it. You're ready to edit that selected part of the clip.

Note the handles that appear at the beginning or ending of the selection. You can make fine changes to the selected section by dragging them. (The arrow keys allow even finer adjustments to the in and out points.)

- **To crop:** Choose Edit⇨Crop. Everything but the selected region is removed.

- **To split:** Choose Edit⇨Split Video Clip at Playhead. The clip is divided into two clips.

- **To trim:** Choose Edit⇨Clear. The selected section disappears.

Transitions for the masses

Many iMovie HD owners approach transitions as *visual bookends:* They merely act as placeholders that appear between video clips. Nothing could be farther from the truth because judicious use of transitions can make or break a scene. For example, which would you prefer after a wedding cere-mony — an abrupt, jarring cut to the reception or a gradual fadeout to the reception?

Today's audiences are sensitive to transitions between scenes. Try not to overuse the same transition. Also weigh the visual impact of a transition carefully.

iMovie HD includes a surprising array of transitions, including old favorites (such as Fade In and Dissolve) and some nifty stuff you may not be familiar with (such as Billow and Disintegrate). To display your transition collection, click the Editing button on the Tools palette and then click the Transitions button in the upper right, as shown in Figure 14-5.

To see what a particular transition looks like, click it in the list to display the transition in the monitor. (If things move too fast, slow down the preview with the speed slider, which appears at the bottom of the Transition list.)

Adding a transition couldn't be easier: Drag the transition from the list in the Transitions pane and drop it between clips or between a clip and a still image. In iMovie HD 6, transitions are usually applied in real time — however, if you're working with an older Mac, the transition may take a few seconds to render. (If rendering time is required, iMovie HD displays a red progress bar in the viewer to indicate how much longer rendering takes.)

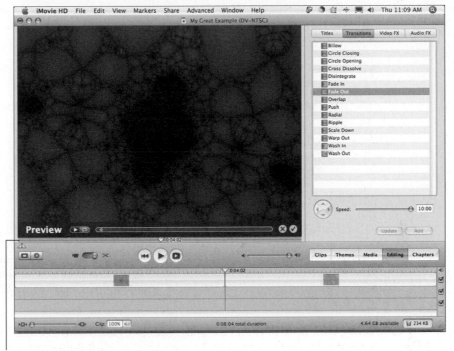

Figure 14-5:
Add
transitions
for flow
between
clips in
iMovie HD.

Scrubber bar

Oh, we got effects!

iMovie HD offers a number of fun visual effects that you can add to your clips and stills. These aren't the full-blown visual effects of the latest science-fiction blockbuster, but then again, your movie already stars Uncle Humphrey, and most people would consider him a special effect.

For example, to immediately change a clip (or your entire movie) into an old classic, you can choose the Aged Film or Sepia effect to add that antique look.

To view the effects, click the Editing button on the Tools palette and then click the Video FX button at the top of the screen. Click an effect from the list in the pane to display the options you can customize for that particular effect. The settings you can change vary for each effect, but most include the Effect In and Effect Out sliders, which allow you to gradually add an effect over a certain amount of time from the beginning of the clip and then phase it out before the clip ends. When you make a change to the settings, you see the result in the monitor window.

To add an effect to a clip or still image in the timeline viewer

1. **Click the clip or image to select it.**

   The selection turns blue.

2. **Click the desired effect.**

3. **Make any necessary adjustments to the settings for the effect.**

4. **After everything looks perfect, click Apply.**

Like transitions, effects take a few seconds to render. The faster your Mac, the shorter the time. Such is the life of a techno-wizard.

Even Gone with the Wind had titles

The last stop on your iMovie HD Hollywood Features Tour is the Titles pane. You find it by clicking the Editing button. You can add a title with a still image, but iMovie HD also includes everything you need to add basic animated text to your movie.

Most of the controls you can adjust are the same for each animation style. You can change the speed of the animation, the font, the size of the text, and the color of the text. You can even add an optional black background, but doing so actually inserts a new clip into your movie to show the text, which may affect the timing of your sound effects or narration.

To add a title, follow these steps:

1. **Select an animation style from the list.**

2. **Type one or two lines of text in the text boxes at the bottom of the Titles pane.**

3. **Make any changes to the settings specific to the animation style.**

   iMovie HD displays a preview of the effect in the monitor with the settings that you choose.

4. **Drag the animation style from the list to the timeline.**

   The title appears in the timeline viewer as a clip.

Automating Your Filmmaking with Magic iMovie

iMovie HD makes things just about as easy as can be with *Magic iMovie,* which you can use to create your movie automatically from the settings you choose from just one dialog. (I know, it sounds like a corny name, but the feature is truly cool.) If you're in a hurry or you want to produce something immediately after an event (and you can do without the creative extras that I discuss earlier in this chapter), a Magic iMovie is the perfect option.

In fact, the close integration of iMovie HD and iDVD 6 can automate the process of downloading video from your DV camcorder and producing a finished DVD. iDVD has a similar feature — *OneStep DVD* — that can create a DVD video from your Magic iMovie!

Follow these steps to let iMovie HD take care of moviemaking automatically:

1. **Connect your DV camcorder to your Mac by using a FireWire cable.**

2. **Turn the camcorder on.**

3. **Set it to VCR (or VTR) mode.**

4. **Launch iMovie HD and then**

   - *If you see the opening top-level dialog,* click Make a Magic iMovie.

   - *If you had a project open and that project appears instead,* choose File⇨Make a Magic iMovie.

5. **Type a project name and choose a location.**

6. **Choose a video format.**

   Typically, you want to use DV, DV widescreen, or the proper HDV resolution format. (Of course, there's always the iSight format, if your Mac has an iSight camera.)

7. **Click Create.**

   iMovie HD displays the Magic iMovie dialog.

8. **In the Movie Title box, type a name for your movie.**

9. **If your tape needs rewound before the capture starts, select the Rewind the Tape before Capturing the Movie check box.**

10. **If you want transitions between scenes, select the Use Transitions check box and then choose the transition you want from the pop-up menu.**

11. **If you want a soundtrack, select the Play a Music Soundtrack check box, and then click the Choose Music button to browse your iTunes music library or to select an audio CD that you've loaded.**

12. **Select the Send to iDVD check box.**

    This ships your finished movie directly to iDVD, which launches automatically.

13. **Click Create.**

Sharing Movies with Your Adoring Public

Your movie is complete, you've saved it to your hard drive, and now you're wondering where to go from here. Of course, you can choose to sync the movie to your Apple TV (see Chapter 8), but what about distributing it to others? iMovie HD has you covered there as well.

Click Share on the application menu bar, and you see that iMovie HD can unleash your movie upon your unsuspecting family and friends (and even the entire world) in a number of ways:

- ✔ **E-mail:** Send your movie to others as an e-mail attachment. iMovie HD even launches the Apple Mail application automatically!

- ✔ **iWeb:** Share your movie with the world at large by using it with iWeb and posting it on your .Mac Web site.

- ✔ **Video camera:** Transfer your finished movie back to your DV camcorder.

- ✔ **iPod:** Truly *the* option to choose if you want to watch your movie on an iPod with video support.

- ✔ **GarageBand:** Export your movie to GarageBand, where you can add it to a podcast for that truly professional look.

- ✔ **iDVD:** iMovie HD can export your movie into an iDVD project, where you can use it to create a DVD video.

- ✔ **QuickTime:** Any computer with an installed copy of QuickTime can display your movies, and you can use QuickTime movies in Keynote presentations as well.

- ✔ **Bluetooth:** If you have Bluetooth hardware installed on your Mac, you can transfer your movie to a Bluetooth device.

When you choose a sharing option, iMovie HD displays the video quality for the option. If you decide to send your movie through e-mail, for example, it's reduced as far as possible in file size, and the audio is reduced to mono instead of stereo. The Videocamera and Bluetooth options give you onscreen instructions for readying the target device to receive your movie.

If you're worried about permanently reducing the quality of your project by sharing it through e-mail or your .Mac Web site, fear not! When you choose a sharing option to export your movie, your original project remains on your hard drive, unchanged, so you can share a better quality version at any time in the future!

After you adjust any settings specific to the desired sharing option, click Share to start the ball rolling.

Chapter 15

Creating Audio Tracks with iTunes

Cast your mind back — back to the misty beginnings of time, when the iPod was new, and mammoths roamed the Earth. (Six years ago or so, to be more exact.) In those ancient days, iTunes was *only* an audio application.

Yes, good reader, it may be hard to believe now, but there were days when our favorite multimedia player–media organizer–light show–content shopping center was centered completely on digital audio: iTunes was all about ripping tracks from CDs, burning new discs, and listening to Internet radio, without video or podcasts or audio books.

And here's the good news: You don't have to be an archeologist to locate those original functions! In this chapter, I show you how to use all the digital audio tools that still form the foundation of iTunes. You find out everything you need to know to expand your iTunes music library . . . and then you can send that music through that Apple TV box of yours!

Selecting an Audio Format

iTunes and your Apple TV can handle these different audio formats:

- ✔ MP3
- ✔ AAC
- ✔ WAV
- ✔ AIFF
- ✔ Apple Lossless

Ah, but which format is best for your iTunes Music Library? Which formats save you space, which offer better sound quality, and which formats offer the best compatibility? Good questions all, and I address all three concerns in this section.

Space savers

Some formats can save you the most space — note that these formats still offer sound quality that's more than acceptable to all but the most demanding audiophile, so don't be concerned about your music sounding like something from a '70s a.m. radio!

I'll prove it to you: The two winners in this category are MP3 and AAC. MP3 is the most popular digital audio format available these days, whereas music you download from the iTunes Store is in AAC format . . . these two audio formats didn't earn that popularity by delivering sub-par sound.

The Bottom Line: Choose MP3 or AAC format if you want to fill your available hard drive space (and your iPod and your Apple TV) with as much music as possible.

Superior sound

iTunes offers three formats with top-quality sound. Two of them, in fact, offer probably the best audio quality you'll find because your music is uncompressed and pristine: WAV and AIFF formats offer the best sound possible in iTunes, but the file sizes created by these formats are huge. I mean *honking* huge. 20 or 30MB for a single song? That's about right! You'll use these two formats only if you want the absolute best quality, and you have literally terabytes of space for your music. (And forget using them for your iPod. Transferring an evening's worth of music to your Apple TV using WAV or AIFF takes considerably longer, even with the unit's wireless connection speeds.)

If you're looking for the best sound quality without all the hard drive space, Apple Lossless is the answer. You get better fidelity than either MP3 or AAC, yet the file sizes are comparable . . . nowhere near the behemoths produced by WAV or AIFF files.

The Bottom Line: If you're looking for audiophile sound quality and you're using an iPod — or you have a sizeable music library — choose Apple Lossless.

Highly compatible

The last category involves compatibility: What audio formats are recognized by the largest number of audio devices, computer applications, and personal music players? The winners are MP3 and WAV, which are supported by practically every piece of audio hardware and software on the planet.

You already know the difference between the two: MP3 files are quite small and are suitable for portable players and wireless streaming. Although WAV files are superior in sound quality, they're outrageously big, and really suitable only for archiving your music on a data DVD-ROM.

The Bottom Line: For the best in compatibility across computers and audio devices, go with MP3 every time.

Ripping Songs from Audio CDs

You can create your own MP3, AAC, Apple Lossless, AIFF, and WAV files from your audio CDs with iTunes, by using a process called *ripping*. (Sometimes you also hear ripping referred to by its more formal name, *digital extraction . . .* but then, techno-nerds have to give everything an exotic name.)

As I mention in the preceding section, you'll likely choose the MP3, AAC, or Apple Lossless format for your Apple TV listening pleasure. Because MP3 is the most compatible, the most common type of ripping is to convert CD audio to MP3 format. (Go figure.) To rip MP3s from an audio CD, follow these simple steps:

1. **Launch iTunes by clicking its icon on the Dock (Mac) or desktop (PC).**

   Alternatively, you can locate it in your Applications folder. Under Windows, choose Start⇨All Programs⇨iTunes⇨iTunes, or if iTunes appears in your Quick Launch icons, just click it on the taskbar.

2. **Choose iTunes⇨Preferences on a Mac or Edit⇨Preferences on a PC.**

3. **In the Preferences window that appears, click the Advanced toolbar button/tab.**

4. **Click the Importing tab.**

5. **Choose MP3 Encoder from the Import Using pop-up menu.**

   Figure 15-1 illustrates these settings within the PC version of iTunes.

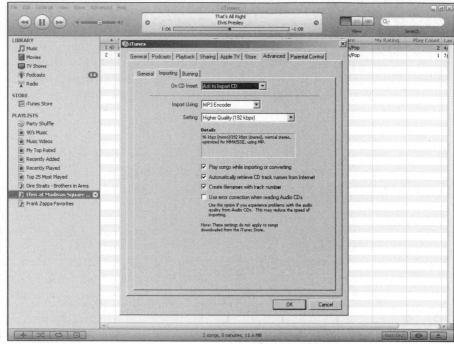

Figure 15-1:
Configuring
your format
settings for
audio CD
importing.

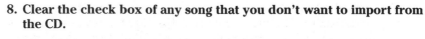

6. **Choose High Quality (160 Kbps) from the Setting pop-up menu and then click OK.**

   This bit rate setting provides the best compromise between quality (it gives you better than CD quality, which is 128 Kbps) and file size (tracks you rip are significantly smaller than "audiophile" bit rates, like 192 Kbps or higher).

7. **Load an audio CD into your Mac or PC.**

   The CD title shows up in the iTunes Source list, which is on the left side of the iTunes window. The CD track listing appears on the right side of the window.

   If iTunes asks you if you want to import the contents of the CD into your Music Library, you can click Yes and skip the rest of the steps; however, if you've disabled this prompt, just continue with the remaining two steps.

8. **Clear the check box of any song that you don't want to import from the CD.**

   All songs on the CD have a check box next to their title by default. Unmarked songs aren't imported.

   Notice that the Browse button changes to Import CD.

9. **After you select the songs that you want added to the Library, click the Import CD button.**

Burning Your Own Audio CDs

Although this book focuses on syncing or streaming content to your Apple TV, I'd be willing to bet the farm that you probably want to do something else very cool with your digital music — the same tracks that you play using Apple TV can be recorded to CD for use in your car stereo, home stereo system, and even a boombox or two!

Sure, just about any computer audio player can burn audio CDs these days, but iTunes makes recording *simple* — plus, you can burn other types of discs, too! iTunes creates CDs in one of three formats:

- ✔ **Audio CD:** This is the typical kind of commercial music CD that you buy at a store. Most typical music audio CDs store 700MB of data, which translates into about 80 minutes of music.

- ✔ **Data CD or DVD:** A standard CD-ROM or DVD-ROM is recorded with the audio files. This disc can't play in any standard audio CD player (even if it supports MP3 CDs, which I discuss next). Therefore, you can listen to these songs only by using your Mac and an audio player, like iTunes or a PC running Windows.

  If you do want to create an archival backup of your most precious music in WAV format, you definitely want to record the disc in data format!

- ✔ **MP3 CD:** Like the ordinary computer CD-ROM that I just described, an MP3 CD holds MP3 files in data format. However, the files are arranged in such a way that they can be recognized by audio CD players that support the MP3 CD format (especially boomboxes and car stereos). Because MP3 files are so much smaller than the digital audio tracks found on traditional audio CDs, you can fit as many as 160 typical 4-minute songs on one disc. (Heck, my technical editor has gotten up to 18 solid *hours* of standup comedy on a single disc! That's because those tracks — a voice recorded in mono — are much smaller in size.) These discs can also be played on your Mac via iTunes.

Keep in mind that MP3 CDs aren't the same as the standard audio CDs that you buy at the store, and you can't play them in older audio CD players that don't support the MP3 CD format. Rather, this is the kind of archival disc that you burn at home for your own collection.

First things first: Before you burn, you need to set the recording format. Open the iTunes Preferences dialog by choosing iTunes⇨Preferences (on a Mac) or by choosing Edit⇨Preferences (on a PC); click the Advanced tab and then click the Burning tab (see Figure 15-2). Select the desired disc format by enabling the corresponding radio button. Click OK to close the Preferences window when you're finished.

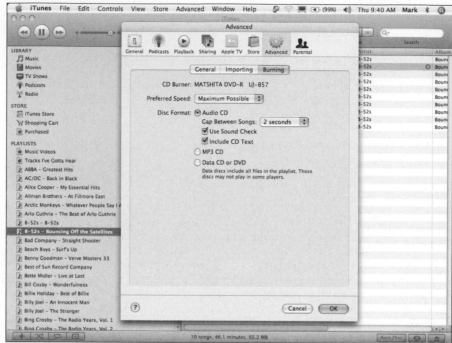

Figure 15-2:
Choosing a
format for
recording
discs.

The next step in the CD creation process is to build a playlist, as I show you in Chapter 11 (or select an existing playlist that you want to record). If necessary, create a new playlist and add to it whatever songs you want to have on the CD. With the songs in the correct order, select the playlist. Click the Burn Disc button at the bottom of the iTunes window to commence the disc burning process. iTunes lets you know when to load the blank disc and alerts you when the recording is complete.

Trimming Tracks Using iTunes

Call it very simple editing, but for most of us the ability to play a portion of a track is likely all the "manual labor" we need to tweak a song. For example, if you've downloaded a hard-to-find song from your halcyon days — only to find that it has static at the beginning or ending — you'll want to trim the offending noise so that you don't have to listen to that annoying crackle every time you play the song.

As a first step, listen to the song and note the start and stop times you prefer on a scrap of paper. Remember, you can drag the diamond in the iTunes playback progress bar to quickly rewind and fast-forward through the track to reach the desired spots.

With the new start and stop times on hand, follow these steps to trim unwanted material from the beginning or end of a song:

1. **Right-click the song you want to edit and choose Get Info.**

   The Info dialog appears.

2. **Click the Options tab.**

   Figure 15-3 illustrates these settings within the PC version of iTunes.

3. **Click the Start Time and Stop Time check boxes to enable them.**

4. **Type the new start and stop times into the corresponding text boxes.**

5. **Click OK.**

Note that iTunes doesn't actually remove the beginning or ending of the track — rather, the trimming you're doing is nondestructive. iTunes just places markers on the track indicating where you want that track to begin and end; if you display the Option tab again and disable the Start Time and Stop Time check boxes, you hear the entire song and you haven't lost a thing.

Do you have a live version of a song that has a lengthy introduction before the music starts or interminable applause afterward from the audience? Trim that stuff with a clear conscience, knowing that you can restore the track to its pristine condition later!

Figure 15-3:
Trimming an audio track to just the right dimensions.

Part V
Apple TV Tricks and Troubleshooting

The 5th Wave   By Rich Tennant

In this part . . .

Would you like a new screen saver for your Apple TV? Or perhaps you want to back up your entire iTunes Library? You find out about those tricks and more, and I've added a troubleshooting chapter with my Should-be-Patented Apple TV Troubleshooting Tree (just in case things don't go as planned).

Chapter 16

Customizing Your Apple TV

*T*he default configuration settings Apple has chosen for your Apple TV have been carefully designed to provide the most pleasant experience for the largest number of happy owners. Highly paid user interface gurus slaved for countless hours to tweak and adjust the menu system to appeal to 99 percent of humanity at large . . . and those same folks argued for who knows how long about *what* the screen saver should display and *when*.

But that still leaves 1 percent that isn't quite satisfied. I'm generally in that group.

In this chapter, I show you how to tweak *your* Apple TV — to toggle the menu system's audio feedback, fine-tune the screen saver, and check for software updates from Apple without leaving the comfort of your couch. I also demonstrate how to repeat playlists, automatically adjust volume between tracks, and work with multiple iTunes libraries residing on your home or office computer.

If you happen to be satisfied with the default settings, stick with me anyway. It pays to know this stuff!

Customizing Your Screen Saver

When I have guests over at my house, I like to fire up my Apple TV to provide music for the folks in my living room. Invariably, I get compliments every time the Apple TV screen saver kicks in on the family's widescreen LCD TV — I think you'll agree that those 3D images are truly a hoot to watch!

However, if you're using the default settings on your Apple TV screen saver, you may be missing out on your own photos. Follow these steps to fine-tune the screen saver and bend it to your will:

1. **From the top-level Apple TV menu, move the highlight cursor to the Settings item and press Play/Pause.**

2. **Move the highlight cursor to the Screen Saver item and press Play/Pause.**

   The Screen Saver screen displays, as shown in Figure 16-1.

3. **Select the Timeout item and press Play/Pause and change the inactivity delay.**

   Your Apple TV can wait 2, 5, 10, 15, or 30 minutes of inactivity (meaning no input from the Apple Remote) before the screen saver starts. If you want to disable the screen saver entirely, choose Never.

Disabling a screen saver on today's expensive LCD and plasma TVs is the very definition of A Bad Thing, because you'll be inviting *burn-in* from a stationary image. (Remember the harsh lesson taught by the screen at your local automatic teller machine location.)

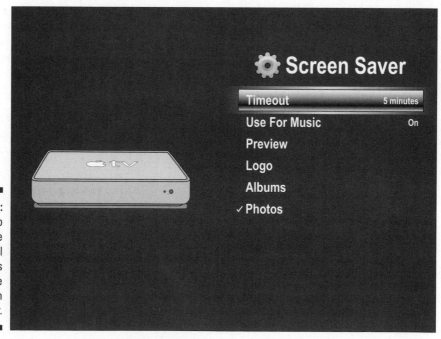

Figure 16-1: Time to configure the visual feast that is your Apple TV screen saver.

4. **Select the Use for Music item and press Play/Pause to toggle the feature on or off.**

   By default, your Apple TV displays the screen saver while playing music — however, if you'd rather keep the album art, title info, and progress bar visible at all times, toggle this setting to off.

5. **Select the visual for your screen saver:**

   - *Logo:* Displays a moving Apple logo

   - *Albums:* Displays random images from the album artwork stored in your iTunes Music library

   - *Photos:* Displays random images from your iPhoto library if you've stored your treasured digital photographs on your Apple TV (Photos are always the right choice at family gatherings!)

   Your visuals choice is identified by a check mark next to it in the menu. In Figure 16-1, I've chosen Photos.

6. **Select Preview to check out the result.**

   C'mon, you know you want to see what the screen saver looks like.

7. **When all is set just so, press Menu to back up to the previous menu.**

Toggling Sound Effects

Personally, I think those designers were spot-on when it comes to the subtle audio feedback from the Apple TV menu system — the sound effects remind me of the Starship Enterprise. However, if you'd rather have silent operation from your Apple TV, follow these steps:

1. **From the top-level Apple TV menu, move the highlight cursor to the Settings item and press Play/Pause.**

   Figure 16-2 illustrates the Settings menu.

2. **Move the highlight cursor to the Sound Effects item and press Play/Pause to toggle it off.**

3. **Press Menu to back up to the previous menu.**

Figure 16-2:
The Settings menu includes the Sound Effects, Repeat Music, and Sound Check items.

Toggling Repeat Music and Sound Check

If you're an iPod owner (or if you've been using iTunes for some time), you're likely already familiar with these two settings: Repeat Music and Sound Check.

With Repeat Music toggled on, your Apple TV plays the contents of a playlist continuously until you stop. The Sound Check feature equalizes the level of all your tracks in your Music library, keeping your KISS at the same volume level as your Cat Stevens — makes for a far better listening experience if your playlists cover a wide range of music.

By default, both these options are disabled. Follow these steps to turn either feature on:

1. **From the top-level Apple TV menu, move the highlight cursor to the Settings item and press Play/Pause.**

2. **Move the highlight cursor to the Repeat Music item (refer to Figure 16-2) and press Play/Pause to toggle it.**

   A tiny circular "loop" appears above the progress bar when you're playing music to indicate that the Repeat Music feature is on. You can see it at the far right of Figure 16-3.

HAWKINS!
ELDRIDGE!
HODGES!
ALIVE!
AT THE VILLAGE GATE!
COLEMAN HAWKINS ROY ELDRIDGE JOHNNY HODGES

Bean and the Boys
Coleman Hawkins
Hawkins! Eldridge! Hodges! Alive...

6 of 7
2:47 ▬▬▬▬▬▬▬▬▬▬▬▬▬▬▬▬▬▬▬▬ -4:06

Figure 16-3:
Your Apple
TV indicates
that Repeat
Music is
turned on.

3. **Move the highlight cursor to the Sound Check item (refer to Figure 16-2) and press Play/Pause to toggle it.**

4. **Press Menu to back up to the previous menu.**

Updating Your Apple TV Software

You already know that your Apple TV has an Intel CPU inside as well as an internal hard drive. Put the two of those together, and you have most of what you need for a computer — and that means that bugs can be fixed and improvements made to the features.

You can check on available updates at any time with your Apple Remote. I check at least once a week. To check for an update (and apply it, if one is available), follow these steps:

1. **From the top-level Apple TV menu, move the highlight cursor to the Settings item and press Play/Pause.**

2. **Move the highlight cursor to the Update Software and press Play/
   Pause to toggle it.**

   Your Apple TV connects to Apple over the Internet and displays any
   updates. It's always a good idea to install any updates offered for your
   Apple TV.

3. **Press Menu to back up to the previous menu.**

Switching betwixt iTunes Libraries

Hey, did you know that you can use multiple iTunes libraries on a single computer? For example, if your kid wants a separate library with nothing but
Avril Lavigne and Foo Fighters, you can create one (I have 'em in my library,
but you may not).

Your Apple TV can switch between those libraries, making it easy to switch
all your music at one fell swoop. (Think of that huge collection of holiday
music . . . after the season is over, you can switch back to your secular
library!)

First, create a separate library in iTunes:

1. **Quit iTunes if it's currently running.**

2. **Hold down the Option key (on the Mac) or the Shift key (on the PC)
   and launch iTunes.**

   iTunes displays a dialog that lets you create or choose a library.

3. **Click Create Library.**

4. **Type a name for the Library in the Save As box.**

5. **Choose a location — for example, an external hard drive — using the
   Where pop-up menu.**

6. **Click Save to create the new library.**

After you create multiple libraries, you can switch your Apple TV over to
another library from the Sources menu. Follow these steps:

1. **From the top-level Apple TV menu, move the highlight cursor to the
   Source item and press Play/Pause.**

   Figure 16-4 illustrates the Sources menu that appears.

2. **Move the highlight cursor to the Syncing item and press Play/Pause.**

   You see two options, as shown in Figure 16-5.

Figure 16-4:
The
Sources
menu.

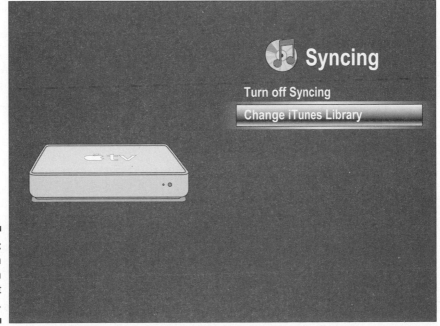

Figure 16-5:
You can
switch
libraries at
any time.

3. **Move the highlight cursor to the Change iTunes Library item and press Play/Pause.**

4. **Move the highlight cursor to Continue and press Play/Pause (see Figure 16-6).**

   Switching libraries means that your Apple TV has to perform a complete synchronization, so the contents of the hard drive are overwritten. (Note, of course, that this doesn't mean you lose the content in the previous iTunes library you were using — that media stays on your computer. Resyncing takes some time, but it *never* causes you to lose any data on your computer.)

5. **Select the desired library and press Play/Pause.**

6. **Press Menu to back up to the previous menu.**

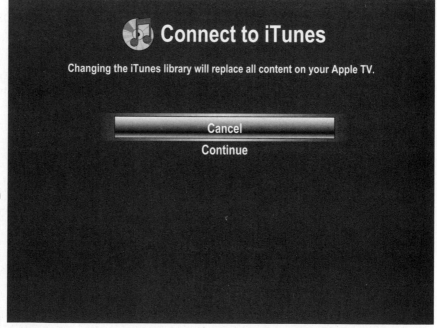

Figure 16-6:
Are you
absolutely
sure you
want to
resync your
Apple TV?

Chapter 17

Maintaining Your Media Library

*T*hroughout most of this book, I discuss your iTunes Library like it's some kind of living organism — your self-maintaining media storehouse, or perhaps your constantly growing CTT (short for *Content Treasure Trove*). It's easy to simply lump everything together and collectively label all those songs, videos, movies, and photographs as content.

Sure, I discussed playlists in Chapter 11 . . . but playlists are just the beginning to arranging your stuff. What if you want to *organize* your CCT? What if you want to actually get a handle on everything you own from Frank Zappa? Can you really launch a rating system that helps you determine what's best in your collection? If you're asking questions like this, you're likely a digital media connoisseur . . . and this is your chapter.

I'm one of those people. I listen, watch, and enjoy a library that spans an entire external hard drive (as well as an audio CD collection of over 1,200 discs). When I click Music in my iTunes source list, I have seven uninterrupted days of listening, with over 3,000 songs taking up well over 15GB of space. (And that's just this week. By the time this book is published, who knows what I'll have?)

In this chapter, I cover the tips and tricks used by myself and your fellow media collectors: not only how to document and tag, but how to back up and automate your library. You're taking iTunes to a totally new level!

Arranging and Cataloging Your Media

At the heart of any truly organized iTunes content library is data: identifying data that you can use to find, rate, arrange, and sort songs. I call it *detailing* your music, providing all the data that iTunes can call upon when you need that mix CD from 1979, or your top ten favorite country hits.

And no, the Data Entry Elves aren't going to enter or edit that data for you. (You probably knew I was going to say that.) Providing all the details to build a truly organized, state-of-the-art media library involves a lot of typing on your part, and even the occasional bit of detective work.

Here's yet another Mark's Maxim that I want you to commit to memory:

Your media library provides you far more enjoyment if you take the time to detail your content!

In this section, I show you how to add the details for your music. (You can also detail your photos with keywords and comments in iPhoto — I show you how in Chapter 13.)

Tagging your songs

Besides organizing your music into Elvis and non-Elvis playlists, iTunes gives you the option to track your music at the song level. Each song that you add to your Music Library has a complete set of information associated with it. iTunes displays this information in the Info dialog (as shown in Figure 17-1), including

- **Name:** The name of the song
- **Artist:** The name of the artist who performs the individual song
- **Composer:** The name of the astute individual who actually *wrote* the song
- **Album Artist:** The name of the artist responsible for a compilation or tribute album
- **Album:** The album where the song appears
- **Grouping:** A group type that you assign
- **Year:** The year the artist recorded the song
- **BPM:** The beats per minute (which indicates the song's tempo)
- **Track Number:** The position of the song on the original album
- **Comments:** A text field that can contain any comments on the song

> ✔ **Part of a compilation:** Enable this check box to indicate that the track is part of a compilation album — Best of the '80s, for example — and the album includes multiple artists

> ✔ **Genre:** The classification of the song (such as rock, jazz, or pop)

You can display this information by clicking a song name and pressing ⌘+I on a Mac or Ctrl+I on a PC — the fields appear on the Info tab.

Setting the song information automatically

Each song that you add to the iTunes Music Library might or might not have song information included with it. If you add music from a commercial audio CD, iTunes connects to a server on the Internet and attempts to find the information for each song on the CD. Songs you buy on the iTunes Store are typically detailed already, with accurate dates.

If you download a song from the Internet, it often comes with some information embedded already in the file; the amount of included information depends on what the creator supplied. (And believe me, it's often misspelled as well — think *Leenard Skeenard.*) If you don't have an Internet connection, iTunes can't access the information and displays generic titles instead.

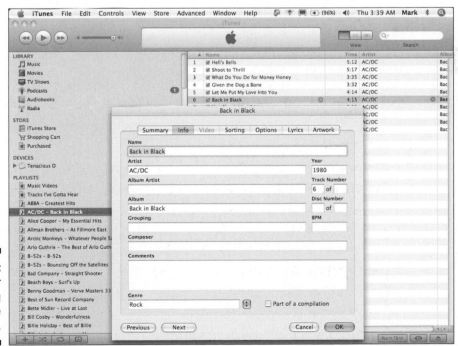

Figure 17-1:
Begin your detailing with the Info menu.

Mark's rant concerning genres

Okay, I have a few pet peeves — we all do — and one of them is any attempt to plaster one of my musical favorites with what I consider an ill-fitting "genre." iTunes offers a far better genre selection than most Web sites and online music stores, but the fact is that only *you* can assign what *you* consider the proper genre to a song. (Told you this was a button for me.)

Here's a great example: Is Benny Goodman's classic *Verve Masters 33* album *Jazz* or is it *Big Band?* One man's *Q: Are We Not Men?* by DEVO is labeled *Alternative* whereas it's another person's

Classic Rock. This means something when you search your iTunes Music Library by *Alternative* and don't see Green Day's *American Idiot* there because it's mislabeled (in my opinion) as *Hard Rock* by someone else.

Who has to make the choice here? You do because you think of certain music as fitting into a certain cubbyhole that others don't see. Therefore, make sure that you label your genres as you see fit, no matter what they're assigned by the iTunes Store or that Web site where you got them.

Setting or changing the song information manually

If iTunes can't find your CD in the online database or someone gives you an MP3 with incomplete or inaccurate information, you can change the information yourself — believe me, you want at least the artist and song name! To view and change the information for a song, perform the following steps:

1. **Select the song in either the Music Library list or a playlist.**
2. **Press ⌘+I on the Mac (Ctrl+I on the PC) or choose File⇨Get Info.**
3. **Edit the song's information on the Info tab.**

Yanking in cover art

Want to add album covers to your song info? I recommend it because the latest versions of iTunes offer a beautiful Browse feature that allows you to flip through your collection, with each album cover reflected as if they're perched on a mirror! (See Figure 17-2 to see what I mean.) iTunes can also use your album art within the Visualizer, and if you have a Mac, you can use your Mac OS X iTunes Artwork screen saver to show off your collection. (Oh, and don't forget the iTunes Print command, which can print a mosaic cover insert with all the album art and a track list!)

You can add cover art in two ways: the automatic method, which is less certain, and the old-fashioned manual method, which requires a little work on your part but always delivers the right results. (Note that adding large images can significantly increase the size of the song file.)

Figure 17-2:
No library
is fully
detailed
without
album
covers!

By the way, if you buy tracks or an album from the iTunes Store, Apple always includes album covers automatically. Thanks, Steve!

After you add artwork with either method, the image appears in the Summary pane, and you can display it while your music is playing by pressing ⌘+G (Mac) or Ctrl+G (PC), or by pressing the Show or Hide Song Artwork button at the lower left of the iTunes window!

The automatic method

iTunes can try to locate artwork automatically for the tracks you select. Follow these steps:

1. **Select the desired songs from the track list.**

2. **Choose Advanced➪Get Album Artwork.**

You can set iTunes to automatically attempt to add album artwork every time you rip tracks from an audio CD, or when you add songs without artwork to your Music Library. Choose iTunes➪Preferences and then click the General button and click the Automatically Download Missing Album Artwork check box to enable it.

Unfortunately, the iTunes Store doesn't carry every album ever to appear on CD, so sometimes the Automatic method of adding artwork doesn't fly. Hence the old-fashioned manual method.

The manual method

Follow these steps to add artwork manually to a single track, or the tracks in a single album:

1. **Select one (or all) of the songs from a single album in the track list.**

2. **Press ⌘+I (Mac) or Ctrl+I (PC) to display the Info dialog.**

   If you select a single song, click the Artwork tab. If you select multiple tracks, the Artwork box appears on the Multiple Item Information dialog.

3. **Launch the Internet browser of your choice, visit Amazon.com, and do a search on the same album.**

4. **Drag the cover image from the Web page right into the Info or Multiple Information dialog and drop it on top of the image well.**

5. **Click OK to seal the deal.**

Many Dashboard widgets that run in Mac OS X can also display your album artwork — visit `www.apple.com/downloads/dashboard` and browse by the keyword *album!* One of my favorites is the Amazon Album Art widget, by Mac Foundry, which displays the Amazon.com artwork for the currently playing track and imports it with one button click. (Kinda makes the manual method almost automatic.)

Assigning ratings

Ratings . . . talk about personalizing your media! The assignment of ratings is probably about as subjective as you can get with your iTunes detailing. You can assign a rating of anywhere from zero to five stars to every track. But what corresponds to a two-star song? And do you only want to assign five-star ratings to save time? Again, it's totally up to you, so rate 'em as you see 'em.

Later, of course, you can use your ratings to create smart playlists (which I discuss in the next section), or display them in the track list so that you can sort by your favorites.

Follow these steps to assign a rating to a track:

1. **Select a song from the track list.**

2. **Press ⌘+I (Mac) or Ctrl+I (PC) to display the Info dialog.**

3. **Click the Options tab.**

   The Options tab displays with the My Rating field (as shown in Figure 17-3).

4. **Click within the My Rating box and choose the desired rating.**

5. **Click OK.**

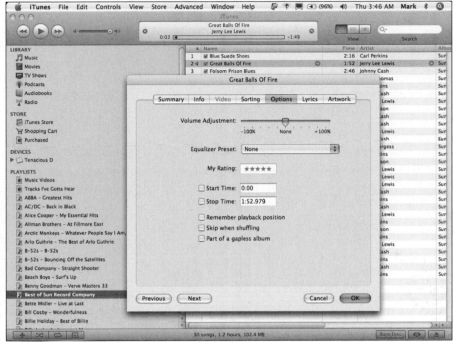

Figure 17-3:
I think this song is one of the best in my collection.

Configuring Smart Playlists in iTunes

Remember, I thrive on definitions, so here comes one: The contents of a smart playlist are automatically created from a specific condition (or rule) that you set via the Smart Playlist dialog. For example, you can limit the track selection by mundane things like album, genre, rating, or artist; or you can get funky and specify songs that were played last, the date you added tracks, the beats per minute, the sampling rate, or the total length of the song. iTunes can create a playlist packed with songs that are shorter than three minutes, so you can fill your iPod Shuffle with more stuff!

You reach the Smart Playlist dialog by choosing File➪New Smart Playlist, or press ⌘+Option+N (Mac) or Ctrl+Alt+N (PC). The Smart Playlist dialog, as shown in Figure 17-4, appears, ready to take your first rule.

That's right, I said "first" rule . . . you're not limited to just one. If you want to add other criteria, click the plus sign at the right side of the dialog and you get another rule, complete with a condition field to refine your selection even further.

Speaking of wireless music . . . .

I know this book honors your Apple TV, but if your Mac has an AirPort Extreme wireless card and you're using an AirPort Express portable wireless Base Station, you can use the AirTunes feature to ship your songs right to your Base Station from within iTunes, and from there to your home stereo or boombox! (Consider it yet another way to share your music.)

After your AirPort Express Base Station is plugged in and you connect your home stereo (or a boombox or a pair of powered stereo speakers) to the stereo mini-jack on the Base Station,

you see a Speakers pop-up menu button appear at the bottom of the iTunes window. (If the Speakers button doesn't appear, choose iTunes⇨Preferences to open the Preferences dialog and click the Advanced tab as shown in the figure. Make sure that the Look for Remote Speakers Connected with AirTunes check box is enabled.)

Click the Speakers button and you can choose to broadcast the music you're playing in iTunes across your wireless network. Ain't technology truly *grand?*

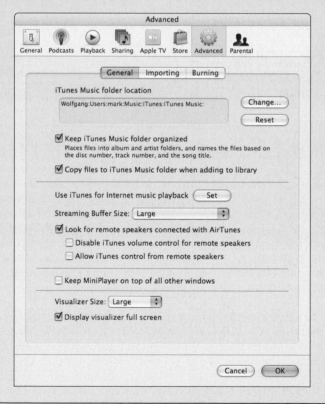

Figure 17-4:
Figure 17-4:
Use smart
playlists to
automate —
*smarten
up* — your
content
library!

This is probably a good place to mention that smart playlists are also available for podcasts (using the Podcast condition), TV shows (using the Season condition), and music videos and full-length movies (using the Video Kind condition). Although I ramble on about audio in this chapter — because music still takes up the majority of most people's iTunes use — smart playlists play the field. (Boy howdy, that was the worst pun so far.) You can choose the maximum songs to add to the smart playlist or limit the size of the playlist by the minutes or hours of play or the number of megabytes or gigabytes the playlist will occupy. (Again, great for automatically gathering as much from your KISS collection that fits into a specific amount of space on a CD or your iPod.)

Mark the Live Updating check box for the ultimate in convenience. iTunes automatically maintains the contents of the smart playlist to keep it current with your conditions at all times in the future. (If you remove items manually from a smart playlist, iTunes adds other items that match your conditions.)

Now think about what all these settings mean when combined . . . *whoa.* Here's an example yanked directly from my own iTunes library. I created a smart playlist that selects only those songs in the Rock genre. It's limited to 25 songs, selected by least often played, and live updating is turned on. The playlist is named *Tracks I've Gotta Hear* because it finds the 25 rock songs (from my collection of 3,184 songs) that I've heard least often! After I listen to a song from this smart playlist, iTunes automatically "freshens" it with another song, allowing me to catch up on the tracks I've been ignoring. Completely, unbelievably *sweet* — and another reason why iTunes is the best music player on Planet Earth!

Backing Up Your Media Library

The last discussion in this chapter may seem out of place — and, in fact, it might not even appear in some books on the Apple TV unit. That, dear reader, would be a major malfunction — because backing up your iTunes library is The Smart Thing to Do. Let me underline that fact:

If you don't back up your content, you *will* eventually *lose* it. This I can guarantee.

I don't claim to know how it will happen: Perhaps your hard drive will take a flying, grinding leap to destruction, or a smaller, less knowledgeable hand than yours will accidentally delete your iTunes music and data from your system. *Only a backup* prevents you from losing everything you've collected, and that's what I demonstrate in this section.

Of course, *your entire PC or Mac should be backed up on a regular basis.* If you're already backing up your iTunes library every few weeks within part of a full system backup, you are A Hero (and I sincerely mean that). Listen to your music with the peace of mind that only a backup can give you.

Oh, and if your CTT is indeed saved by a restore from your backup, please send me an e-mail at mark@mlcbooks.com — use the subject "I Saved My Content, Mark!" We can celebrate together!

In fact, I go one step further than just the built-in backup features within iTunes: I discuss how to back up any of your files and folders, on both Macs and PCs. (I told you I was committed to spreading the Lesson of the Backup!)

How often is often enough when it comes to backing up your content? That depends completely on how often your media library changes. The idea is to back up often enough so that you always have a recent copy of your media files close by.

Backing up within iTunes

iTunes offers a built-in backup feature for your media library — I told you this was the best media player ever designed! Choose File⇨Back Up to Disc to display the iTunes Backup dialog, as shown in Figure 17-5. You can choose to back up your entire iTunes library and all your playlists (which I recommend) or just the content you've purchased from the iTunes Store.

Personally, if I lost everything in my collection except for what I've bought from the iTunes Store, I'd be just as crushed . . . back it all up, and you won't be sorry.

Click Back Up, and iTunes prompts you for blank CDs or DVDs. If you need to restore from your completed backup, launch iTunes and load the first backup disc into your drive.

Backing up on a PC

Microsoft Vista offers a backup utility under several of its flavors — in this section, I use Vista Ultimate to demonstrate how to back up your files. I recommend that you use rewriteable DVDs as your backup media — alternatively, you can always use CD-RWs, but you'll need several more discs. If you're using Windows XP Professional Edition, you'll find the Backup utility by choosing Start➪All Programs➪Accessories➪System Tools.

Figure 17-5:
Preparing to back up my media collection.

If you'd rather not use Vista's Backup (or you're using Windows XP Home Edition, which doesn't have a backup utility), either buy a commercial backup application or consider copying your iTunes folder (and most important documents) to a CD-RW or DVD-RW disc on a regular basis. You'll still have to reinstall Windows and your major applications if you have a crash or your computer is stolen, but at least your irreplaceable stuff is safe. *Do not use a floppy disk* for this important job because floppy disks are unreliable and might not be readable on another PC. (I hate floppies, really I do.)

To back up files and folders under Vista, follow these steps:

1. **Click Start and click Computer to display the hard drives on your system.**

2. **Right-click the hard drive that contains the files you want to back up and choose Properties from the pop-up menu that appears.**

3. **Click the Tools tab.**

   Vista displays the buttons, as shown in Figure 17-6.

4. **Click the Backup Now button to run the Backup and Restore Wizard.**

   The wizard displays the options that you see in Figure 17-7. Decisions, decisions.

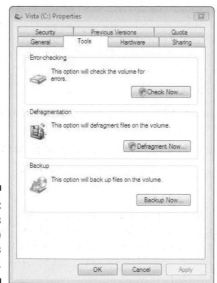

Figure 17-6:
Vista's backup utility hides here.

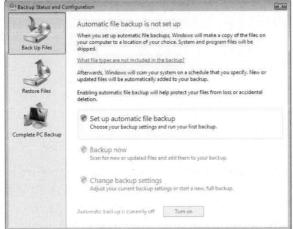

Figure 17-7:
Time to
set up
automatic
backups!

5. **Click the Set Up Automatic File Backup button.**

6. **Click the On a Hard Disk, CD or DVD radio button, choose your CD or DVD drive from the pop-up menu and click Next.**

7. **Make sure all the file type check boxes are enabled (see Figure 17-8) and click Next to continue.**

   Technically, the only boxes you need to check for your iTunes library (and the other content you may have that's not organized by iTunes) are Music, Pictures, Videos, Documents, TV Shows, and Additional Files — but what the heck, that's practically the entire list anyway! I say throw caution to the wind and back up it all.

8. **Choose a schedule, date, and time for your backup.**

   Naturally, your PC has to be on when the automatic backup is scheduled for everything to kick off correctly, so keep that in mind.

9. **Click Save Settings and Start Backup, and the backup process begins.**

   You're done! Windows Vista prompts you for CD or DVD rewriteable discs as necessary.

To restore from a backup that you've made, load the backup media, follow the preceding Steps 1–4, and then click the Restore Files button. The wizard leads you through the process of restoring your stuff from the backups you've made. Breathe a sigh of relief . . . and shoot me that e-mail!

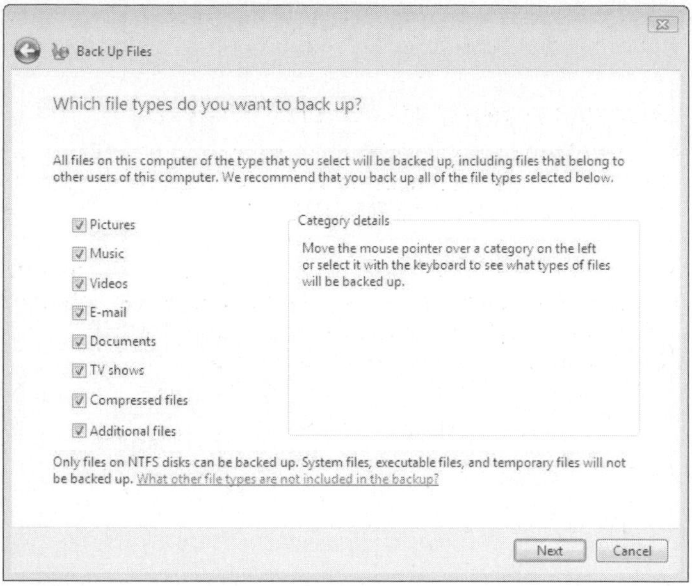

Figure 17-8:
I recom-
mend you
leave all
these check
boxes
enabled.

Backing up on a Mac

I used to tell readers that Mac OS X didn't have a comprehensive backup program — and if you're using Mac OS X Tiger 10.4, my statement is still true. However, the upcoming late 2007 release of Leopard (version 10.5) includes *Time Machine,* an integrated backup system. If you're upgrading to Leopard later, keep Time Machine in mind for your backup needs . . . but for now, you can manually back up your stuff, use the .Mac Backup application, or invest in a commercial backup utility.

Doing things the simple way

Again, if you're running Tiger and you simply want to safeguard files and folders, you can copy up to about 4GB of items directly from your hard drive onto a rewriteable DVD (or about 700MB to a rewriteable CD). Follow these steps:

1. **Load a blank DVD-RW or DVD+RW disc into your drive.**

2. **Double-click the disc icon when it appears on your Mac desktop.**

3. **Drag whatever you want to hang onto that fits into 4GB to the disc window.**

4. **Choose File⇨Burn Disc when you're ready to go.**

To restore your stuff (after your Mac is running well again), load the disc and drag the files back to their original location.

Using .Mac or a commercial backup application

If you've subscribed to Apple's .Mac service, a backup utility is included, and it has a built-in feature that backs up your iTunes library. This application runs like a top, and it does a great job.

If you're not a .Mac member, however, you can turn to a commercial backup application for your salvation — my personal recommendation is EMC Retrospect, from EMC (www.emcinsignia.com). This well-written "software bungee cord" has saved my posterior more than once.

Chapter 18

Okay, It's Not Working . . .

Most of my books that deal with computer hardware — PCs, Macs, printers, and such — have a hands-on troubleshooting chapter. This chapter *should* be pretty similar to those.

But it's not . . . and that's because your Apple TV is a closed universe. You'll likely void your warranty from Apple if you try to open it, upgrade the hard drive, or even use the USB 2.0 port that's hanging out at the rear of the box. (Follow those glossy magazine articles about "supercharging" your Apple TV at your own risk.) Therefore, there's nothing to unscrew, no cards to pull, and doggone little to accomplish with the hardware other than reading the indicator light and checking cable connections.

That's why Apple TV troubleshooting revolves around things like software, networks, cabling, and batteries: Things that fit outside the plastic sandwich protector. This chapter is devoted to my should-be-patented Apple Troubleshooting Tree, which is another piece of refrigerator-quality display material.

Here's hoping your sandwich protector runs like a top for many years!

Who Needs a Tech to Troubleshoot?

That's an easy one to answer. *Anyone* can troubleshoot — if you installed your Apple TV, you can probably figure out at least where the problem lies, if not fix it on the spot.

Unfortunately, a number of myths about computer troubleshooting just aren't true. For example:

- ✔ **It takes a college degree in computer hardware.** Tell that to my trouble-shooting kid in junior high. She'll think it's a hoot because she uses her own Apple network and has streamed her iTunes library to our Apple TV countless times now. You can follow all the steps in this chapter without any special training.

- ✔ **I'm to blame.** Ever heard of viruses? Failing hardware? Buggy software? Any of those things can be causing the problem. Heck, even if you do something by accident, I'm willing to bet it wasn't on purpose. It's Mark's Maxim time:

  Don't beat yourself up — your Apple TV can be fixed.

- ✔ **I need to buy expensive utility software.** Nope. A third-party utility isn't a requirement for troubleshooting; you can use the Disk Utility that ships with Mac OS X or the Windows repair tools that accompany Windows.

- ✔ **There's no hope if I can't fix it.** Parts fail, and as I said earlier it's prob-ably not a good idea to crack open your Apple TV case. However, your Apple Service Center can repair just about any problem. Even if some-thing catastrophic has happened to your PC or Mac, if you've backed up your iTunes library and other important data (as I demonstrate in Chapter 17), you'll keep your stuff even if a new computer hard drive is in your future.

- ✔ **It takes forever.** Wait until you read the number one step in the trouble-shooting tree; the first step takes but 30 seconds and often solves the problem. Not all problems can be fixed so quickly, but if you follow the procedures in this chapter, you should fix your Apple TV (or at least know that the problem requires outside help) in a single afternoon.

Now that I've squashed the myths, you can get down to business and troubleshoot!

Basic Troubleshooting Rules to Remember

Although you can't delve deep into the guts of your Apple TV — at least without voiding your warranty — keep in mind a few important rules while you work with my Troubleshooting Tree. Following these rules saves you time and helps you avoid missing a clue to what's causing the problem.

✔ **Keep your serial number handy.** Your Apple TV serial number is printed on the bottom of the unit, and also appears on the Summary pane within iTunes, as shown in Figure 18-1 (click your Apple TV under the Device heading in the iTunes source list). If you need to call Apple for technical support, you're asked for your serial number — you can also use it to check on your warranty coverage on the Apple Web site.

✔ **Take your time.** You're not being evaluated for your speed, so don't feel rushed. Troubleshooting isn't a race!

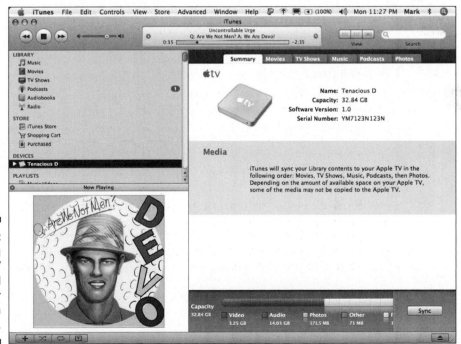

Figure 18-1: Displaying my Apple TV serial number within iTunes.

✔ **Keep track of what you've done.** If you're following the Troubleshooting Tree, jot down which steps you've performed on a sheet of paper — in case you talk to an Apple support technician, you can list the things you've tried already and save quite a bit of time on the phone.

✔ **Ask for help if it's handy.** Got a computer guru among your friends or family? Perhaps someone who's adept at networking or knowledgeable about that forest of cables sprouting from the back of your A/V receiver? If so, recruiting them adds another set of eyes and another mind on the problem . . . and may be worth far more than the price of a dinner.

✔ **Don't skip any steps.** Skipping steps can result in a solution "falling through the cracks." If you're not absolutely sure that something has been verified, don't count that step as complete.

The Apple TV Indicator Light

Sure, it's tiny, but the indicator light on the front of your Apple TV can tell you something about what's going on inside. Here's the rundown on what the different status lights mean:

✔ **Solid white:** Simply an indication that your Apple TV is on and is receiving AC power.

✔ **Single white flash:** Your Apple TV is receiving a command from the Apple Remote.

✔ **Turned off:** Your Apple TV is in standby mode, or it's been unplugged from an AC socket.

✔ **Blinking amber:** The unit is powering on — making the network connection, loading the Apple TV operating system. During this phase, you may not get a signal from your TV.

✔ **Single amber flash:** The Apple Remote command being sent to your Apple TV has a problem — this typically happens when you're attempting to use a remote that hasn't been paired with your unit.

✔ **Alternating blinking white and amber:** There's an internal hardware or software problem with your Apple TV, and you may need to bring it in for warranty service.

Mark's Should-Be-Patented Apple TV Troubleshooting Tree

Your Apple TV and iTunes are irrevocably tied together, as I mention elsewhere in this book — that's why this troubleshooting guide includes steps covering them both. Follow the steps in order, and you should be able to correct the problem with your Apple TV or pinpoint it as something only Apple can handle.

Unfortunately, I can't cover all the solutions I suggest here in depth — Wiley has entire books devoted to just troubleshooting (whereas I have room for only one big troubleshooting chapter because I'm concentrating on your Apple TV and how to use it). However, you can find ample documentation and help on the Apple and Microsoft Web sites, as I discuss at the end of this chapter. Search these online resources using the solution as a search phrase, and you're very likely to get the whole story.

Step 1: Reboot and restart!

Yep, it sounds silly, but the fact is that rebooting your computer and restarting your Apple TV can often solve a number of problems. If you're encountering the following types of strange behavior with your hardware, a reboot or restart might be all you need:

- Intermittent problems communicating over a network
- A garbled screen, strange colors, or screwed-up fonts
- A "busy" icon that won't go away after several minutes
- An application that locks up
- An external device that seems to disappear or can't be opened

To put it succinctly, here's a modest Mark's Maxim:

Always try a reboot and restart before beginning to worry. *Always.*

Try to save all open documents before you reboot your computer. That might not be possible, but try to save what you can. Also, it's best to put your Apple TV into standby mode before you unplug it from the AC socket. Note that if you have a wireless base station, router, or Internet sharing device, it's a good idea to restart that as well along with your Apple TV.

Why is rebooting so darn effective?

Rebooting and restarting fix hardware problems because they *reset* everything. Your network connection, for example, might be acting up or might have timed out, and rebooting restores it. Rebooting also fixes problems due to brownouts or those notorious AC power flickerings that we all notice from time to time. Such interruptions in constant juice might not bother you or me (or your less-intelligent toaster), but they can play tricks on your computer and Apple TV that rebooting and restarting can correct.

Restarting your Apple TV is as easy as putting it in standby mode (by holding the Play/Pause button on your Apple Remote for six seconds, until the TV signal drops) and then unplugging it from the AC socket. Wait five seconds and then plug your Apple TV back into the wall.

If your Mac or PC simply won't shut down normally, do what must be done:

1. **Press and hold your computer's Power button until it shuts itself off.**

   You have to wait four or five seconds for your computer to turn off.

2. **Wait five seconds to allow your hard drive to spin down.**

3. **Press the Power button again to restart the computer.**

After everything is back up, check whether the problem is still apparent. If you use your Apple TV for an hour or two and the problem doesn't reoccur, you've likely fixed it!

Step 2: Investigate recent changes

This is a simple step that many novice computer owners forget. Simply retrace your steps and consider what changes you made recently to your system, and what setting changes you may have made to your Apple TV. Here are the most common culprits:

✔ **Did you just finish installing a new application when things went haywire?** Try uninstalling it by removing the application directory and any support files that it might have added to your system. (And don't forget to keep your applications current with the most recent patches and updates from the developer's Web site.)

On a Mac, an application's *preference file* — which stores all the custom settings you make — can become corrupted. Although the application itself is okay, it might act strangely or refuse to launch. To check your preference files, try scanning your Mac's applications with Preferential Treatment, a freeware AppleScript utility by Jonathan Nathan, available from his Web site at www.jonn8.com.

✔ **Did you just apply an update or patch to an application?** Uninstall the application and reinstall it without applying the patch. If your computer suddenly works again, check the developer's Web site or contact its technical support department to report the problem.

✔ **Did you just update your OS using Software Update?** Updating Windows or Mac OS X can introduce problems in applications that depend on specific routines and system files. Contact the developer of the application and look for updated patches that bring your software in line with the latest operating system updates. Under Windows, display the Control Panel and choose Add and Remove Programs to uninstall a system update you applied using Microsoft Update.

✔ **Did you just make a change in System Preferences (on the Mac) or Control Panel (on the PC)?** Return the options that you changed back to their original settings. (I always recommend searching your Mac OS X or Windows online help or the Apple support Web site for more clues.)

✔ **Did you just connect (or reconnect) an external device?** Try unplugging the device and rebooting/restarting to see whether the problem disappears. Remember that some peripherals need software drivers to run — and without those drivers installed, the device won't work correctly. Check the device's manual or visit the company's Web site to search for software that you might need.

If you haven't made any significant changes to your system before you encountered the problem, proceed to the next step.

Step 3: Check your cables

It's a fact that cables work themselves loose, and they fail from time to time. Check all your cables to your external devices — make sure that they're snug — and verify that everything's plugged in and turned on. (Oh, and don't forget to check your cables for crimps or even Fluffy's teeth marks.)

Step 4: Check your TV input and video mode

Small fingers can press your TV's remote control in exactly the wrong spot . . . take my word for it, I know. Make sure that your TV is set to the proper input signal and follow the steps in Chapter 3 to select the proper video mode on your Apple TV.

Step 5: Is your Apple TV a stacker?

Never stack anything on top of your Apple TV — the unit heats up, and it may cause overheating if you use it for a pedestal. Also, a wireless network may suffer performance problems (or even have trouble connecting) if you stack stuff on your Apple TV. (Speaking of networking . . . .)

Step 6: Consider the Apple Remote

If your Apple Remote seems kaput — if the indicator light isn't flashing white when you press a button — here's a list of possible problems and solutions that may get you back on track:

- **Are you using the correct remote?** If you've paired an Apple Remote with your Apple TV, only that remote is recognized. (For more information on pairing remotes, see Chapter 9.)

- **Is the receiver lens blocked?** Although the IR (infrared) receiver on the front of your Apple TV can function even if line-of-sight is blocked, you should never place anything in front of your Apple TV. Oh, and don't forget to clean the lens at the front of your Apple Remote.

- **Is your Apple Remote battery dead?** See Chapter 9 for the details on changing the battery in your Apple Remote.

Step 7: The dreaded network problems

Next, consider possible networking problems — because your Apple TV is so dependent upon networking for syncing and streaming, even the smallest glitch in your wired or wireless network can wreak havoc. Other than cable connections (for a wired network) and power cords (for a base station, switch, or router), things to check include

✔ **Are you connected to the Internet?** Check to be sure that your cable or DSL connection is up and running. You should be able to connect to the Apple Web site using your computer's Web browser, for example — if not, your Internet Service Provider (ISP) may be having problems with its DNS server.

✔ **Is your base station or computer off, or is your computer in sleep or hibernate mode?** If your hardware ain't on . . . well, you know the rest. In fact, if you're using an Ad Hoc connection or sharing an Internet connection with your PC or Mac (without a base station) and the computer goes to sleep or hibernates, the connection is lost.

✔ **Is your firewall open for business?** Check to make sure that your operating system firewall isn't blocking ports 3689 and 5353, which are the "holes" in your firewall that your Apple TV needs to access iTunes. (Don't worry, opening these ports doesn't render your computer a target for hackers and malicious software.)

If you're using a Mac, open System Preferences, click Sharing, and then click Firewall. Now check to make sure that Apple TV Sharing, iTunes Music Sharing, and iPhoto Bonjour Sharing check boxes are enabled.

✔ **Are you using the wrong encryption standard or invalid characters in your wireless password?** If you installed your Apple TV on a wireless network and the unit isn't accepting your password, check to make sure that your computer or base station isn't using WPA-Enterprise encryption. Your Apple TV accepts WPA2 or WEP encryption. It's always a good idea to use only uppercase and lowercase letters and the numbers 0 through 9 in your password (for the best compatibility).

✔ **Is your network using a proxy server?** If so, I have bad news: You can't see trailers, download updates for your Apple TV, or play content you've purchased on the iTunes Store. There's currently no work-around for this.

✔ **Have you set iTunes to look for your Apple TV?** Run iTunes and choose iTunes⇨Preferences (Mac) or Edit⇨Preferences (PC). Click the Apple TV tab and make sure that the Look for Apple TV check box is enabled.

If your Apple TV is still experiencing problems, it's time to resort to diagnostics and the factory defaults.

Ach, Cap'n, It Dinna Work . . . What Now?

If you followed the entire Troubleshooting Tree without locating a problem, it's time to dig a little deeper (using the diagnostic utility built in to your Apple TV). You can also try resetting your Apple TV or restoring its factory defaults.

I also cover how to reach Apple's technical support and how you can find help on the Web (if you can access the Internet).

Running the Apple TV diagnostics

It's a good idea to run the Apple TV Diagnostic any time you notice "flaky" or "strange" behavior from your Apple TV. (Gotta love those technical terms.) Anyway, follow these steps to run the diagnostic set:

1. **Hold the Menu and minus buttons on your Apple Remote until the indicator light flashes amber and then release the buttons.**

   The language screen appears.

2. **Move the highlight cursor to the desired language and press Play/Pause.**

   The Apple TV Recovery screen appears.

3. **Move the highlight cursor to the Run Diagnostics item and press Play/Pause.**

   You see a message and progress bar displayed while the diagnostics are performed. If an error message is displayed, write it down — otherwise, you receive a message stating that your Apple TV is working correctly.

4. **Press Play/Pause to back up to the previous menu.**

5. **Move the highlight cursor to Restart and press Play/Pause.**

   Your Apple TV restarts — and you get to see that cool introductory video again. *W00t!*

Resetting Apple TV

You can reset all the configuration changes you've made to your Apple TV Settings menu very easily, returning it to factory settings.

A reset doesn't change your network configuration.

And, unlike a Factory Restore, which I cover in the next section, you don't lose any content stored on the unit's hard drive — this makes it A Good Thing to try a reset before you must resort to a Factory Restore.

From the top-level Apple TV menu, follow these steps:

1. **Move the highlight cursor to the Settings item and press Play/Pause.**

   The Settings menu appears.

2. **Move the highlight cursor to the Reset Settings item and press Play/Pause.**

   Your Apple TV displays the Reset Settings screen, where you're prompted for confirmation before all your user settings are returned to their defaults.

3. **Move the highlight cursor to Reset Settings and press Play/Pause.**

   If your Apple TV begins working correctly again, you can customize your settings as before, but make sure that you carefully review each setting change you make (especially to the video mode)!

Restoring factory defaults

A Factory Restore is The Big Kahuna — in effect, you're returning your Apple TV's hard drive to exactly the same state as it was when you first took the unit out of the box. You lose your network configuration as well as the content stored on your Apple TV's hard drive (although, of course, the original media files stored in your iTunes library on your PC or Mac remain, so you can resync them later).

Generally, you want to perform a Factory Restore as a last step before calling Apple for support.

From the top-level Apple TV menu, follow these steps:

1. **Move the highlight cursor to the Settings item and press Play/Pause.**

   The Settings menu appears.

2. **Move the highlight cursor to the Reset Settings item and press Play/Pause.**

   Your Apple TV displays the Reset Settings screen, where you're prompted for confirmation.

3. **Move the highlight cursor to Factory Restore and press Play/Pause.**

Do not unplug your Apple TV while the Factory Restore operation is performed!

Contacting Apple support

Remember, just because you've reached the end of my Apple TV Troubleshooting Tree doesn't mean you're out of luck. In this section, I discuss the online help available on Apple's Web site as well as local help in your own town.

If you haven't visited Apple's Support site, run — don't walk — to `www.apple.com/support/appletv`. There you find

- ✔ The latest patches, updates, and how-to tutorials for your Apple TV
- ✔ The Apple TV discussion boards, which are moderated by Apple
- ✔ Tools for ordering spare parts, checking on your remaining warranty coverage, and searching the Apple knowledge base

Local service, at your service

In case you need to take in your Mac for service, an Apple Store or Apple Authorized Service Provider is probably in your area. To find the closest service, launch your Web browser, visit the Apple TV support site, and then click either

- ✔ **Find an Apple Store Near You,** where you can ask a tech for advice or help in testing your Apple TV.
- ✔ **Find an Apple Authorized Service Provider,** where you can bring your Apple TV if it has suffered a hardware failure that you can't fix yourself.

Always call your Apple service provider before you lug your (albeit lightweight) Apple TV all the way to the shop.

Part VI
The Part of Tens

"Oh, I like Apple TV, too. Except when David shows photos of my mother's visit while playing 'A Night on Bald Mountain' over the speakers."

In this part . . .

Ah, what book in the *For Dummies* series is truly complete without The Part of Tens? Here you find lots of this author's raw opinion: my best tips for improving your computer's performance, a discussion of attractive multimedia peripherals, and my top utility applications for both PC and Mac — as well as my *infamous* "Top Ten Things to Avoid Like the Plague."

Chapter 19

Top Ten PC and Mac Performance Tweaks

• •

*H*ere's The Dumb Question for this book: Do you want your Macintosh or PC to run faster? (No need to answer.)

In this Part of Tens chapter, I detail my ten favorite tips for turning your computer into a hot rod. One or two involve changes to your hardware, but most of them are simple modifications to system settings or utilities that you should use on a regular basis. Of course, anyone can increase the performance of his computer by buying and installing a faster motherboard and processor, but that's not an option most of us want to take.

Consider this the cheaper route to faster computing!

Add RAM for a Speedier PC

This same Mark's Maxim has appeared in every book on PCs and Macs that I've written for the last decade:

Add as much RAM to your computer as you can afford.

I think I'll put this maxim on T-shirts that I can sell at computer user group meetings.

RAM modules are inexpensive, and they're easy to install. No hardware addition that you make to your PC speeds up everything as much. Games, image and video editors, and even Windows and Mac OS X themselves — they all benefit from extra memory.

Remember, however, that your motherboard has a maximum amount of memory that it can handle, and there are many types of memory for different computers. If you're unsure what you're doing when you decide to upgrade, consider taking your PC or Mac to your local computer shop (or enlisting the aid of an uber-tech family member or friend) to help.

Although this book doesn't go into the details of PC system RAM — after all, I'm on your Apple TV unit — my best-selling books, *PCs All-in-One Desk Reference For Dummies* and *Mac OS X All-in-One Desk Reference For Dummies* (both published by Wiley), cover selecting and installing RAM modules in your computer like a blanket. I've got your back, no matter which type of system you're using!

Give Spyware the Boot

If your PC is riddled with *spyware* — that atrocious "hidden" software that both riddles your Web browser with pop-ups and tracks your personal information and e-mail contacts — you'll find that your computer runs significantly slower and uses the Internet almost constantly. (Dialup Internet users with modems know what I'm talking about because their PCs are always connecting for no obvious reason.)

Make sure that your PC is free of spyware by using Spybot - Search & Destroy (www.safer-networking.org).

Make Room on Your Hard Drive

As I mention earlier, your computer's system RAM is exceptionally important when it comes to performance. However, your motherboard can hold only so much. When you run Windows Vista or Mac OS X and you use a memory-hog application, like a video editor or a cutting-edge 3D design package, your computer can run out of available RAM in a hurry. What happens when your system RAM is completely used up?

That's when Windows and Mac OS X use *virtual memory.* In other words, your operating system temporarily plops the data that it'd normally store in system RAM on your hard drive instead. Of course, your hard drive is many times slower at storing and retrieving data than your computer's RAM modules (yet another reason to max out your system RAM), but this solution actually works pretty well — unless you don't have the necessary room on your hard drive. If you have only a few megabytes of empty space left, your computer slows to a crawl while it desperately tries to juggle the stuff your applications need with the stuff it needs to put somewhere. Your machine might even lock up if the situation gets too dire.

I always recommend that you reserve at least 8GB of free hard drive space. If you notice that your drive has less than 8GB free, do the right thing and delete stuff you don't need. (Don't forget to empty your Windows Recycle Bin or Mac Trash, and uninstall demo software and applications you know you won't use again.) Your computer thanks you with less waiting and more fun.

Adjust Your Windows XP Performance Options

If you're a PC owner running Windows XP, it's time to take a trip. Right-click My Computer on your desktop (or from your Start menu) and then choose Properties to display the Windows System Properties dialog. Next, click the Advanced tab and then click the Settings button of the Performance area.

In the Performance Options dialog that opens, you see a list of "eye candy" features that help make Windows more attractive but also use system RAM, CPU time, and video card horsepower. (These features include fancy graphic fun, like animations, fading ToolTips, and drop shadows.) If you want to strip Windows XP of its eye candy and speed up the graphics your operating system displays, select the Adjust for Best Performance radio button, which turns off all these extras. (If you like, you can enable individual graphics features by selecting the check box next to that particular item. For example, I keep the Smooth Edges of Screen Fonts feature turned on because that makes text look better on my fancy, flat panel LCD monitor.)

But wait, you're not finished yet! Still in Performance Options, click the Advanced tab, and make sure that both Processor Scheduling and Memory Usage are set to Programs. This ensures that your applications receive priority service from your system's CPU and RAM.

Now you can click OK to return to faster graphics and improved application speed.

Time to Defrag Your Hard Drive

Don't confuse *defragging* with fragging your enemies in a 3D game. When you defrag a hard drive, you optimize it for the best performance, which is indeed A Good Thing. Defragging helps keep all the data that makes up your programs and documents in a contiguous block on your hard drive, allowing your operating system to read them more efficiently and faster.

Unfortunately for Mac owners, Mac OS X Leopard doesn't come with a defrag application. I can personally recommend both Drive Genius (from Prosoft Engineering, www.prosofteng.com) and TechTool Pro (from Micromat, www.micromat.com). Both are full-fledged hard drive utilities that offer excellent defragmenting features.

Microsoft actually gives you the utility you need for free! (That got your attention, didn't it?) Yep, both Windows XP and Vista come with a defragging program. Open Windows Explorer, right-click the icon representing your PC's hard drive, and then choose Properties. Click the Tools tab and then click the Defragment Now button.

Two things to remember:

✔ Have at least 15 percent of the space on your hard drive free and empty before you try defragging that drive. Otherwise, a defrag takes forever and a day.

✔ Avoid running any other applications while your drive is defragging because they'll slow to a crawl, and the defrag takes longer by far.

Kill Off Background and Hidden Applications

Take a look at the right side of your Windows taskbar — the system tray — where a lot of VNCPUHs can reside. (That's short for *Very Nasty CPU Hog*. Sorry, all the acronyms finally got to me.) Mac owners, check your Dock for the same animals.

On the PC side, some of the icons you see in the system tray are simple indicators, like a wireless network connection or your system's volume control. Other icons, however, belong to programs that are running, and you might not necessarily need those programs. An unneeded program that puts an icon in the system tray can sap your CPU time or use system RAM that could better be used for your applications. Disable these hogs whenever possible.

Most of these icons display either a disable or quit command when you right-click them. Alternatively, you can check the settings for the program that spawned the system tray icon and see whether you can turn off the unwanted icon. If you don't want the program at all, choose Start⇨Control Panel⇨Add or Remove Programs and remove the offending program once and for all. Good for you!

On the Mac side, applications you see running in the Dock may be hidden — they don't show a window on your Leopard desktop, yet they're running all the same. Quitting a hidden application that you don't need saves overhead, just like a background task on a PC; if the application returns in hidden mode when you reboot and you don't need it, uninstall or remove it. Your Mac's CPU will thank you.

Scan Your Hard Drive for Errors

It's a fact: Errors slow down your hard drive. Although Windows and Leopard can continue to run with a corrupted file structure, your hard drive efficiency slows down considerably, and it's only a matter of time before you actually start to lose data or experience lockups while using your programs and applications.

Like the Defragment tool, the Error-Checking tool hangs out on the Properties dialog. From Windows Explorer, right-click the icon for your hard drive and then click Properties. Click the Tools tab and then click the Check Now button. If you're using a Mac, open your Utilities folder (inside your Applications folder) and run the Disk Utility to check for hard drive and permission errors.

I recommend that you check your drives for errors at least once a week.

Use USB 2.0 or FireWire Stuff

If your PC or Mac is old enough to sport USB 1.1 ports, you're holding yourself back from the fastest possible speeds when you connect an external hard drive, DVD burner, or scanner. Sure, USB 2.0 hardware works with the older USB 1.1 ports, but it's like riding a bike with only one pedal. (Kinda.)

Anyway, the fix is both easy and inexpensive: Install a USB 2.0 adapter card in your PC and start living the good life. If your Mac can accept a PCI expansion card, you can also add a USB 2.0 adapter card . . . otherwise, stick with FireWire whenever possible.

Dialup Modems Are Bad

Well, dialup modems didn't *used* to be bad. Heck, for about a decade there, dialup modems were cool. I still have three or four occupying a closet in my office.

These days, however, dialup service is rapidly going the way of the dodo. It's just not convenient enough. (All those horrible modem noises, and having to dial out every time you want to connect.) Plus, a dialup connection seriously slows down every type of communication you make through the Internet — not only Web surfing but also file transfers, multiplayer gaming, and instant messaging.

As long as either cable or DSL Internet service is available in your area, you no longer have any reason to hold back. Prices have dropped, hardware is standardized, and installation is usually free. You'll thank me for it.

Keep Your Drivers Up-to-Date

This last tip is a no-brainer, and here's why. When you keep your drivers up-to-date, your applications get upgraded, you install new applications and games, and both Windows and Leopard get updated all the time. In order for your PC or Mac to perform its best in every situation, you *must* make sure that your hardware drivers are up-to-date once per month.

Each manufacturer's Web site should have a driver download section where you can verify the latest version number. Of course, you don't need to download and reinstall a driver that's the same version as the one you're using. The point is that you should check for updates, once per month, like the PC or Mac power user you are!

Chapter 20

Top Ten Utilities You Can't Do Without

. . . .

*N*othing can start a spirited discussion between computer techno-types as fast as a comparison of favorite utility software. Why? Because no two computer owners are likely to agree on The Right Way to save time and trouble behind the keyboard!

Take the example of the operating system itself. Even though most computer owners tend to perform the same tasks in Windows and Mac OS X — things like running programs and applications, copying and moving files, and recording CDs and DVDs — we all tend to do them differently. (For example, on the PC some folks still use Windows Explorer to copy and move stuff — I, on the other hand, eschew drag and drop and the entire Explorer interface and depend instead on the Total Commander utility program.)

Well, good reader, this is my book; and in this Part of Tens chapter, I introduce you to *my* ten favorite utilities! Not all are directly multimedia-related (after all, the earlier chapters of this book cover most of the bases for graphics, audio, and video applications for Macs and PCs), but you're likely to find them tremendously helpful every time you use your computer.

Oh, and if you disagree, feel free to write your own book and present your utility lineup!

Organize in Windows with Total Commander

What would you think if I told you that you could increase your efficiency within Windows XP and Vista tenfold? It's true: By installing Total Commander (from Christian Ghisler), you can practically forget about clunky old Windows Explorer. With a two-pane display, Total Commander makes all those management chores a breeze — you can copy, move, delete, and modify a single file or folder to any other location on your system, including your network. You can easily select multiple items and perform the same operations either with the mouse or your function keys. Double-click a program to run it, just like you would from the Explorer window.

Ah, but things really get slick when you need to sort your files by size, creation date, or type — a single click does the job. If you work with files in ZIP or RAR compressed format, you can easily see the contents of those archives. You can even choose an FTP site as your source or destination so that you can copy or move files across the Internet with the same screen! Such is the very definition of *sassy*.

For more information on Total Commander and all the features it includes, visit www.ghisler.com. For $34, you won't find a better file manager on the planet.

Archive Data for the Internet with WinRAR

Sure, Mac OS X, Windows XP and Vista have *limited* built-in support for the ZIP archive format, but yours truly is never impressed by the word *limited!* Instead, I use the archive format that's firmly entrenched as the standard on Internet newsgroups, Linux Web sites, and anywhere else where the smallest compressed file sizes and powerful features are preferred. The RAR archive format is superior to the ZIP format in many ways.

To create, expand, and modify RAR archives, look no further than WinRAR from www.rarlab.com. This archive utility is highly configurable, fast as all get-out, and even acts as a backup utility in a pinch. Naturally, you can protect your RAR archives with passwords, and WinRAR can handle large files and folders with aplomb. (I wouldn't use anything else for compressing the contents of an entire VIDEO_TS folder into a single file!)

There are also RAR utilities for Mac OS X that offer a graphical interface, like UnRarX (from www.unrarx.com).

WinRAR is only $29 — a bargain, indeed.

Your Mac OS X Toolbox: TechTool Pro

My favorite native Mac OS X disk repair application is TechTool Pro from Micromat (www.micromat.com).

More than just about any other type of application, it's important for a disk maintenance program to be built "from the ground up" for Mac OS X. *Never* attempt to repair a Mac OS X disk in Classic mode, nor should you try to use an older repair utility that was written for use under Mac OS 9.

With TechTool Pro 4, you can thoroughly check a hard drive for both *physical* errors (such as faulty electronics or a bad sector on the disk surface) and *logical* errors (incorrect folder data and glitches in the file structure). The Disk Utility that's included with Mac OS X does a fine job of checking the latter, but it doesn't perform the physical testing — and TechTool Pro does both.

I should note, however, that TechTool Pro doesn't take care of viruses. Pick up a copy of VirusBarrier X4 (www.intego.com) to protect yourself against viral attack.

TechTool Pro also takes care of disk optimization, which is a feature that's been conspicuously absent from Mac OS X ever since the beginning. As I explain in Chapter 19, defragmenting your disk results in better performance and a faster system overall.

TechTool Pro 4 (which sets you back about $100) comes on a self-booting DVD-ROM for both G-series and Intel Macs, so you can easily fix your startup volume by booting your system from the installation disc.

Protect Your PC with avast! antivirus

"What? You're not going to plug The Big Antivirus Program like everyone else?" Well, I do. I use Norton AntiVirus on most of my machines, and it's a wonderful utility. However, if you're a little short on funds at the moment, why should you just leave your PC an open target if you can't afford a commercial PC antivirus program? Hmmm. . . . That's a question that needs answering.

Never leave any computer without antivirus protection. Repeat, never. *Never ever.*

Fortunately, I can heartily recommend avast! antivirus from ALWIL Software (www.avast.com). The Home edition of the program is free for download, and it's one of the few, fully featured antivirus applications that runs under both the 64-bit version of Windows XP Professional and Windows Vista. avast! Home has all the features you've come to appreciate from any good antivirus program — real-time scanning, timely automatic virus data updates, scanning of your entire system on demand (as well as specific folders and drives), and repair of infected files. Oh, it looks cool, too.

To unlock the full potential of avast!, you can upgrade to the commercial Professional version for $40 per year.

Burn CDs and DVDs with Nero

If you're looking for a comprehensive CD and DVD recording application for the PC, look no further than Nero 7 Ultra Edition from www.nero.com. I use this great burning software for just about everything, including audio CDs, archival data discs, scheduled PC backups, and DVD-Video movie discs. (You can even create a bootable restore disc for your PC.)

Nero 7 Ultra Edition can record and edit HD video and Dolby Digital 5.1 audio, and it comes with *Nero ShowTime,* which is a full-featured software video player. Nero can produce slideshows, catalog your media, and even master DVD-Audio discs.

Nero 7 Ultra Edition is $80 in downloadable form. I highly recommend it!

Catalog Your DVD Movie Collection with DVD Profiler

When your DVD movie collection reaches 100 movies (what I call *The Magic Triple Digit of DVD Collecting*), consider a cataloging utility that helps you keep track of what you have, how much your collection is worth, and what you've loaned out to others (if you do that sort of thing).

For me, the clear choice for Windows is DVD Profiler, from InterVocative Software. With the free version that you can download from www.inter vocative.com, you put the Internet and the company's incredible database to work. Entering a movie into your collection is as simple as typing the UPC code number. Each movie description includes a plot synopsis, cover image, cast and crew list — and so much more that I can't cover it all here. Oh, and you want that online on a Web site so that you can show your collection to others? Done!

Any video lover will tell you: DVD Profiler is the best in the business.

Defend against Spyware with Spybot

Spyware. It's almost as bad as viruses and Trojan horses. If you don't want your system surreptitiously invaded, your personal information and Web surfing data *collected* (another great word), and then sent to a company halfway across the world, you need an anti-spyware utility. *Now.*

Spybot - Search & Destroy from Patrick M. Kolla (`www.safer-network ing.org`) is my spyware eradicator of choice; it's *donationware* (meaning that it's free, but the author appreciates a donation if you like his work). Spybot downloads the latest spyware detection data files from the Internet and can scan your entire system for thousands of different hidden spyware vermin. I also like the Immunize feature, which actually blocks many types of spyware from installing themselves via Internet Explorer!

With avast! Home edition and Spybot - Search & Destroy on your PC at the same time, you're delivering a knockout punch to just about every malicious piece of software on the Internet. (Don't hesitate to pat yourself on the back.)

Yes, It's Really Called "Toast"

Ready to record all sorts of data CDs, audio CDs, and DVDs on the Macintosh? I do a lot of that . . . in fact, I cover Mac recording in detail in another of my *For Dummies* books, *CD & DVD Recording For Dummies,* 2nd Edition (Wiley). Of course, Mac OS X can burn basic data CDs that you can share with your Windows and UNIX friends without any add-on software, and iTunes can burn a fine audio or MP3 CD. If you have a Mac equipped with a SuperDrive, you can also create standard, cross-platform data DVDs, too. But what if you need an exotic format, like CD Extra, where data and digital audio tracks can coexist peacefully on one disc? Or perhaps you need a self-booting disc?

Here's one clear choice: When you're ready to seriously burn, you're ready for *Roxio Toast 8 Titanium* (`www.roxio.com`), the CD and DVD recording choice for millions of Mac owners. (No snickering about the name, please.)

This powerhouse of an application presents an elegant design that's both simple to use and perfectly Aqua. Files, folders, and digital audio tracks that you want to record are simply dropped into the application window.

As for exotic formats, here's a list of what types of discs you can record with Toast:

- ✔ Standard data CDs and DVDs
- ✔ Standard audio CDs
- ✔ Video CDs, SuperVideo CDs, and DivX video discs
- ✔ MP3 discs (which store MP3 audio tracks)
- ✔ Discs recorded from an image file
- ✔ Mac volumes
- ✔ Hybrid PC/Mac discs
- ✔ ISO 9660 discs
- ✔ Multisession discs
- ✔ CD Extra discs

Toast works with both internal and external CD and DVD recorders, taking advantage of the latest features on today's drives — in particular, *burn-proof* recording, which can practically eliminate recording errors. You can also copy existing discs, using one or multiple drives.

Toast is quite affordable at $100. You can buy it directly from the Roxio online store at `www.roxio.com`.

Talk Trash in Multiplayer Games with Ventrilo

Ah, you're taking a break from Apple TV, using your multimedia PC for a bit of multiplayer Internet relaxation. If you're playing *World of Warcraft* or *Quake 4* (my personal favorites) over a broadband DSL or cable modem connection, your fingers can start to hurt from all that typing you do in the chat window. Cooperation among the members of a team is hard enough in these games without trying to do everything through the keyboard. Why not communicate with your voice instead?

With Ventrilo Internet voice communication software and a USB headset microphone, you can keep your hands free to play while swapping commands and jokes with your teammates. In order to use Ventrilo, you must download, install, and configure the Ventrilo public server software (`www.ventrilo.com`), but the software is free, and the process is very easy. After your server is set up, your friends can install the Ventrilo client program and sign in using a password you choose and then you're ready to chat!

Read Usenet Newsgroups with Xnews

My final award for outstanding utility application goes to _Xnews,_ the outstanding freeware Usenet newsgroup reader from master programmer Luu Tran (`xnews.newsguy.com`). For those who haven't ventured into newsgroups, you'll find that Usenet is a great source for discussion, opinion, downloads, arguments, and proselytizing. It includes literally tens of thousands of newsgroups on subjects large and small, and most Internet ISPs offer a free Usenet newsgroup server for customers. (In other words, I bet you already have access to Usenet.)

Xnews allows you to subscribe to specific newsgroups that interest you and also download any binary files that may be attached to those messages. You can post replies by using an online persona that you create, or just read and enjoy the opinions you see without participating. (By the way, if you're a passive reader and don't participate directly, you're _lurking._ I love that word.)

Chapter 21

Top Ten Multimedia Gadgets

I know, I know, this book covers Apple TV like a blanket . . . but is streaming media really the *only* use for your multimedia computer? In earlier chapters, I focus on required things, like the Apple TV itself, along with TVs, speakers, iTunes, and Front Row — these hardware and software elements are The Necessary Side of installing and using Apple TV, so they come first.

In this Part of Tens chapter, however, I introduce you to a number of gaming and multimedia entertainment gadgets that no digital lifestyle should do without. (In other words, stuff that you do when you're not watching Star Trek movies or listening to your iTunes playlists.)

The Joystick That Joggles

The Logitech Force 3D Pro joystick (www.logitech.com) is a gaming power user's play toy. What sets this piece of hardware apart from the pack is its ability to provide actual tactile feedback. In other words, when something happens in the game, you can feel an authentic sense, force, or impact through the joystick. For example

- ✔ If you're flying a light plane with a flight simulator, you feel the stick resist your movements when you begin a turn and then relax gradually while the turn continues.

- ✔ If you're driving a tank, you feel the impact of each hit on your tank's armor as well as the recoil of each shot you fire.

- ✔ If you're piloting a space fighter, the joystick explodes when your spaceship breaks up. Okay, I lied; it doesn't explode, but it likely kicks pretty hard.

As a dyed-in-the-wool hardcore PC gamer, I can tell you that this kind of feedback adds that extra touch of realism. Much like how a sound card with 3D support enhances the audio experience of a game, the Force 3D Pro enhances physical sensations of your game-playing experience. After all, a game becomes much more realistic when your World War II fighter plane gets harder to control when you're dodging bullets with an enemy on your tail.

The Force 3D Pro reflects every hit on your plane as well as the force required to pull out of a power dive.

Like most of the more expensive joysticks on the market, you can program each button to perform a keyboard command. And the stick itself is specially designed for hours of hazardous flying through the enemy-filled skies of Planet SpeedBump without cramping your hand.

Before you tense your muscles to leap out of your chair and run to your local computer store for a Force 3D Pro, don't overlook the downside:

- **Pricey:** Compared with a standard joystick that costs $15 or $20, the Force 3D Pro is significantly pricier at about $70.

- **Game-dependent:** The game that you're playing must explicitly support force feedback controllers to enable the tactile-feedback feature. So, for older games, like the original *Quake* or *Wing Commander,* the Force 3D Pro becomes just another joystick.

The Zen of the iPod

If you're the proud owner of an Apple iPod portable audio player, I salute you. You can choose from all sorts of models: Some cost less than $75, and others can display photos, movies, and video (and podcasts to boot) for under $300. My old 15GB music-only model is still chugging away and still has a little room left for a few more songs. (It dates back to the days when there were only a couple of iPod versions to choose from. Progress marches on.)

Each time you plug your iPod into its cradle or a handy USB connector, iTunes automatically updates your iPod's internal storage with any changes, additions, or deletions you make to your main audio and video iTunes library. It's all pretty automatic.

Because iTunes and the iPod both support the MP3-format audio files and MPEG-format video files, you can also enjoy the media you create on-the-go.

If you want a comprehensive guide to *everything* that you can do with iTunes and iPod, *iPod & iTunes For Dummies,* 4th Edition (by Tony Bove and Cheryl Rhodes; Wiley) devotes a full 432 pages to the dynamic duo.

Converse with Quake

I'm the first to admit that I need another set of hands when playing the 3D games *Doom 3* or *Half-Life 2* or flight simulators, such as *Falcon* or *Apache Longbow.* Just because you're an ace typist doesn't make you better at fragging your buddies in a hot-and-heavy multiplayer game. You have to control your weapon with your mouse, trackball, or joystick, but moving around, selecting weapons, and using special commands normally entails a quick leap toward the keyboard! Getting confused is easy when you can't take your eyes off your monitor without being blown to your component atoms.

Although you can solve the problem with a programmable joystick, it's an expensive solution. You have to create a button configuration by hand for each game, and you'll spend more than a few days teaching yourself all those button assignments. I suggest an alternative for your entertainment system: If you're like me, you'd rather use your voice to control your character!

With Game Commander 3 from Mindmaker (`www.gamecommander.com`), you can program as many as 256 keystrokes that your Windows PC automatically "presses" when you speak a single command. To change to the next weapon in *Quake 4,* for example, you'd say, "Next," instead of reaching for the bracket key on your keyboard. Plus, voice commands in a game, such as *MechWarrior* or *Freelancer,* seem much more realistic than pecking at your keyboard. With a little imagination, you feel like you're talking to your ship's computer or your copilot! I've been using Game Commander 3 for several years now, and the program has helped increase my scores.

You can easily configure Game Commander for new games with templates that you can download for free from the Mindmaker Web site. These templates can be loaded within Game Commander 3 to provide you with a complete ready-made set of spoken-command assignments.

To use Game Commander 3 under Windows, you need a full-duplex sound card (all modern sound cards made in the last three or four years are full duplex, but you can check the manual for your card to make sure) and a headset microphone.

Play Poker with Media Cards

Most of the digital toys that people carry these days use one type of removable media card or another — CompactFlash, SmartMedia, Memory Stick, SD (Secure Digital), MultiMediaCard, what have you — and they get strewn all over your desk. If your PC has a built-in set of card reader slots, you're set to go.

What if your computer isn't quite that advanced? Heck, each one of those media cards needs its own stand-alone reader or cable. (I guess you could stack them and make a conversation piece.) Or, you could pick up a single media reader peripheral that handles them all! That's the idea behind a USB 2.0 reader like the Lexar Multi-Card Reader, which you can buy directly from Lexar at `www.lexar.com` for $35. If your computer is equipped with an open USB 2.0 port, you can download video, audio, and photos at a fast clip from any of the card types I mention earlier, and some that are less common to boot.

By the way, using an external card reader isn't just convenient: It conserves the battery power in your DV camcorder, digital camera, or mobile phone because you don't have to download the media directly from the device itself.

Run Your Home with Your Computer

With the Apple Remote, you can control your Apple TV remotely — but can you turn down the lights from your couch as well?

Home automation and remote control through your PC are easy with X10 technology, from www.x10.com. Just plug in special modules into your home's AC outlets and connect them to your home's lighting system and appliances; then hook your computer into the system with another module. Now you can set up an automated schedule for turning on your lights and starting that pesky coffeemaker first thing in the morning. If you're away on vacation, you can set up a schedule that turns certain lights on at random intervals, making your house look "lived in" and thus less inviting to thieves.

If you can add one more remote control to your den, you can also turn off electrical devices and lighting from your couch. (Popcorn for that movie, anyone?)

X10 compatible products are all over the Internet and eBay, but a visit to www.x10.com is a great place to start.

Add a Bigger Screen to Your Video iPod

Today's generation of video iPods are great devices, but they lack two important features that today's discerning media maven demands: a decent-sized portable widescreen display and a pair of speakers that you don't shove in your ears. That's where the iFlip Mi8000 from Memorex comes in — it's my favorite portable display for the iPod. Simply plug your iPod into the iFlip, and you suddenly gain a superb 8.4-inch widescreen LCD display as well as built-in stereo sound from the iFlip speakers. And all this from a unit that's not much bigger than a hardcover book!

In case you want to share your audio or video with others, the iFlip Mi8000 includes dual headphone jacks for you and your significant other, as well as both an audio line-out jack (to hook to a stereo system) and an S-Video out port to connect to an external TV. Along with video and audio, you can use the iFlip as a still image "picture frame," showing your iPhoto images or slideshows.

If you like watching multiple movies in one sitting while you're on the road, the iFlip's high-capacity internal rechargeable battery can extend the playback time offered by the video iPod by several hours. In fact, if the iFlip is plugged in an AC outlet, it can charge your iPod while you watch.

You can buy the iFlip directly from Memorex at www.memorex.com for $199 . . . your family's appreciation is a free bonus.

A Printer Worthy of Your Designer DVDs

A hundred bucks is practically pocket change when it comes to today's high-end hardware for your entertainment computer, but that's all you'll pay for an Epson Stylus Photo R280 printer, from Epson America (www.epson.com).

But is a printer really an integral part of your entertainment system? (Well, I wouldn't use a Mac or PC as my primary computer if it didn't have a printer, but that's beside the point.) What's special about this particular Epson printer is its ability to print on inkjet-printable CDs and DVDs. Forget sticky labels and print directly on the discs you burn instead! Your friends and family will be impressed not only with the videos, movies, and audio CDs you've created but with the slick, professional-looking discs as well.

The software you need to put your own designs on your discs (including full-color photo quality graphics and text effects) comes with this printer, and I can heartily recommend the Epson package. I've been using my Stylus Photo R200, an earlier model, for years now.

Create Your Own Musical Masterpiece

With a MIDI (Musical Instrument Digital Interface) keyboard, you can play directly into your PC or Mac and record your music automatically. Then your computer can play your song at any time for you as well as thousands of popular songs that you can download from sites all over the Internet. MIDI support is offered for all sorts of instruments, including electronic horns and drum sets.

If your sound card doesn't have support for a MIDI port built in, look for a MIDI USB instrument, which plugs directly into your computer's USB port instead.

For example, the USB Prodikeys PC-MIDI keyboard from Creative Technology (www.creative.com) is only $50, but it can act as both your PC keyboard (for work) and a 37-key piano keyboard as well! (However, it might be hard for aspiring musicians to get a book report finished in Word when they can play jazz piano instead.)

You Want 3D? This Is 3D!

You've probably tried on a pair of cellophane 3D glasses at the movies. Not very satisfying. And neither were the old-fashioned, first-generation "shutter" 3D headsets that gamers have tried in the past.

If you're willing to spend the $550 for the best 3D available, however, you can join the select group of hardcore gamers who play in immersive 3D. Games that support the eMagin Z800 3DVisor offer *head-tracking* (move your head in the game, and your view actually changes, as if you're looking that way in the game environment, without using a mouse or keys). You get true optical stereo vision, with a separate micro screen for each eye, providing the equivalent of a 105-inch screen at 12 feet in true 3D. *Whoa.*

You can also use the 3DVisor to watch DVD movies in private, or you can work on proprietary documents without anyone else looking over your shoulder.

For more information, check out the product Web site at www.3dvisor.com.

The Less-than-Sexy but Still Gotta-Have Gadget

Okay, this last item is not just a good addition to an entertainment computer: It's a must-have for *any* computer system that stores your irretrievable work! Take this example: You just finished the last transition of your new film — you know, the one that you've been working on for the past year — when someone on your block decides to juice up a new electric car, and every transformer within three miles goes up in smoke. You get hit with a power failure, and the final scene that you've been working on is suddenly headed to that home for unfinished classic movies in the sky. Even worse, your video editor project file is corrupted!

What can you do? Unfortunately, the answer is a big, fat "nothing." If you save your work often, you can at least back up to the last revision, although the loss of power might have resulted in lost clusters on your computer's hard drive. (Or you have to resort to your backup from three weeks ago.) If you're burning a CD or DVD on your computer and the recording process is interrupted by a power failure, you just created a dandy coaster for your cold drinks.

However, you can prevent such a catastrophe by adding an uninterruptible power supply (UPS) to your entertainment system. A *UPS* is essentially a giant battery that automatically provides power within a few milliseconds in case of a power blackout or brownout. A typical UPS provides your computer with another priceless 15 minutes or so of operation before it's fully exhausted, which should give you ample time to save your work and shut down your system normally (or finish recording that DVD movie). Believe me, it's a weird feeling to see your computer monitor alive and well with every other light and appliance in your home as dead as a doornail. (After you're finished saving your work, gather the family around for a computer game or two!)

Note that a UPS is different from a *surge protector,* which is essentially just an extension cord that self-destructs if it gets hit by a massive power surge. You don't get any additional power in case of a blackout with a surge protector.

A UPS is constantly recharged from your wall socket, so it's always ready. Most of these power supplies also filter AC line *noise* (small variations in line voltage caused by some appliances, such as vacuum cleaners and televisions) and provide some measure of protection against lightning strikes.

Chapter 22

Top Ten Things to Avoid Like the Plague

*I*f you've read other books that I've written in the *For Dummies* series, you might recognize the title of this chapter — it's a favorite Part of Tens subject of mine. I don't like to see *any* computer owner fall prey to pitfalls (no matter which side of the field they choose). Some tips I cover here are hardware warnings, such as avoiding a Pentium III CPU, and other tips help you prevent downright catastrophic software mistakes, such as ignoring backups or overwriting an original image.

All these potential mistakes, however, share one thing in common: They're *easy to solve or prevent* with a little common sense as long as you're aware of them! That's my job, and I take it very seriously. In this chapter, I fill in what you need to know. Consider these pages as hard experience gained easily.

The Creaking CPUs

Don't get me wrong. In their time, the Pentium III (on the PC side) and the G3 (on the Mac side) were grand chips, but their days are *long* past us now. Unfortunately, many computer owners have held onto these relics through sheer tenacity and strength of will. If you've invested in a new Apple TV and a 42-inch LCD TV fit for a king, don't saddle them to a slow Pentium III or G3 processor (and all the antique hardware that accompanies an older CPU)!

Applications, like video editing, image editing, and 3D gaming, demand much more than a Pentium III or G3 can provide, so upgrade and save yourself the headaches!

Overclocking Your Video Card

Many techno-types will grill me over hot coals for saying this, but avoid over-clocking your video card. *Overclocking* a PC motherboard or video card involves running the CPU (or GPU) significantly faster than it was meant to run via hardware settings, software utilities, or a combination of both.

The Good Side is obvious: You get better performance from your existing video card and motherboard, so your applications run faster. However, the Bad Side is hidden and quite insidious: random lockups, video glitches, memory problems, and (because of the extra heat generated by overclocking) a shorter life expectancy in general for your silicon-based friends.

Avoid overclocking, and operate both your entertainment PC and your multi-media video card within the engineer's designed speeds. You'll appreciate the reliability of your system, and your PC's components will last far longer.

The Evils of Media Compression

The old truism that "you don't get something for nothing" is alive and well, especially when it comes to producing or converting digital images, video, or music. Typically, the best quality media requires the most hard drive space — which translates into the longest download times.

I know, I know — a longer download time is rarely the shining advantage that you're striving for when producing Internet media. However, the massive amounts of compression that you need to shrink your files produce blurry video, fuzzy images, and tinny-sounding music, too. What's to be done?

Here's the general rule that holds fast with professional video editors, pho-tographers, and musicians, deftly translated into a Mark's Maxim:

Use media compression only when necessary. If you *must* compress, experi-ment to find the best compromise between file size and quality.

Whenever possible, use formats that offer lossless compression, like TIFF and PNG (for images) and Apple Lossless (for audio). Before you save or convert using a compressed format, don't forget to keep archival originals of your work, which is the perfect segue into the following section.

Editing without a Safety Net

You have the photo of a lifetime: three generations of your family, and not a single face not smiling, and no one missing! You decide that you need to edit the photo and then resize it to something that can be easily downloaded from Aunt Harriet's e-mail (meaning less than 300K in size). After you crop the photo slightly and reduce it to 640 x 480, you're ready to go, so you click Save, and. . . .

Hold it right there. *Do not* click Save.

"But why, Mark? I have my photo just like Aunt Harriet needs it! I have to save it to send it to her, right?" Yes, dear reader, you do need to save it — *but not by overwriting the original file!* I wish I had a dime for every time I commiserated with a client, family member, or friend who accidentally or intentionally destroyed the *original* version of an irreplaceable photo, video, or audio recording. Suddenly, you lose the high-resolution photo you originally had, and if you try to use it in a DVD slide show or print a larger copy of the image, you realize that it's now the size of a postage stamp. *Forever.*

Instead, click **Save As** and create a copy of the original image that's specifically named for Aunt Harriet. Or, use a program, like Photoshop Elements, that includes built-in "copy from original" protection to make sure that the original media source stays pristine and ready for use in the future.

Media professionals refer to *archival copies* of their work: namely, a CD or DVD with everything they've ever produced that can both act as a backup and a source for the original media. (I create a full DVD backup of my entire digital image, video, and MP3 audio collections every month.) With such an archival set handy, you can easily copy an original video clip from the set and edit it, safe in the knowledge that you're working with a safety net!

"Borrowing" Copyrighted Media

The Internet is indeed a smorgasbord of video clips, photos, and music, but how much of that bounty can you legally use in your business and personal projects? The answer is, "Not very much at all." Unfortunately, it's too easy to cut and paste or import your way to plagiarism and copyright violations. If an image, song, or video clip isn't your original work, you *must* be careful.

Make sure that any media you use from another source is explicitly released as one of the Big Three:

- ✔ Public domain
- ✔ Free for reproduction and use
- ✔ Royalty-free for use

If you're not sure about the source of a clip, photo, or song, act conservatively and don't use it or modify it for your use.

I'm not a lawyer. (Although I know a lot of lawyer jokes, that doesn't qualify me for the bar.) Therefore, the guidelines you read about copyrights in this book are exactly that — suggestions and recommendations. *Only a copyright lawyer can make a final determination of the legality of a specific image, video clip, or audio recording!*

Ancient Monitors from Eons Past

Boy, howdy, do folks love their monitors. Of all the components that computer owners can't seem to get rid of, monitors are the last to be upgraded. Imagine a state-of-the-art entertainment PC or Mac connected to an old CRT 1024 x 768 monitor — you know, the kind of relic that belongs in one of those archeological adventure movies! (Believe it or not, I've seen that very setup.)

Heed my words: You can't produce your best work or play your best game on an inferior monitor! Today you can pick up a stunning 19-inch LCD flat panel monitor with superb resolution and a fast 8-millisecond display speed for far less than $300 anywhere on the Web. Why saddle yourself with the 15-inch CRT that came with your parent's PC?

Along the same lines, make sure that the dimensions of the monitor you're using fit your applications. Primary on the list, of course: Forget a monitor with a standard aspect ratio for use with your Apple TV, and go widescreen!

Pokey Dialup Connections

As I mention elsewhere in the book, I strongly recommend using a broadband connection for your Internet travels! Dialup connections aren't fast enough for streaming Internet media, and downloading any media of merit becomes an epic quest lasting hours. (Literally.)

Switch to a DSL or cable modem Internet provider if you're within shouting distance of a populated area. These days, the cost is minimal compared with the benefits of a broadband connection. If you're living in a rural area, consider a satellite Internet connection.

The Video Editing Circus Effect

Every once in a while, a relative or reader sends me a movie to critique (or enjoy) that suffers from what I call the *Circus Effect:* the overuse of effects and transitions that are available in today's video editing applications.

Whether you're using Apple's iMovie, Studio from Pinnacle Systems, Premiere Elements from Adobe, or a more powerful video software package, resist the impulse to try out everything that the software has to offer in a single film! Remember, it's easy to shock or amuse your viewer *away* from the message you're trying to deliver in a movie. For example, avoid using transitions too often (like between every scene!) or using audio effects that distract the viewer's ear from the dialog.

Use restraint and place effects and transitions where they'll do the most good in your film, and you'll produce a more effective and enjoyable work.

Recording Rewritable DVD Video Discs

This one really drives folks up the proverbial wall. You've burned a DVD-video of your latest work — perhaps a practical joke slide show disc, or your dramatic *exposé* of college dorm life — and you bring it to your friend's place to show it off. The disc checked out fine on your computer's DVD drive before you left, but when you load the disc into your buddy's innocuous DVD player, it seizes up and spits the disc back, saying that it can't read your DVD. What gives?

Good reader, you've fallen prey to one of those ridiculous alphabet-soup acronym problems that still plague PC owners with DVD recorders. You burned your work onto a DVD-RW or DVD+RW rewritable disc, but your friend's DVD player doesn't recognize discs created with either of these rewriteable formats. (That's why your disc worked fine on your PC's DVD drive — it recognizes the format.)

Older DVD players are usually compatible only with DVD-R and DVD+R discs, which are write-once. Unfortunately, some DVD players don't even recognize DVD+R discs, so your best bet for the best possible compatibility is DVD-R.

Ignoring Your Backups

My final entry in this chapter is so predictable that even my cats knew it was coming: Back up your projects and your media on a regular basis. **DO IT.**

Without a comprehensive backup on hand, you'll eventually lose everything on your hard drive. It's just a matter of time. The cause could be a hardware failure, a hiccup within Windows, a virus, or your ten-year-old grandson, but the effect is the same.

When readers ask about my backup recommendations, I suggest using an external hard drive that's specifically designed for backups (and comes bundled with the backup software so you don't end up spending money on that as well). If you'd rather use your computer's internal DVD recorder to back up your system, invest in a good backup application, like True Image from Acronis (www.acronis.com) or Retrospect from EMC Corporation (www.emcinsignia.com).

If you're using Mac OS X Leopard, just pick up a good FireWire or USB 2.0 hard drive and use the new Time Machine feature to perform your backups automatically.

Back up your computer. Not next week, but *today*.

Part VII
Appendixes

The 5th Wave   By Rich Tennant

"Wait a minute... This is a movie, not a game?! I thought I was the one making Keanu Reeves jump kick in slow motion."

In this part . . .

You want a glossary that helps cut through the fog of engineer-speak and marketing terms? You got it! I also include a discussion of Apple TV-related software that can help you convert file formats, exercise with your Apple TV, and even use your widescreen wonder as an office presentation device! (Hmm . . . perhaps *your* boss would spring for that 40-inch plasma after perusing this stuff!)

Appendix A

Apple TV Software

· ·

After you've set up your Apple TV — using all the helpful information in this book, of course — a part of you may yearn for more. You want to expand what Apple has given you and push the boundaries of your Apple TV farther than the norm.

I hear that. Heck, I *love* taking hardware up a notch.

However, you can't really upgrade the hardware in your Apple TV without voiding the warranty. (No user-serviceable parts inside, as the saying goes.) Therefore, the techno-wizard in you has to use another outlet: software!

In this appendix, I describe the best and the brightest software applications and utilities that you can add to your media collection and help you minimize the amount of space on your Apple TV's hard drive.

I spend the lion's share of time on QuickTime Pro because it's one of the least expensive, media format conversion, "Swiss Army Knives" on the market — and it's from our favorite company — but you'll see that there are several alternatives. Who knows, perhaps you use your Apple TV for presentations. Or even *workouts?*

They Call It QuickTime Pro

- ✔ **Developer:** Apple (www.apple.com)
- ✔ **Operating system:** Mac OS X and Windows
- ✔ **Claim to fame:** Media player and format converter

"Oh, isn't that the media player that's installed with iTunes?" True, QuickTime's main claim to fame is playing all sorts of media on the Mac and PC — and I do mean *all* sorts. (Figure A-1 illustrates the content browser that appears each time you run the PC version of the Player as a stand-alone application.)

Figure A-1:
The familiar
face of the
QuickTime
content
browser.

Table A-1 lists the most popular of the media types that QuickTime supports. But playing media is just the tip of the iceberg . . . for Apple TV owners, QuickTime's attraction is its ability to *convert* media formats. (Which is why you need QuickTime Pro — more on this in a few paragraphs.)

The world of multimedia includes all kinds of file formats — so many, in fact, that it can take a rocket scientist to figure them all out. Fortunately, beyond its abilities as a world-class media player, QuickTime also has a full suite of conversion tools at its heart. QuickTime can import many kinds of media and spit them back out into practically any other format that it supports. QuickTime handles the messy details behind the scenes for you. You don't need to know a `.mov` file from an `.mp4` file to import and export to and from either format. QuickTime has you covered.

Table A-1	QuickTime Supported Formats
Media Type	*File Types*
Movie	`.mov`, `.avi*`, `.mpg`, `.dv`, `.mp4`, `divx`, `3g` (cellphones), `h.263`, `h.264`
Audio	`.aiff`, `.wav`, `.mp3`, `.au`, `.sfil`, `.aac`, `.amr`
Graphics	`.jpg`, `.tif`, `.pct`, `.bmp`

Media Type	File Types
Music	`.mid, .kar`
3D	`QTVR` (QuickTime Virtual Reality)
Animation	`.swf`

Movies in AVI format use a wide range of compression schemes, many of them proprietary (DivX, for example). For this reason, QuickTime might not be able to play some AVI movies that you download, but you can add support for additional schemes using third-party products. (DivX support for QuickTime, for example, is available from `www.divx.com`.)*

But you've gotta upgrade

QuickTime has two versions: free or Pro. The main differences between the free and Pro versions of QuickTime lie in the QuickTime Player application itself. The free version just plays media, and the Pro version adds extra features to QuickTime Player, such as converting 'twixt different media formats and full-screen playback. If you're using QuickTime Pro, all items listed in this section work as I describe.

If, however, you notice that a feature is dimmed out or missing altogether, you might be using the free QuickTime license. To find out whether you're using a free or Pro license on a Mac, open the System Preferences and navigate to the QuickTime panel. If you've registered as a QuickTime Pro user, you can find its registration information here, as shown in Figure A-2. If you're not a registered user, you can purchase the upgrade at `www.apple.com/quicktime`. The upgrade costs $29.99 at the time of this writing.

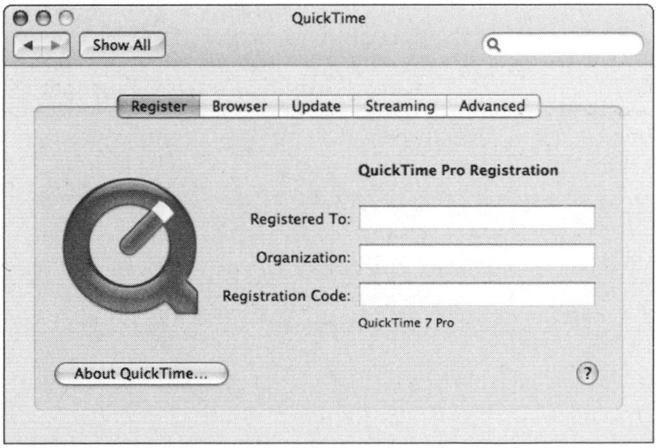

Figure A-2:
Check
System
Preferences
to see
which
license you
have.

On a PC, choose Start⇨Programs⇨QuickTime⇨QuickTime Player. Then in QuickTime, choose Edit⇨Preferences⇨QuickTime Preferences to display the dialog, as shown in Figure A-3. Again, if you're not registered, the price for the Windows upgrade is the same, and you can also get it at www.apple.com/quicktime.

Figure A-3: The QuickTime Pro registration screen under Windows.

Unsure about the format or file size of a movie? To see more information about a movie that you're playing using QuickTime Player, choose Window⇨Show Movie Info or press ⌘+I (or Ctrl+I on a PC). The resulting window displays data, like the compression standard used, the pixel dimensions of the file, the file size, and the duration. These bits and pieces of information are *read-only,* so you can't change them from the Movie Info window.

Exploring movie properties

In addition to general movie information, you can also peek inside a QuickTime movie to see what makes it tick. To display the Movie Properties window, choose Window⇨Show Movie Properties or press ⌘+J on the Mac (Ctrl+J on the PC).

The Movie Properties window (as shown in Figure A-4) displays the audio and video tracks in the list at the top of the window. Select a track and click one of the panel buttons to display things, like the Audio Settings, for the track or the general settings you can change. (The panel buttons you see depend on what type of item you select in the list.)

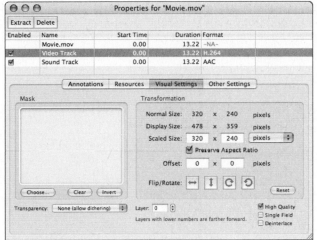

Figure A-4:
Altering
movie
properties
with
QuickTime
Pro.

Yep, that's correct, these settings you *can* change because they're not read-only. For example, to rotate or flip a movie's video track, follow these steps:

1. **With QuickTime Player, open a QuickTime movie.**

2. **Press ⌘+J/Ctrl+J to open its Movie Properties window.**

3. **From the Tracks list at the top of the Properties window, choose the first available Video Track.**

4. **Click the Visual Settings panel button.**

5. **Click the Flip or Rotate buttons.**

6. **After you adjust the track's orientation to your liking, close the Movie Properties window.**

If you want to save your movie with the new video track, press ⌘+S on the Mac or Ctrl+S on the PC.

Every file that you open with QuickTime Player consists of one or more tracks. A *track* contains one (and only one) type of media. For example, a typical QuickTime movie might comprise two tracks:

✔ **Video track:** Stores the video data of the movie

✔ **Sound track:** Stores the audio data of the movie

In contrast, opening an audio file with QuickTime Player might have only a single sound track. Other files don't have a video or sound track at all: Shockwave and Flash (.swf) files, for example, usually contain only one Flash track. MIDI files have yet another type of track. Luckily, QuickTime makes it simple for you to ignore these technical trivia facts altogether (which most of us prefer).

Converting files

Now, about converting stuff: When your collection of multimedia grows, you'll eventually find yourself wishing that certain files were in a different format for use on your Apple TV. For example, you might want to convert a digital video (DV) file to a QuickTime movie (MOV) for use with Apple TV. With a few clicks, QuickTime Pro can open a media file in one of dozens of formats and convert it to almost any other format that QuickTime understands. To do so, you must import the file into QuickTime and then export it into the format that you prefer.

Loading (or *importing*) a file in QuickTime Player is as easy as choosing File⇨Open or simply double-clicking the file icon. (No need to wait until a file has finished playing . . . you can begin converting it immediately.)

After you open or import a media file, QuickTime Pro lets you export it to one of many formats. For example, you might export a QuickTime movie to an AVI movie for those Windows users who don't have QuickTime installed. To export a movie, choose File⇨Export. In the dialog that appears, select the desired output format from the Export pop-up menu. Each export type also has a set of options, like those shown in Figure A-5. To view them, click the Options button on the right side of the Export dialog. You can also choose to rename the file or specify a different location on your system where the exported file should be saved.

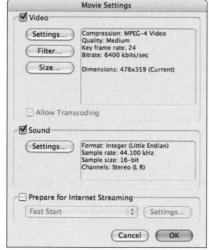

Figure A-5:
Preparing to
convert a
H.264 video
clip to
MPEG-4
video.

Recording with QuickTime Pro

Most folks don't think of QuickTime as a recording application . . . that's because Apple provides applications like Photo Booth, iMovie, and iTunes that have long been the recording tools of choice in the Mac universe. However, you can indeed record audio and video with QuickTime Player as long as your computer is equipped with the proper hardware (a microphone or line-in device for audio and an iSight camera or external video camera for video).

If you're recording video (sorry, PC owners, only the Mac version of QuickTime Pro allows video recording), you should first set the Recording preferences in the QuickTime Player Preferences dialog:

1. **Press ⌘+, (comma) or choose QuickTime Player⇨Preferences.**

2. **Click the Recording tab.**

3. **Set your recording input source, the quality of the video, and the default location where the video files are stored.**

When you're ready to record, choose File⇨New Movie Recording (on the Mac) or New Audio Recording (on both Mac and PC). This is a one-click operation: Click the Big Red Button to start and stop recording. QuickTime displays both the recording time and the approximate hard drive space used so far. 'Nuff said.

Converting with Crunch

✔ **Developer:** Sonic Solutions (www.roxio.com)

✔ **Operating system:** Mac OS X

✔ **Claim to fame:** Format converter extraordinaire

Roxio Crunch (see Figure A-6) hails from the same family tree as Roxio Toast, which I cover in Chapter 20. Like QuickTime Pro, many Apple TV and iPod owners look to Crunch for format conversions — but unlike QuickTime Pro, Crunch was created from the ground up with iTunes in mind, so it automates the conversion process for your Apple TV or your iPod.

The features that stand out include

✔ **More supported formats:** Crunch can handle DivX and MPEG-2 video, as well as non-encrypted DVD movie discs (like an iDVD project that your friend has burned and loaned to you).

✔ **Conversion from files or disc:** Crunch can use a VIDEO_TS folder on your hard drive or a Mac OS X image file as the source for your stuff.

✔ **Batch conversion:** Need to convert a large number of files for use on your Apple TV? No problem, Crunch can do it.

✔ **Video quality presets for Apple TV:** Crunch comes pre-configured to produce converted content that's optimized for your Apple TV.

Figure A-6:
Roxio
Crunch
works
wonders as
a format
converter.

After you convert your video to the right format, Crunch automatically moves it to your iTunes Library, where — as you know because you're now an Apple TV expert — iTunes syncs it to your Apple TV, according to the syncing rules you've set up. (Visit Chapter 8 if you missed that discussion.) In fact, you could even stream it . . . I won't tell anyone.

Grabbing More Video with TubeTV

✔ **Developer:** Chimoosoft (www.chimoosoft.com)

✔ **Operating system:** Mac OS X

✔ **Claim to fame:** Copies YouTube and Google Video clips to iTunes

TubeTV (as shown in Figure A-7) allows you to copy video clips from YouTube and Google Video and save them in your iTunes Library. It's *donationware* (freeware with a requested donation) and works on any Mac running Mac OS X Tiger or Leopard.

Figure A-7:
For a donation-ware application, TubeTV is impressive at grabbing video.

TubeTV offers

- ✔ **A built-in browser:** You don't even have to open your Web browser to search for clips! TubeTV includes a search bar, too.
- ✔ **H.264 conversion:** Produces high-quality video.
- ✔ **Conversion presets for Apple TV:** It's easy to optimize your clips for your Apple TV.

An Apple TV . . . Workout?

- ✔ **Developer:** Helmes Innovations (www.helmesinnovations.com)
- ✔ **Operating system:** Mac OS X and Windows
- ✔ **Claim to fame:** A fitness trainer for iPod and Apple TV

Yep, you read right: iWorkout, as shown in Figure A-8, provides a video health trainer for cardio, free weights, machines, stretching, and more. It's share-ware, so you can try it out first, and it works on your iPod, Apple TV, and even on your Mac with Front Row.

iWorkout features include

- ✔ **Workout videos:** Watch your exercises done the right way.
- ✔ **Trainer tips and fitness guides:** Documentation with illustrations.
- ✔ **An exercise metronome:** Let your Apple TV keep your tempo during exercising!

Figure A-8:
iWorkout
brings your
health
training to
Apple TV.

Presenting Your Presentations

✔ **Developer:** ZappTek (www.zapptek.com)

✔ **Operating system:** Mac OS X and Windows

✔ **Claim to fame:** Presentation converter for Apple TV and iPod

iPresent It converts Keynote, PowerPoint, and PDF presentation slides to
Apple TV and iPod-compatible formats. It can produce widescreen
slideshows that look great on an Apple TV display.

iPresent It offers

✔ **Track changes and updates your slideshow:** When you change your
presentation, iPresent It can update your slideshow.

✔ **Drag and drop support for presentations:** iPresent It is very intuitive
to use.

✔ **Automatic iPhoto albums:** Your Mac can create iPhoto albums from
your presentation files.

Moving Your DV to Disk

✔ **Developer:** Square Box Systems (www.squarebox.co.uk)

✔ **Operating system:** Mac OS X

✔ **Claim to fame:** DV tape-to-hard drive capture utility

CatDV Live Capture Plus is a heavy-duty application for professional video work, allowing you to capture the video stream in raw DV format, MPEG-4, or any format recognized in QuickTime. An extensive set of advanced options (see Figure A-9) allows the video professional to create automated workflows for digital video.

Figure A-9:
CatDV Live
Capture
Plus offers
professional
video
capture with
Apple TV
presets.

CatDV Live Capture Plus features include

✔ **Apple TV presets:** Save video as clips optimized for Apple TV viewing.

✔ **Automatic splitting:** Capture and save each scene as a separate file.

✔ **Automatic background compression:** Automatically pause incoming video stream to allow for compression during capture.

Calling Upon Your Widgets

✔ **Developer:** Jeffrey Holcombe

✔ **Operating system:** Mac OS X

✔ **Claim to fame:** Dashboard Widget that automatically details your TV shows

As you now know, I'm a stickler for detailing my iTunes Library files with as much identifying information as possible, and *Descriptor* — a freeware offering from Mr. Holcombe — can take care of that chore for your TV episodes. Because it's a Dashboard Widget, it's onscreen with a single press of your F12 key. You can get it from the Apple Widget download area at www.apple.com/downloads/dashboard.

Descriptor reads the episode and season number from the filename and then adds information to the file's tags, like

- ✔ Show Name
- ✔ Year Released
- ✔ Episode Description
- ✔ Episode and Season Number

Moving EyeTV Video to Apple TV

- ✔ **Developer:** Elgato Systems (www.elgato.com)
- ✔ **Operating system:** Mac OS X
- ✔ **Claim to fame:** Capturing cable and over-air broadcasts to video and then to your Apple TV

If you've been a Mac owner for long, you've probably heard of Elgato's EyeTV software, which works with its EyeTV line of TV display and personal video recording hardware devices. The EyeTV hardware and software package, which resembles (you guessed it) *another* remote control, have been well-known in the Mac community for reliable operation and a wealth of features.

The latest version of EyeTV includes an Apple TV button, which exports recorded video directly to iTunes in Apple TV-compatible format. Your syncing rules take care of things from there.

Other EyeTV software features include

- ✔ **Complete control over broadcast TV:** Fast-forward and pause live broadcasts on your Mac.
- ✔ **PVR mode:** Record your favorite shows direct to your Mac's hard drive.
- ✔ **Use the Program Guide to schedule recording:** Automate the recording process for your favorite shows.

Appendix B

Glossary

• •

802.11b: The original wireless networking standard, also called Wi-Fi. 802.11b, hardware provides the slowest transfer speeds, but it's still compatible with your Apple TV. (Note that streaming video isn't supported by your Apple TV when using an 802.11b connection.)

802.11g: Currently the most common wireless networking standard, 802.11g offers much faster speeds than 802.11b and fully supports all the streaming and syncing features offered by Apple TV.

802.11n: The latest and fastest wireless networking standard. Your Apple TV includes 802.11n hardware (as does the current generation of Mac computers and the latest AirPort Extreme Base Station). 802.11n is compatible with both 802.11b and 802.11g hardware — however, for the best performance, your network must use all 802.11n hardware.

AAC: Apple's digital audio format, which offers compressed file sizes comparable to the well-known MP3 format — however, AAC files are smaller than MP3 files of the same quality. All the audio you purchase from the Apple iTunes Store is in AAC format. *See also* AIFF, MP3, and WAV.

access time: The amount of time that a hard drive, DVD drive, or memory module takes to read data. The faster the access time, the better.

adapter card: A circuit board that plugs into your motherboard to provide your computer with additional functionality. For example, a wireless adapter card plugs into your motherboard and enables your computer to connect to your wireless network.

AIFF: The original Apple digital audio format developed for the Macintosh. Like WAV files, AIFF files offer very high quality sound reproduction, but they're huge in size and are generally used only for archival storage. *See also* AAC, MP3, and WAV.

Apple Lossless: A digital audio format developed by Apple that offers significant compression with no loss in sound quality — although audio tracks in Apple Lossless format are larger than AAC or MP3 files, they're far smaller than WAV or AIFF files. Apple Lossless is the preferred format for audiophiles with iTunes, iPod, and Apple TV.

application: A program that performs a task on your computer. For example, an Internet application is a program that performs some useful function while your computer is connected to the Internet.

Blu-ray: One of the two latest optical disc standards, providing high-definition video and high-capacity storage (up to 25GB for a single-layer disc and 50GB for a dual-layer disc). *See also* HD-DVD.

BMP: Microsoft's Bitmap image format was developed for Windows and provides the best quality digital photographs — however, it's uncompressed, so bitmap images are much larger than JPEG or PNG images. *See also* JPEG, PNG, and TIFF.

bps (bits per second): A common method of measuring the speed of a modem. Today's high-speed modems are usually measured in kilobits per second (Kbps), as in 56 Kbps.

broadband: A high-speed Internet connection that delivers data much faster than a traditional dialup analog modem connection. Common Internet broadband connections include DSL, cable, and satellite. *See also* DSL.

bus: A slot on your computer's motherboard that accepts adapter cards. Bus slots on PC motherboards are generally 32-bit PCI slots, AGP slots, or PCI Express slots. *See also* PCI and PCI Express.

cable modem: An external device that connects your computer to your cable TV company's coaxial cable. A cable modem is a requirement for connecting to the Internet through cable access. Although a cable modem really isn't anything like a traditional analog modem, it looks like one.

case: The metal enclosure that surrounds your computer and holds all its parts. The case, typically held on with screws or thumbwheels, might have a separate cover that you can remove to add or remove parts; other cases are one piece and simply open up.

CD-ROM drive: An internal device that can read both CD-ROMs (which store computer programs and files) and audio CDs (which store music). A typical CD-ROM can hold as much as 700MB of data. CD-ROM drives can't write to the disc; they can only read data.

CD-RW drive: Also called a *CD recorder;* enables you to record (and re-record) CDs. Discs made with a CD-RW drive can hold computer data and music. CD-Rs can be read on any CD-ROM drive but can be recorded only once. CD-RWs can be read on most CD-ROM drives and can be re-recorded.

client-server: A network in which computers act as clients and retrieve information or services from a central server computer. In the case of a home entertainment network, a media server would store all your video, music, and photos for viewing on your entertainment PC. Server computers can also hold common shared resources, such as modems or CD-ROM drives, or provide shared access to Internet services, like e-mail and a Web site.

color depth: A reference to the number of bits used to represent the colors in an image. Popular color depths are 256 colors, 64,000 colors, and 16 million colors.

component: The technoid word for a piece of computer hardware; a computer part.

component video connectors: Also called *RGB cables* (for their red, green, and blue signals and cable colors); component video cables are a common connection between video equipment and today's high-definition televisions. Although a component video connection isn't as high quality as an HDMI connection (and doesn't carry audio like HDMI does), the Apple TV includes a set of component video jacks for compatibility. ***See also*** HDMI.

compression: The use of a mathematical formula to reduce the amount of disk space taken up by a file, a video clip, or an image. Some compression schemes can reproduce the original exactly; other compression schemes lose some detail from the original. Modems also use compression to reduce the time necessary to transfer a file.

CPU (central processing unit): The chip that acts as your computer's brain. The CPU performs the commands provided by the programs that you run.

CRT (cathode ray tube): A traditional PC monitor or TV that uses a glass tube and magnetic gun. CRT displays are typically bulky, but they're inexpensive and offer great color reproduction.

digital cable-ready: A standard that guarantees that your new monitor or TV is already capable of displaying a signal from your cable box (without using an external tuner). Most satellite receivers can also work with a digital cable-ready display.

digital camera: A camera that looks and operates much like a traditional film camera except that its finished images are uploaded directly to a computer rather than processed into photographs. Digital cameras are more expensive than their film cousins.

DirectX: An extension to Windows XP, Windows Vista, and Windows 2003 Server that enables fast animation and graphics display in game and multimedia programs.

dot pitch: The amount of space between pixels on a monitor. The smaller the dot pitch, the clearer and more detailed the display.

DPMS (Display Power Management Signaling): A feature that enables your computer to power down your monitor after a specified period of inactivity. This feature helps save energy and money.

DSL (digital subscriber line): A high-speed connection to the Internet offering top speeds of around 4–8 Mbps. Although DSL uses regular copper telephone line and is always on, it's still not available in some rural areas of the country. *See also* broadband.

DSL modem: An external device that connects your computer to a DSL line. The modem looks like a traditional analog telephone modem but delivers data much faster.

DVD (Digital Video Disc or Digital Versatile Disc): The replacement for the older CD-ROM format. A single DVD can hold from 4.7–17GB. DVDs can hold computer data, full-length movies, and several hours of audio in MPEG format.

DVD-RW/DVD+RW drive: A DVD recorder that enables you to record (and re-record) DVDs. DVD-Rs and DVD+Rs can be read on any DVD drive (and virtually all DVD players designed for use with your TV set), but they can be recorded only once. DVD-RWs and DVD+RWs aren't as compatible as DVD-R and DVD+R discs, but they can be re-recorded.

DVI (Digital Visual Interface or Digital Video Interface): A high-performance port that connects your video card to flat-panel LCD and CRT monitors as well as to many LCD, plasma, and projection TVs. A DVI connection provides the best-quality video signal and the fastest data transfer between your PC and your monitor — digital end-to-end, as the techs say.

Ethernet: The most common networking design for home and small office use, where data is broadcast across the network between computers. Although Ethernet is generally less efficient than other network architectures, it's less complex and less expensive to maintain. Ethernet networks can use cabling or wireless hardware.

external peripheral: A type of peripheral or device that sits outside your computer's case and is connected by a cable — for example, an external modem.

female connector: A cable connector with holes that accept the pins on a male connector. *See also* male connector.

firewall: A program or device designed to protect network data from being accessed by a computer hacker. Most Internet and Web sites use a firewall to provide security for company data, and both Vista and Mac OS X have their own internal firewalls.

FireWire: The popular name for the IEEE 1394 high-performance serial bus connection standard developed by Apple. A FireWire connection is similar to a USB connection. Devices can be added or removed without rebooting the computer, and you can daisy-chain as many as 63 FireWire devices from a single port. Because of a FireWire port's high data-transfer rate of 400 Mbps and ability to control digital devices, it's especially well suited for connecting digital camcorders and external hard drives to your PC. The latest FireWire 800 standard (which is now available for PCs) can transfer data at a mind-boggling 800 Mbps.

Flash drive: An external solid-state removable storage drive that connects to your USB port. These drives store data using the same technology as the memory cards that you find in digital cameras.

flat-panel display: A monitor or TV that uses LCD and plasma technology instead of a traditional tube. LCD monitors have been used on laptop computers for years and are now just as popular for full-size desktop computers. A flat panel is much thinner than a traditional tube monitor, uses less electricity, and emits very little radiation. *See also* plasma display.

game port: A port for connecting joysticks and game peripherals. Game ports can be installed separately, although most sound cards have a game port built in.

GB (gigabyte): A unit of data equal to 1024MB (megabytes).

GHz (gigahertz): The frequency (or speed) of a CPU as measured in billions of cycles per second.

GPU (Graphics Processing Unit): Performs the complex rendering and 3D display tasks on today's video cards.

H.264: A video compression algorithm that offers far smaller file sizes than the older MPEG compression used on DVD movie discs. H.264 (or *AVC*) compression is supported by both Vista and Mac OS X, and movies that you buy from the iTunes Store are downloaded with H.264 compression.

hard drive (or hard disk): A component that usually fits inside your case. Your hard drive acts as permanent storage for your programs and data, enabling you to save and delete files. Unlike the RAM in your computer, your hard drive doesn't lose data when you turn off your PC.

HDMI (High-Definition Multimedia Interface): The standard connector for carrying both a high-definition video signal and multichannel audio from your PC's video card (or an A/V receiver) to your display and speaker system. *See also* component video connectors.

HD-DVD: One of the two latest optical disc standards, providing high-definition video and high-capacity storage (up to 15GB for a single-layer disc and 30GB for a dual-layer disc). *See also* Blu-ray.

high-definition: A video signal that provides higher resolution; a widescreen aspect ratio and digital quality far superior to older analog broadcast TV. High-definition video can be broadcast, provided by your cable or satellite connection, or provided by a Blu-ray or HD-DVD player.

integrated video card: Video card hardware that's built into a PC's motherboard. An integrated video card can't be removed but can usually be upgraded by using a standard video card in an adapter card slot on the motherboard.

interface: A technoid term that refers to the method of connecting a peripheral to your computer. For example, printers use a parallel port interface or a USB interface; hard drives use EIDE, FireWire, or SATA (Serial ATA). Some interface types refer to adapter cards; others refer to ports and cables. *See also* FireWire and USB.

interlaced: A video signal (either high-definition or analog) that is displayed in two sets of alternating rows (instead of being displayed in a continuous line-by-line form, like a progressive image). *See also* progressive.

internal component: A component that you install inside your computer's case — for example, a hard drive or an internal modem.

iTunes Store: Apple's online digital media store, where you can browse and purchase audio and video content. The files you buy are downloaded automatically to your computer and stored in your iTunes media library.

joystick: An input device (for games) that's similar to the control stick used by many pilots. Predictably, joysticks are usually used by game players who enjoy flight simulators.

JPEG: The most popular digital photograph format in use today, JPEG images are the norm on the Web and are produced by most of today's digital cameras. JPEG is a compressed format, providing very good quality with small file sizes. *See also* BMP, PNG, and TIFF.

K (kilobyte): A unit equal to 1024 bytes.

LAN (local area network): *See* network.

LCD (liquid crystal display): *See* flat-panel display.

male connector: A cable connector with pins that fit into the holes on a female connector. *See also* female connector.

MB (megabyte): A unit equal to 1024K.

MHz (megahertz): The frequency (or speed) of an older CPU as measured in millions of cycles per second.

MIDI (Musical Instrument Digital Interface): The hardware standard that enables computers of all types to play MIDI music and enables interaction between the computer and the instrument. MIDI music files are common on the Internet.

MIDI port: Enables you to connect a MIDI-compatible musical instrument to your computer. Notes that you play on the instrument can be recorded on your computer, or your PC or Mac can be set to play the instrument by itself.

modem: A computer device that converts digital data from one computer to an analog signal that can be sent over a telephone line. On the opposite end, the analog signal is converted back to digital data. Modems are widely used to access the Internet, online services, and computer bulletin board systems.

monitor: An external component that looks something like a TV screen. Your computer's monitor displays all the graphics generated by your PC.

motherboard: Your computer's main circuit board. It holds the CPU, the RAM modules, and most of the circuitry. Adapter cards plug into your motherboard.

mouse: The standard computer pointing device. You hold the mouse in your hand and move it in the desired direction to create movement on your screen. A mouse also has buttons that you can press to select items or run a program.

MOV: Apple's QuickTime video format is the standard for Mac OS X, offering excellent quality with compression. MOV files are common on the Web and can be synced and streamed with Apple TV. QuickTime movies can also be viewed on PCs using the Windows version of QuickTime.

MP3: A popular digital sound format used to download CD-quality music from the Internet. Your computer can play MP3 files through its speaker system, you can listen to them with a portable MP3 player, or you can record MP3 files to a CD-ROM and play them in any standard audio CD player. Like the AAC format, MP3 files can be compressed at different bit rates, allowing better quality with larger file sizes, or smaller files with acceptable quality. *See also* AAC, AIFF, and WAV.

MPEG (Motion Pictures Expert Group): A popular digital video format and compression scheme often found on the Web. MPEG-format video is used on commercial DVD movies and is supported by Apple TV.

network: A system of computers connected to each other. Each computer can share data with other computers in the network, and all computers connected to the network can use common resources, such as printers and modems.

PCI (Peripheral Component Interconnect): A local bus standard designed by Intel. A PCI bus slot can hold a 32-bit adapter card to add functionality to your computer. PCI slots are faster than older ISA slots, so they're used for everything these days: for example, Ethernet cards and sound cards.

PCI Express: The high-performance successor for a standard PCI slot. The PCI Express bus is most commonly used these days for adding the latest and fastest video cards to your PC.

pixel: A single dot on your monitor. Text and graphics displayed by a computer on a monitor are made up of pixels.

plasma display: A monitor or TV that uses phosphorescent plasma sandwiched between two sheets of glass. Plasma displays are very expensive and have a shorter operating life, but they provide the best detail and image quality for today's home theater systems. *See also* flat-panel display and projection display.

PNG: A relative newcomer, the PNG digital image format offers somewhat smaller file sizes than JPEG. Most of today's cellphones take and display images in PNG format, and your Apple TV can display them as well. *See also* BMP, JPEG, and TIFF.

port: A fancy name for a connector that you plug something into. For example, your USB scanner plugs into a USB port.

progressive: A digital video signal that is drawn line by line across your display (instead of being displayed in two sets of alternating rows, like an interlaced image). Progressive high-definition signals are superior in quality to interlaced high-definition video. *See also* interlaced.

projection display: A monitor or TV that projects an image onto either a sheet of glass or a separate screen. Projection displays offer the largest size and reasonable prices but with mediocre detail and image quality. *See also* flat-panel display and plasma display.

RAM (random access memory): The type of chip that acts as your computer's short-term memory. This memory chip holds programs and data until you turn off your computer.

refresh: The number of times per second that your video adapter card redraws the image on your PC's monitor. Higher refresh rates are easier on the eyes.

rendering: A technoid term for creating 3D objects and full 3D scenes on your computer. The classic films *Toy Story, Finding Nemo,* and *A Bug's Life* feature rendered 3D characters. Many 2D images are rendered as well.

resolution: The number of pixels on your screen measured as horizontal by vertical. For example, a resolution of 1024 x 768 means that there are 1024 pixels across the screen and 768 lines down the side of the screen.

rpm (revolutions per minute): The speed of the platters in a hard drive. The faster the RPM, the faster the drive can access your data.

scanner: A device that converts (or captures) text and graphics from a printed page into a digital image. Scanners are often used to "read" pictures from books and magazines; the digital version of the picture can be edited and used in documents or placed on a Web page.

sound card: An adapter card that enables your computer to play music and sound effects for games and other programs. Sound cards can also record audio from a microphone or stereo system.

static electricity: The archenemy of all computer circuitry, especially computer chips. Before you install anything in your computer, you should touch the metal chassis of your computer to discharge any static electricity on your body.

streaming: The process of sending digital media from iTunes running on your computer to your Apple TV, which then sends the signal directly to your TV. Unlike syncing, streaming content is not saved on your Apple TV's internal hard drive. You can also receive streaming audio or video over the Internet from another computer.

subwoofer: A separate speaker that you can add to a standard two-speaker computer sound system. Subwoofers add deep bass response and can bring realistic depth to sound effects.

SVGA (Super Video Graphics Array): The most common graphics standard for PC video adapter cards and monitors. The SVGA standard allows for more than 16 million colors (24-bit or true color).

syncing: The process of sending digital media from iTunes running on your computer to your Apple TV, which then stores the content on your Apple TV's internal hard drive until you send the command to play the video or audio.

TIFF: A popular digital image format offering a good tradeoff on image quality and compressed file sizes, TIFF images are supported across many different computers and operating systems, and TIFF images can be displayed on your Apple TV. *See also* BMP, JPEG, and PNG.

TOSLINK: A standard optical fiber cable for carrying a digital audio signal between an A/V receiver, and external devices like a DVD player or speaker system. Your Apple TV includes a TOSLINK port.

twisted-pair cable: A form of network cable that looks much like telephone cord. Twisted-pair cable is commonly used on Ethernet networks with a central router or switch.

USB (universal serial bus): A standard connector that enables you to daisy-chain a whopping 127 devices, with data transfers at as much as 12 Mbps for USB standard 1.1 (and a respectable 480 Mbps for USB standard 2.0). USB connectors have become the standard of choice for all sorts of computer peripherals, from computer videocameras and scanners to joysticks and speakers. (By the way, a USB 1.1 device works just fine when connected to a USB 2.0 port.)

VGA (Video Graphics Array): The IBM PC graphics standard that featured 256 colors. Replaced on most of today's computers by the SVGA standard. *See also* SVGA.

video card: An adapter card that plugs into your motherboard and enables your computer to display text and graphics on your monitor. Advanced adapter cards can speed up the display of Windows programs and 3D graphics.

WAV: The original Microsoft standard format for a digital sound file. WAV files are common across the Internet and offer the best quality (like AIFF files, they're uncompressed) but are far too large for efficient streaming or storing on a portable device like the iPod — hence the popularity of sound formats like MP3, AAC, and Apple Lossless that produce much smaller file sizes. *See also* AAC, AIFF, and MP3.

wireless mouse: A pointing device similar to a standard mouse but without the cord that connects it to the computer. Wireless mice require batteries but are a little more convenient without the cord.

Index

• *B* •

(continued)

BUSINESS, CAREERS & PERSONAL FINANCE

0-7645-9847-3   0-7645-2431-3

Also available:
- Business Plans Kit For Dummies
  0-7645-9794-9
- Economics For Dummies
  0-7645-5726-2
- Grant Writing For Dummies
  0-7645-8416-2
- Home Buying For Dummies
  0-7645-5331-3
- Managing For Dummies
  0-7645-1771-6
- Marketing For Dummies
  0-7645-5600-2

- Personal Finance For Dummies
  0-7645-2590-5*
- Resumes For Dummies
  0-7645-5471-9
- Selling For Dummies
  0-7645-5363-1
- Six Sigma For Dummies
  0-7645-6798-5
- Small Business Kit For Dummies
  0-7645-5984-2
- Starting an eBay Business For Dummies
  0-7645-6924-4
- Your Dream Career For Dummies
  0-7645-9795-7

HOME & BUSINESS COMPUTER BASICS

0-470-05432-8   0-471-75421-8

Also available:
- Cleaning Windows Vista For Dummies
  0-471-78293-9
- Excel 2007 For Dummies
  0-470-03737-7
- Mac OS X Tiger For Dummies
  0-7645-7675-5
- MacBook For Dummies
  0-470-04859-X
- Macs For Dummies
  0-470-04849-2
- Office 2007 For Dummies
  0-470-00923-3

- Outlook 2007 For Dummies
  0-470-03830-6
- PCs For Dummies
  0-7645-8958-X
- Salesforce.com For Dummies
  0-470-04893-X
- Upgrading & Fixing Laptops For Dummies
  0-7645-8959-8
- Word 2007 For Dummies
  0-470-03658-3
- Quicken 2007 For Dummies
  0-470-04600-7

FOOD, HOME, GARDEN, HOBBIES, MUSIC & PETS

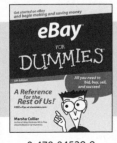 

0-7645-8404-9   0-7645-9904-6

Also available:
- Candy Making For Dummies
  0-7645-9734-5
- Card Games For Dummies
  0-7645-9910-0
- Crocheting For Dummies
  0-7645-4151-X
- Dog Training For Dummies
  0-7645-8418-9
- Healthy Carb Cookbook For Dummies
  0-7645-8476-6
- Home Maintenance For Dummies
  0-7645-5215-5

- Horses For Dummies
  0-7645-9797-3
- Jewelry Making & Beading For Dummies
  0-7645-2571-9
- Orchids For Dummies
  0-7645-6759-4
- Puppies For Dummies
  0-7645-5255-4
- Rock Guitar For Dummies
  0-7645-5356-9
- Sewing For Dummies
  0-7645-6847-7
- Singing For Dummies
  0-7645-2475-5

INTERNET & DIGITAL MEDIA

 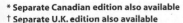

0-470-04529-9   0-470-04894-8

Also available:
- Blogging For Dummies
  0-471-77084-1
- Digital Photography For Dummies
  0-7645-9802-3
- Digital Photography All-in-One Desk Reference For Dummies
  0-470-03743-1
- Digital SLR Cameras and Photography For Dummies
  0-7645-9803-1
- eBay Business All-in-One Desk Reference For Dummies
  0-7645-8438-3
- HDTV For Dummies
  0-470-09673-X

- Home Entertainment PCs For Dummies
  0-470-05523-5
- MySpace For Dummies
  0-470-09529-6
- Search Engine Optimization For Dummies
  0-471-97998-8
- Skype For Dummies
  0-470-04891-3
- The Internet For Dummies
  0-7645-8996-2
- Wiring Your Digital Home For Dummies
  0-471-91830-X

* Separate Canadian edition also available
† Separate U.K. edition also available

SPORTS, FITNESS, PARENTING, RELIGION & SPIRITUALITY

0-471-76871-5

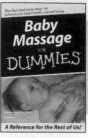

0-7645-7841-3

Also available:

- Catholicism For Dummies
  0-7645-5391-7
- Exercise Balls For Dummies
  0-7645-5623-1
- Fitness For Dummies
  0-7645-7851-0
- Football For Dummies
  0-7645-3936-1
- Judaism For Dummies
  0-7645-5299-6
- Potty Training For Dummies
  0-7645-5417-4
- Buddhism For Dummies
  0-7645-5359-3

- Pregnancy For Dummies
  0-7645-4483-7 †
- Ten Minute Tone-Ups For Dummies
  0-7645-7207-5
- NASCAR For Dummies
  0-7645-7681-X
- Religion For Dummies
  0-7645-5264-3
- Soccer For Dummies
  0-7645-5229-5
- Women in the Bible For Dummies
  0-7645-8475-8

TRAVEL

0-7645-7749-2

0-7645-6945-7

Also available:

- Alaska For Dummies
  0-7645-7746-8
- Cruise Vacations For Dummies
  0-7645-6941-4
- England For Dummies
  0-7645-4276-1
- Europe For Dummies
  0-7645-7529-5
- Germany For Dummies
  0-7645-7823-5
- Hawaii For Dummies
  0-7645-7402-7

- Italy For Dummies
  0-7645-7386-1
- Las Vegas For Dummies
  0-7645-7382-9
- London For Dummies
  0-7645-4277-X
- Paris For Dummies
  0-7645-7630-5
- RV Vacations For Dummies
  0-7645-4442-X
- Walt Disney World & Orlando
  For Dummies
  0-7645-9660-8

GRAPHICS, DESIGN & WEB DEVELOPMENT

0-7645-8815-X

0-7645-9571-7

Also available:

- 3D Game Animation For Dummies
  0-7645-8789-7
- AutoCAD 2006 For Dummies
  0-7645-8925-3
- Building a Web Site For Dummies
  0-7645-7144-3
- Creating Web Pages For Dummies
  0-470-08030-2
- Creating Web Pages All-in-One Desk
  Reference For Dummies
  0-7645-4345-8
- Dreamweaver 8 For Dummies
  0-7645-9649-7

- InDesign CS2 For Dummies
  0-7645-9572-5
- Macromedia Flash 8 For Dummies
  0-7645-9691-8
- Photoshop CS2 and Digital
  Photography For Dummies
  0-7645-9580-6
- Photoshop Elements 4 For Dummies
  0-471-77483-9
- Syndicating Web Sites with RSS Feeds
  For Dummies
  0-7645-8848-6
- Yahoo! SiteBuilder For Dummies
  0-7645-9800-7

NETWORKING, SECURITY, PROGRAMMING & DATABASES

0-7645-7728-X

0-471-74940-0

Also available:

- Access 2007 For Dummies
  0-470-04612-0
- ASP.NET 2 For Dummies
  0-7645-7907-X
- C# 2005 For Dummies
  0-7645-9704-3
- Hacking For Dummies
  0-470-05235-X
- Hacking Wireless Networks
  For Dummies
  0-7645-9730-2
- Java For Dummies
  0-470-08716-1

- Microsoft SQL Server 2005 For Dummies
  0-7645-7755-7
- Networking All-in-One Desk Reference
  For Dummies
  0-7645-9939-9
- Preventing Identity Theft For Dummies
  0-7645-7336-5
- Telecom For Dummies
  0-471-77085-X
- Visual Studio 2005 All-in-One Desk
  Reference For Dummies
  0-7645-9775-2
- XML For Dummies
  0-7645-8845-1

HEALTH & SELF-HELP

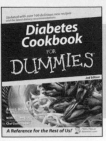

0-7645-8450-2

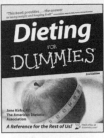

0-7645-4149-8

Also available:

- Bipolar Disorder For Dummies
  0-7645-8451-0
- Chemotherapy and Radiation
  For Dummies
  0-7645-7832-4
- Controlling Cholesterol For Dummies
  0-7645-5440-9
- Diabetes For Dummies
  0-7645-6820-5* †
- Divorce For Dummies
  0-7645-8417-0 †

- Fibromyalgia For Dummies
  0-7645-5441-7
- Low-Calorie Dieting For Dummies
  0-7645-9905-4
- Meditation For Dummies
  0-471-77774-9
- Osteoporosis For Dummies
  0-7645-7621-6
- Overcoming Anxiety For Dummies
  0-7645-5447-6
- Reiki For Dummies
  0-7645-9907-0
- Stress Management For Dummies
  0-7645-5144-2

EDUCATION, HISTORY, REFERENCE & TEST PREPARATION

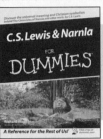

0-7645-8381-6

0-7645-9554-7

Also available:

- The ACT For Dummies
  0-7645-9652-7
- Algebra For Dummies
  0-7645-5325-9
- Algebra Workbook For Dummies
  0-7645-8467-7
- Astronomy For Dummies
  0-7645-8465-0
- Calculus For Dummies
  0-7645-2498-4
- Chemistry For Dummies
  0-7645-5430-1
- Forensics For Dummies
  0-7645-5580-4

- Freemasons For Dummies
  0-7645-9796-5
- French For Dummies
  0-7645-5193-0
- Geometry For Dummies
  0-7645-5324-0
- Organic Chemistry I For Dummies
  0-7645-6902-3
- The SAT I For Dummies
  0-7645-7193-1
- Spanish For Dummies
  0-7645-5194-9
- Statistics For Dummies
  0-7645-5423-9

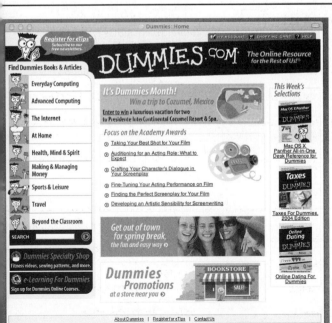

Get smart @ dummies.com®

- **Find a full list of Dummies titles**
- **Look into loads of FREE on-site articles**
- **Sign up for FREE eTips e-mailed to you weekly**
- **See what other products carry the Dummies name**
- **Shop directly from the Dummies bookstore**
- **Enter to win new prizes every month!**

* Separate Canadian edition also available
† Separate U.K. edition also available

Available wherever books are sold. For more information or to order direct: U.S. customers visit www.dummies.com or call 1-877-762-2974.
U.K. customers visit www.wileyeurope.com or call 0800 243407. Canadian customers visit www.wiley.ca or call 1-800-567-4797.